SCHOOL POLITICS
CHICAGO STYLE

Paul E. Peterson

SCHOOL POLITICS
CHICAGO STYLE

THE UNIVERSITY OF CHICAGO PRESS
Chicago and London

PAUL E. PETERSON is associate professor in the Departments of Political Science and Education at the University of Chicago. He is coeditor of *Urban Politics and Public Policy: The City in Crisis* and coauthor of *Race and Authority in Urban Politics*. He has contributed many articles to scholarly journals.

THE UNIVERSITY OF CHICAGO PRESS, CHICAGO 60637
THE UNIVERSITY OF CHICAGO PRESS, LTD., LONDON
© 1976 by The University of Chicago
All rights reserved. Published 1976
Printed in the United States of America

Library of Congress Cataloging in Publication Data
Peterson, Paul E
    School politics, Chicago style.

    Includes index.
    1. Collective bargaining—Teachers—Chicago.
I. Title.
LB2842.2.P44   331'.89'041'371100977311   76–603
ISBN 0–226–66288–8

To my mother
and to the memory
of my father

CONTENTS

ILLUSTRATIONS

ix

PREFACE

Public policy is formulated through bargaining and negotiation among a plurality of individuals, groups, agencies, and interests. No single proposition in the literature on American domestic policy formation has been so convincingly argued, elaborated, and documented. Bargaining takes place on Capitol Hill, amid executive bureaus, within state legislatures, between national and local governmental entities, and among competing municipal agencies. Even our system of justice is marked by pervasive *plea* bargaining. Elected officials, bureaucrats, lawyers, group leaders, union officials, and politically aroused citizens and parents all bargain whenever they seek to shape the exercise of governmental authority. If politicians often bear the opprobrium that comes from brokering these transactions, political scientists have, in their scholarly work, done much to rehabilitate the reputation of this highly skilled craft.

Useful as the concept of bargaining has proved to be in analyzing political life, its widespread applicability limits its discriminating capability.[1] If bargaining can at the same time characterize relations between guards and prisoners, on the one hand, and the president of the United States and the premier of the Union of Soviet Socialist Republics, on the other, then much remains to be said after one has defined an interaction as bargaining. Accordingly, in this study of policy making for Chicago's school system, we have sought to distinguish between two patterns of bargaining sufficiently differentiated in their origins, processes, and consequences that their inclusion under one broad heading called simply bargaining was entirely inadequate. *Pluralist bargaining* occurs when participants are primarily concerned about preserving or enhancing their immediate electoral or organizational interests. Narrowly based groups and agencies concentrate their energies on limited aspects of the issue, develop new alliances as issues and tactics change, migrate from one electoral candidate and political faction to another over time, and compromise their differences out of respect for the legitimacy of competing interests participating in the policy-making process. Numerous studies of both national and local politics have identified such a pattern of political bargaining. *Ideological bargaining* occurs when participants are motivated by broader, more diffuse interests, such as those of a racial or class faction or of a political regime, which are regarded as of such an enduring significance that the participant becomes deeply, ideologically, committed to them.[2] This pattern of bargaining is marked by intense conflict, where groups find similar allies across a range of policy questions, link themselves in a more or less permanent manner with a particular partisan faction, and seek to defeat their opposition whenever they have the political strength to avoid a compromise. Of course, these two patterns of bargaining are seldom found in pure form in American politics; instead, they represent the two extremes of a continuum of highly variegated bargaining patterns. In the pages that follow we thus treat these contrasting bargaining patterns as models; in any given case, we shall see whether the pluralist or ideological bargaining model best fits the political interactions observed.

Bargaining models of policy formation have their critics.[3] Especially during the tempestuous decade of the sixties, students of political life felt that such models overlooked the controlling, stratifying, stultifying elements in the American social system. Since the concept of bargining implied openness, exchange, and mutual satisfaction, many felt that it could only display a Panglossian view of a system marred by racism, sexism, rigid class stratification, and control of all from the commanding heights of corporate capitalism. In their opinion, one should not study bargaining over policy, but the ways in which the system keeps citizen concerns from becoming political demands, social problems from becoming political issues, individual desires from becoming racial and class struggles. Like Sherlock Holmes, the investigator of political relations should attend to what did *not* happen, not to overt interactions among recognized political participants.

In some instances this injunction has led to fruitful research.[4] But most critics of bargaining models have simply abandoned the study of policy formation for generalized, rhetorical accounts of the structure of American politics. To consider alternatives to bargaining models of policy making, therefore, I was forced to turn to two quite different research traditions: organizational theory and the study of international relations.

In contrast to bargaining theory, the two models that I have borrowed from these traditions assume an essential unity within the policy-making organ under study. If fundamental to the notion of bargaining is the assumption that diversity must be accommodated, the competing constructs treat their subject as a monistic unity. In applying organizational theory to policy making, I have treated the bureaucracy under study, in this instance a school system, as an interdependent whole, with a single set of interests, values, and operating routines. Whatever internal differences may exist among organizational members, these are as nothing in comparison with the differences between "insiders" and "outsiders." Accordingly, policies dominated by a single organization such as the Chicago Public Schools are not the outcome of a bargaining game but the output of a large, complex, autonomous bureaucratic structure. The second model, drawn from the literature of international relations, considers actors as rational, value-maximizing, goal-oriented decisionmakers. Graham Allison, whose study of the Cuban missile crisis has greatly influenced my conceptualizations, convincingly demonstrates that foreign policy-making analysts typically treat governments as unitary decision makers who rationally choose among tactical alternatives in order to maximize their strategic objectives.[5] Even though these analysts are aware of great internal differences among political leaders, governmental agencies, and foreign policy advisers, they nonetheless find it useful, for analytical purposes, to treat the nation-state as a single undifferentiated unit.

Although debates between pluralists and elitists have dominated much of the research concerning domestic policy making, no comparable unitary models have been constructed. Rather, elitists and neo-elitists have simply obtained estimates of the individuals with the most power in a community or identified the social backgrounds of those in official positions of power and authority.[6] What I attempt to demonstrate here is that policy making can be viewed simultaneously from bargaining and unitary perspectives, that the causal factors that seem to shape policy vary according to which model is utilized, and that choosing among the models depends in part on the analyst's purposes. In short, I employ bargaining models—both pluralist and ideological—to demonstrate the plurality of forces shaping urban school policy. But I also apply unitary models to the same sets of policies to illustrate the extent to which a single set of factors constrain the alternatives considered.

ACKNOWLEDGMENTS

This study of policy making was set in Chicago's school system during the late 1960s, shortly after a new superintendent, James Redmond, had been asked to administer its schools. As is usual in case study research, we used a wide variety of research techniques to collect vast quantities of information on Chicago school policy formation, only a small portion of which is reported in the pages that follow. During the 1967–70 period, when the bulk of the data collection took place, school board meetings were regularly attended, transcriptions of board meetings were examined, newspaper articles on school affairs were clipped and filed, board members and community leaders were interviewed, and a number of policy makers were invited to meet with the research team in group sessions. In addition, one research assistant served as an intern for a year in various positions within the administrative staff of the school system. He supplemented extensive field notes on this participation-observation experience with extensive, semistructured interviews with a sample of administrators. Another research assistant was given full access to nearly all records of the Chicago Teachers Union. Information on all nonunanimous votes of the Chicago school board was collected and analyzed, the results providing the empirical foundation for chapter 3. Community-level data on patterns of voter support for three tax and bond referenda were also compiled. Other specific data sources are noted at appropriate points in notes to the text.

The debts accumulated in the undertaking are manifold. The Danforth Foundation generously agreed in 1966 to finance a large, comparative study of school board decision making in response to an initiative taken by Luvern Cunningham, then director of the Midwest Administration Center at the University of Chicago. When Professor Cunningham assumed the deanship of the School of Education at Ohio State University, he asked me to assume direction of the Chicago phase of the study. Together with Roald Campbell, then Chairman of the Department of Education at the University of Chicago, he proceeded to assist me in providing access to the Chicago school system, which was generously accorded by Superintendent James Redmond.

When the Danforth grant ran out, the resources of the Department of Political Science of the University of Washington, where I visited during the 1973–74 academic year, and of the Social Science Research Committee of the University of Chicago helped see the project through to completion.

The monograph was researched and prepared with the assistance of Thomas R. Williams. Professor Williams collaborated with me in supervising the research effort during the period 1967–70, when the bulk of data collection was undertaken. While I took primary responsibility for looking at political forces external to the school system, he concentrated on the internal functioning of the system's administrative staff, which he, as a specialist in educational administration, was particularly equipped to analyze. During the 1968–69 academic year I was out of the country, and Professor Williams supervised, with the help of Professor Donald Erickson, the entire research operation. I remain deeply indebted to Professor Williams. Besides assuming burdensome administrative tasks of the study, he contributed valuable information about and insights into the workings of the school board's staff and other aspects of Chicago school politics. He collaborated directly in the preparation of chapter 5, parts of which were published in an earlier version under the title "Models of Decision-Making," in Michael Kirst (ed.), *State, School and Politics* (Lexington, Mass.: D. C. Heath, 1972), pp. 149–62.

A large number of students in the Departments of Education and Political Science at the University of Chicago provided research assistance. The reader can partially determine the extent of my dependence on their efforts by noting the numerous references to student papers and theses throughout the book. I am particularly indebted to James Cibulka, John Elson, Edward Gilpatrick, Michael Holzman, J. David Hood, Jane Hughes, Francis Landwermeyer, William McAllister, James Rabjohn, Carl Struby, Richard Townsend, Joseph Weeres and Robert White. I also appreciate the comments and criticisms of the succession of students in Education 388/ Political Science 329 at the University of Chicago, who suffered through cruder, longer, but still incomplete versions of the analysis presented here. The chapter on the politics of political decentralization was written in collaboration with James Cibulka, whose doctoral dissertation was the primary data source for the material presented there.

Although some of my friends and colleagues may have forgotten their perusals of earlier drafts, I have profited from their criticisms. In this regard I am grateful to Charles Bidwell, Roald Campbell, Terry Clark, Raphael Nystrand, Joseph Cronin, Alan Thomas, Laurence Iannaccone, Leonard Fein, Richard Flathman, Duncan MacRae, William Boyd, and David O'Shea. I owe special thanks to David J. Olson, who has carefully criticized crudely written pages time and again, and to J. David Greenstone, with whom I have discussed many of these ideas for so many years that I can no longer determine their origins.

Many typists helped prepare drafts of this manuscript, but two, Lorraine Dwelle and June Hull, contributed beyond measure.

My greatest debt is to my wife, Carol, whose support and encouragement I needed to complete this enterprise. Although these and other obligations have been incurred, the responsibility for what ensues rests with the author.

Part One

BARGAINING OVER
SCHOOL POLICY

One

MACHINES, REFORMERS, AND
RACIAL CHANGE

Chicago's board of education, deeply divided in its educational philosophy, struggled in the late sixties with the problems of teacher unionization, school desegregation, and administrative reorganization. The power struggle between machine and reform factions on the board crucially affected educational policy. At the same time policy was powerfully influenced by the shape proposals took in the hands of the board's administrative staff. Both factors not only influenced the significant policies upon which the bulk of this study focuses but affected trivial matters as well. Both the contrasting ideological perspectives of board members and the critical impact of staff work on board behavior can be illustrated by an apparently insignificant matter that appeared on the agenda of the September 27, 1967, meeting of the board.

Item 67–998 provided $1,800 to light a trophy case at Kelvyn High School. Ordinarily, the item would have been passed simply by having one board member respond, "Omnibus," which, if no one else objected, would place it in a catch-all category that would then be put to a vote when all such items had been called. But on this occasion, the board's forty-six-year-old insurance executive, Harry Oliver, objected. "I can understand the importance of displaying the trophies," he conceded. But he went on to argue:

> Presumably, these are probably athletic trophies, but I can't help but remember our public hearings last winter, hearing about many schools that had most inadequate lighting on the inside and sometimes dangerously poor lighting on the outside, and I would like to ask a question: May we suggest that we skip lighting trophy cases this time, with the thought that we might divert that $1,800 to some classroom or hallway lighting or classroom lighting elsewhere?[1]

3

Mrs. M. Lydon (Marge) Wild moved that Oliver's proposal be accepted. But Dr. Bernard Friedman, a chemist with Sinclair Oil Company, hesitated: "Let's make sure it is just trophies. It might be for a display of scientific apparatus and experiments." When the responsible staff member stated that the light was, indeed, just for athletic trophies, Friedman joined Oliver in opposition. The scientist apparently felt sports were not so worthy of support as academic activities.

The debate was far from ended, however, for here was a problem which, amid all the complexities of race relations, teachers' salaries, and the management of a multimillion dollar budget, was clear, simple, and could be grasped by *almost* (as we shall see) any board member. One could thus draw on personal experiences in considering the matter:

> WILD: Isn't it possible to get a handyman to put a little reflector in like I did at home and just light it up?
> WARREN BACON: Not without Tom's union.
> WILD: Oh, Tom's union wouldn't like that. (To Thomas Murray): I was going out and do it, Tom. I did it at home.

Warren Bacon had struck a blow at Thomas Murray, and the comment may have reflected the great social and cultural chasm separating them. Bacon was a successful forty-four-year-old black vice-president of Inland Steel Company. He was an able and articulate civil rights enthusiast, publicly aligned with antimachine candidates in the black community. Thomas Murray epitomized in many ways the forces in Chicago school politics that most disturbed Bacon. Murray was an elderly (seventy-five years of age) leader of the Chicago local of the International Building and Electrical Workers and one of the leading union statesmen who had the confidence of Mayor Richard J. Daley. In terms of race, class, political affiliations, and educational philosophy, no two board members could have been more different than Warren Bacon and Thomas Murray.

Murray thus responded to the conversation in injured tones:

> Can you imagine what kind of a controversy this is going to create out in the Kelvyn Park School when those kids feel— the whole staff, they are proud of their trophies, they want them exhibited. That is the reason why they want the trophy case lit, and we say, "No, you can't have it."

Even though Marge Wild was often aligned with Murray in board conflicts, this time she was not persuaded by his argument.

> I just lit two so-called trophy cases for some stuff I have at home and I put it in myself and it didn't cost me $1,800.

MURRAY: Let me tell you something, Lord help you when the electrical inspector gets out and finds out what kind of job you did.

WILD: I did a fine job.

MURRAY: Don't forget this job has to be put in in accordance with the city code.

WILD: So is mine.

President Frank Whiston, though on friendly terms with both Wild and Murray, now acted in his role as chairman of a meeting that had been diverted by an apparently small matter:

We are now talking about the school, and let's keep our homes and rendezvous and other places out of it.

At this point, when several board members, acting on a rule that permits any two board members (unless overruled by a two-thirds majority) to defer an item until the next meeting, moved that the matter be passed over, Superintendent James Redmond sought to protect his administration from this unusual board interference into its routine affairs:

Is there anything that is expected of your staff . . . between now and the next time it comes up?

Wild gave what seemed to be the only appropriate response: "Go out and light the trophy case." But Redmond, expertly using an appeal to efficiency to bulwark his position, retorted: "I would hesitate delaying the work in the switchboard feeders and the distribution of the emergency lighting and the relighting of the auditorium and the study hall. . . ."

With this intervention the board decided to resolve the issue immediately, and after some additional discussion a roll call vote was taken. Oliver, Wild, Bacon, and Friedman all cast their votes in favor of deleting the trophy case item. Apparently, they not only resented the apparently excessive wages paid to skilled workers but also regarded sports activities as peripheral to the main responsibilities of the educational system. For three of these four board members— Marge Wild was the exception—their attitude toward the trophy case was consistent with their voting record elsewhere.[2] Oliver, Bacon, and Friedman all were generally opposed to the pay currently received by skilled workers employed by the schools, opposed to settlements with the Chicago Teachers Union that required a temporarily unbalanced budget, and favored further school integration. Integration, in fact, may be related to the trophy question, and not simply because Kelvyn Park was a 95 percent white high school on the Northwest Side of the city. These reformers, as we shall call them, seemed to regard the schools not as a community institution in which the athletic program played a major role but as an economic investment and an avenue of social mobility which provided children —black and white—an opportunity to learn to read, write, carry on scientific projects, and train themselves for an increasingly complex, technological society. Consistent with this view of the functions of schools, lighting a trophy case was a waste of funds, school integration a valuable educational objective.

Thomas Murray gained the support of three other board members, enough to save the Kelvyn Park trophies. President Whiston, a seventy-three year old, wealthy, self-made Irish businessman, voted for the trophy case, as did Judge Edward Scheffler, an elderly Polish leader and formerly the chief justice of Chicago's municipal court. Whiston and Scheffler may have voted with Murray simply out of friendship. But Murray's appeal also made some sense to these members of the board's "machine" faction. If a school is something one is "proud of," something one "belongs to,'" and not simply an agent of economic expansion and social mobility, then the athletic program, even including trophy cases, are important to the maintenance of school spirit and community stability. Those members' support of the neighborhood school in the face of strong civil rights pressures might well be explained in just these terms, for the in-migration into local schools of strangers with different physical characteristics and cultural values could undermine the "way of life" in many of Chicago's white neighborhoods.

Cyrus Adams III, a vice-president of Carson Pirie Scott and Company, one of Chicago's finest department stores, provided the fourth vote in favor of the trophy case. Adams's educational orientation could best be understood in terms of his business affiliations. He was dedicated to the prosperity of Chicago, and, of course, that prosperity was, for Adams, inextricably linked to the future of the downtown business district. Adams believed community institutions should be conducted in a fiscally responsible fashion, that community leaders should strive for racial peace and harmony, and that the city's schools deserved more financial support than they had received in the past. Ordinarily, one might have expected him to vote against the trophy case, but Adams felt the athletic program had generally not been well supported. And he recognized that for Chicago to prosper, its neighborhoods had to be stable. Athletic programs gave "spirit" to community schools.

One board member, Mrs. Wendell Green, passed her vote on the issue. A black octogenarian, Mrs. Green had often opposed plans for school integration because these made distinctions on racial grounds. When alive, her husband had been an important figure in the Democratic organization, and Mrs. Green usually backed mayoral preferences, thus becoming an ally of Whiston and Murray. As the vote was about to be taken, she intervened for the first time.

> Mr. President, what are we voting on, to delete, may I ask, to delete this report, this one item, line item?
> WHISTON: Yes, ma'am.
> GREEN: And ask Dr. Redmond to bring further information, or are we simply eliminating the lighting of the trophy case?
> WHISTON: At the moment we are eliminating this item, and if Dr. Redmond wishes to come back with it next meeting or a subsequent meeting, of course, he may do so. It is being deleted from this board report.

Mrs. Green, apparently satisfied with this explanation, cast her vote: "On *this* board report, I vote aye"—to delete the item, apparently suggesting that she might vote in favor of lighting the trophy case in the future. Murray, recognizing that Mrs. Green's initial confusion betrayed indecision, seized the opportunity to make one last appeal—this time specifically to her:

> I would like to point out to Mrs. Green they are deleting this from this Board report, and they are not doing anything about spending it any place else to improve the lighting in any other school. They are merely taking away from Kelvyn Park High School the right to light their trophy cases so they can display their awards, awards they are proud of winning, they are really proud of.

The appeal had its impact, for subsequently Mrs. Green changed her mind, registering her confusion once more:

> I still do not understand the import of this motion. If this means that you are simply taking $1,800 off of what is otherwise a large electrical bill and the electricians will be there doing the other work and we are probably getting $1,800 worth because they are there—you see, it is quite complicated.
> PRESIDENT WHISTON: How do you vote, Mrs. Green?
> GREEN: I think I will pass, Mr. President.

With that reversal the vote was tied, and the trophy cases were lit. Interestingly, board procedures required that the superintendent receive only 50 percent and not a majority of the votes cast on matters such as the trophy case. The superintendent and his staff prepared the agenda, of course, and the motion was made to delete the item from the agenda. Since it failed on a tie vote, the trophies were illuminated even though there was no board majority for such action.

The absence of two board members from the meeting probably did not change the result, for in all probability they would have split their votes. The Parent-Teacher Association representative, Louise Malis, could have been expected to favor deletion, because she often opposed union demands and was not a steadfast proponent of the neighborhood school. John Carey, on the other hand, was an executive with the United Steel Workers and would not have taken kindly the insults to working men implied in some of the discussion. In sum, the close division on this minor issue reflected the forces that divided the board and influenced its decisions on far more important matters.

Forces in Chicago school politics can in fact be divided into three parts: the machine, the reformers, and the black community. Although it is an oversimplification to collapse the city's interests and centers of power into just three categories, in the late sixties these three forces not only provided most of the fuel that generated school controversy, but the balance of power among them went far in explaining the political settlements shaping educational policy. A preliminary examination of each of these constituent elements in Chicago school politics helps provide the framework for understanding board policy making.

THE POLITICAL MACHINE

Renowned for its power, internal organizational efficiency, and the shrewdness of its political leadership, Chicago's machine structured the pattern of school politics, as it did all other political relationships in the city. The success of the Democratic party organization in Chicago politics was due, first of all, to its association in the voter's mind with the national Democratic party, which since the thirties had been the party of the urban masses.[3] Irish, Italians, Poles, blacks, labor, "wets," and urban working men generally, had flocked to the Democratic banner in the thirties and had remained loyal ever since. In Chicago the movement began around 1930, as Anton J. Cermak pulled together the competing elements of the party into one cohesive coalition.[4] For Cermak, the liquor issue was central, and it proved to be a powerful magnet for bringing voters to the support of Al Smith and Franklin Roosevelt.[5] Cermak was assassinated at President-elect Roosevelt's side in 1933, and power in Chicago politics returned to the hands of the Irish where it has remained ever since.

The Chicago Democratic party was particularly favored by the events of the depression years, for it contained no serious internal divisions complicating the flow of patronage and federal money which the New Deal provided the cities. As a result, the party was able to build an enormous, disciplined army of workers with the city, county, state, and federal resources available to it. The organization was said to control twenty to thirty thousand government positions, which were allocated in a complex manner to various aldermen and ward committeemen, who in turn awarded them to precinct captains and workers.[6]

The machine has always done better in the poor inner-city communities than in more middle-class fringe areas.[7] In fact its influence in most Cook County suburbs is marginal, which means that county-wide elections are often closely contested, with Republicans emerging victorious from time to time. The reasons for this geographical differentiation in the vote are well known. The poor and the working class living close to the central business district are predisposed to support the local representative of a liberal, labor-oriented national Democratic party. Moreover, the favors the machine can supply to them are particularly valuable. Poorer people are more likely to have fires to endure or sons to get out of jail, they are grateful for moderately well-paying, stable city jobs, and they need more help in negotiating the bureaucratic maze when they must deal with city officials. For example, if they are in need of welfare assistance, they appreciate the help of a precinct worker in seeing that they obtain it. Sometimes this simply means that the worker secures the welfare checks from the mailman when he comes to the housing project, so that the checks are not stolen from the mail boxes. At other times the precinct worker may intercede on the welfare recipient's behalf in direct contacts with bureaucratic officials. Thus, in the 1950s, when poor blacks were migrating to the cities, Chicago's welfare rolls steadily increased, whereas the rolls in other cities did not reflect the increased need for welfare assistance.[8] Since the state paid for most of the welfare assistance, urban Democrats did not hesitate to recruit welfare recipients, knowing that on election day they would be grateful for the assistance.

Machine Strength

The success of the machine in Chicago politics in the postwar period was remarkable. Perhaps the single best quantitative measure of the strength of the Democratic organization was the extent to which it controlled access to the party nomination for a political office. Chicago's machine was seldom challenged in primary elections by dissidents in races for local offices. From 1958 to 1964, 78 percent of the Chicago Democratic primary elections for state representative were uncontested, and in only 8 percent of the races did the opposition candidate receive as much as 20 percent of the vote.[9] In no other city of comparable size were Democratic primaries so well controlled.

James Wilson said it bluntly: Chicago had "the strongest big-city Democratic machine in the United States."[10]

The power of the organization was evident in other, less quantifiable ways. Loyal organization Democrats dominated the fifty-member city council; even in the late sixties only three or four independents and a similar number of Republicans managed to achieve the office. As a result, the council, though it had substantial formal powers, appeared to observers as a rubber stamp, approving all the proposals of Mayor Daley, who doubled as chairman of the Democratic organization.[11] In the state legislature, the organization had the unflinching loyalty of virtually all the city Democrats and even a few of the Republicans from the West Side of Chicago. Because his lieutenants were willing to vote as a bloc on issues important to party leaders, Mayor Daley had great bargaining powers in state politics even when his party was in a legislative minority or failed to control the governor's office. Even downstate Democrats would ordinarily cooperate with Chicago Democrats on matters important to Chicago, anticipating reciprocal support for downstate concerns.[12] The Chicago Democrats had clout in Washington also. Although in 1968 one independent Democrat, Abner Mikva, was elected to the House of Representatives, the Chicago delegation was otherwise known for its propensity to move unanimously on legislative issues. The delegation's unity not only helped secure special legislative benefits for the Chicago area,[13] but local Democratic power could influence federal administrative policies as well. When in 1965 the Office of Economic Opportunity, ignoring Mayor Daley's wishes, sought to impose "participation of the poor" on Chicago's community action program, the director of the regional OEO office was replaced with one loyal to the local party.[14] That same year the Office of Education announced it would cut off federal aid to Chicago schools until the system complied with the Civil Rights Act of 1964. After local officials voiced their displeasure, President Lyndon Johnson ordered the Office of Education to release the funds immediately.[15]

Machine-Labor Relations

The machine's influence was not limited to governmental institutions. Its impact on the black community, businessmen, the press, and the Republican party is discussed below. But its relationships with organized labor were particularly close. Although these were rooted in the alliance between labor and the Democratic party in national politics, the symbiotic local relationship was also important. The machine solidified its alliance with labor by paying high wages for skilled labor in city government, writing building codes requiring union labor, protecting unions in strike situations, appointing union representatives to mayoral commissions and other public bodies, and sponsoring union legislation in the state legislature.[16]

Mayor Daley appointed two representatives of organized labor to the school board, one from craft unions formerly associated with the more conservative American Federation of Labor and the other from industrial unions once associated with the more militant Congress of Industrial Organizations. Although the two wings of the labor movement had joined together in 1953, the differences between craft and industrial unions were still sufficiently great that this pattern of representation continued into the seventies. Thomas Murray of the International Building and Electrical Workers served on the board from 1958 to 1970, giving craft unions stable and influential representation. Raymond Pasnick of the United Automobile Workers (UAW) served on the board during the most controversial days of Benjamin Willis's superintendency. Reflecting the liberal tradition of the UAW, Pasnick himself was a leading advocate of school integration. When he resigned from the board to accept a position in Pittsburgh, he was replaced by John Carey of the United Steelworkers, a less militant industrial union. Carey, who in 1970 became president of the board, was also liberal on racial matters, but his greatest concern as a school board member seemed to be the protection of union rights and privileges.

Union members of the board sought to preserve the prevailing wage rate for skilled workers employed by the school system, the highest rate paid in private industry for comparable work. Critics of this method of payment claimed that public employment provided less arduous, more dependable maintenance work than the seasonal construction work in private industry with which it was compared. But union members of the board were able to preserve the prevailing wage arrangement. The other concern of union members of the board, particularly after 1966 when the Chicago Teachers Union gained collective bargaining rights, were teacher contract negotiations. Murray served on the collective bargaining committee as long as he remained on the board, and for a time Carey served on the committee as well. The significance of the machine-labor alliance for the politics of collective bargaining is explored in greater detail in chapter 8.

Organizational Leadership

The unity and strength of the Democratic machine is in part a function of the character of the organization itself. The numerous rewards available to the party faithful and the great difficulty of achieving success in the face of party opposition combine to induce loyalty from a wide range of political actors. But machine politics has not always meant great centralization of power; factions both within parties and across the Republican and Democratic parties provided great conflict and competition in Chicago politics prior to the 1930s. The impressive achievements of the Chicago machine must be attributed in part to the leadership of its county chairman, Mayor Richard J. Daley.

In 1946 the Democratic party had endured its most severe challenge, when a scandal involving Chicago schools damaged the prestige of Mayor Edward J. Kelly, an event which we shall later see had a great impact on the subsequent pattern of school politics. To prevent the rise of a major reform movement, the party organization slated Martin C. Kennelly, an upstanding local businessman with minimal political connections, as its mayoral candidate. Kennelly governed honestly though without distinction for the next eight years; greater power was held in the hands of the "Big Boys," five key aldermen who through the organization controlled the city council.[17] Nonetheless, without close control of the mayor's office, the machine began to weaken—until Richard Daley assumed its chairmanship in 1953. Two years later he challenged Kennelly in the Democratic primary, defeated him with the help of labor and most of the party organization, and went on to defeat Alderman Robert Merriam, the last strong candidate the Republicans have run for mayor. Once in office Daley steadily strengthened the party organization.

Daley's leadership has been characterized in contrasting ways by two equally astute observers of his reign. Admittedly, Edward Banfield's political science treatise, *Political Influence,* was written a decade before the more journalistic analysis, *Boss,* written by Mike Royko, and perhaps the difference between them is due simply to changes in Chicago politics.[18] Yet, since their perspectives, both so persuasive, differ so markedly, the chronological explanation seems inadequate, and an alternative one, developing one of our major themes, will be proposed.

In Banfield's analysis Daley was portrayed as a shrewd, calculating politician who searched for compromises that reflected the balance of interests mobilized on the issues before him. Daley never initiated programs; instead, he waited for civic organizations, large economic enterprises or the newspapers to suggest them. Nor did Daley do much to promote one or another version of a proposed undertaking. Instead, he waited to see the variety of interests that would express themselves on the matter, the intensity with which each would push its demands, and the problems that might reveal themselves in the discussion of proposals. In the end, he would reach a compromise, fashioned out of the various alternatives others presented.

From this view, even though Daley played a leading role in the decisions that emerged, he used his influence cautiously, seldom imposing his own preferences on the settlement. Daley, it seemed, was a politician interested in his political future, in the extension of Democratic power throughout the city, county, and state, and in the preservation of his Democratic organization. Any policy goals were merely instrumental to this power-focused purpose. Daley fashioned his compromise after all interests had been articulated in order to reach a decision that minimized his political costs.

Banfield did not judge this tough-minded political calculation harshly. Instead, he argued that simply because politicians were oriented toward reelection to office and expansion of their power base, their policies approximated the public interest. The public interest, said Banfield, could be served only by balancing the many partial interests in the community—whose relative importance could be determined only if each was given an opportunity to state its case with the intensity appropriate to its stake in the matter—and then leaving the resolution of the matter to a politician, who had to win the confidence of the community in future elections. In other words, Daley's very lack of policy commitments made him a capable servant of the community.

Royko's perspective on Daley's leadership is presented anecdotally in accord with journalistic fashion. The argument is not stated as clearly as Banfield's, but the selection of material conveys the author's message. Royko dwells in the opening chapters on the culture that nourished Daley. He was raised in a devout Irish Catholic home, attended a nearby Catholic school, joined a local teenage gang which (when the future mayor was seventeen years old) participated prominently in Chicago's infamous race riots of 1919, later became the gang's president, the first step in his long, slow rise through the ranks of the Democratic party. He became in turn a precinct worker, personal secretary to his ward committeeman, state representative, state senator, a losing party candidate for county sheriff in the disastrous elections of 1946, ward committeeman, revenue director for Governor Adlai Stevenson, county clerk, and finally, in July 1953, chairman of the Cook County Democratic organization.

In childhood and early adolescence he was a clean, good boy— almost, Royko suggests, excessively so.[19] In Springfield, as throughout his political career, he apparently remained remarkably free from the corrupt backroom deals and the extramarital affairs that at times enlivened legislative sessions for Illinois assemblymen. His faithfulness to his religious background was expressed by daily attendance at mass even during his many, increasingly arduous years as mayor. His private morality corresponded to a fervent committment to his public obligations. Long hours, meticulous scrutiny of the many matters requiring his judgment, only short scattered holidays: these were the mark of a political leader with a high sense of public responsibility, indeed almost a grim determination to fulfill his duties.[20]

In contrast to Banfield's diagram of an almost artificial political automaton, Royko develops a portrait of a particular man with a specific cultural and psychological background who has been recruited in a distinctive manner to the office of mayor. In the interstices of Royko's tales, one can see how the mayor's character has affected his political decisions. A man without some of the ordinary vices may be too virtuous in defending the values and institutions that make his world meaningful. Excessively dutiful behavior may control strong, almost violent passions that find release when appropriate objects are identified. Royko thus stresses the times that Daley's temperament, usually under strict control, is unleashed. America's year of violence—1968—offers the most widely known examples: the mayor's orders to police that they should "shoot to kill" rioters and looters, his apparent sanction of an unwarranted police attack on peaceful demonstrators against the Vietnam war, and, of course, the incredible confrontations that accompanied the Democratic convention in Chicago.

From the perspective strongly implied by Royko's material, Daley emerges as anything but a neutral bargainer. Blacks, particularly dissident blacks, political leftists, and antiwar demonstrators were attacked with a virulence and viciousness that cannot be attributed simply to political calculation. Rather, it is as though the mayor perceived a threat to the values of the Irish Catholic political hegemony that provided Chicago, the great city of Chicago, with what he saw as the best possible political regime. When the values of home, family, church, ethnic group, and party so central to a man's life are criticized, attacked, and challenged in fundamental ways, a man whose passions are typically under careful control can lash back with extreme measures of his own.

Although the portrait is sharpest in the context of great political controversy, Royko suggests that it clarifies less visible aspects of Chicago politics as well. In an important early passage, Royko discusses a supposedly prototypical visit by a neighborhood group to the mayor's office. Mayor Daley, says Royko, will come out from behind his desk all smiles and hand-shakes and charm. Then he returns to his chair and sits very straight, hands folded on his immaculate desk, serious and attentive. . . .

Now it's up to the group. If they are respectful, he will express sympathy, ask encouraging questions, and finally tell them everything possible will be done. . . .

But if they are pushy, antagonistic, demanding instead of imploring, or bold enough to be critical of him, . . . Then he'll blow, and it comes in a frantic roar:

"I want *you* to tell *me* what to do. *You* come up with the answers. *You* come up with the program. . . . It's easy to criticize. It's easy to find fault. But *you* tell me what to do. . . ."[21]

Such was Royko's Mayor Daley.

Pragmatism As an Ideology

Banfield's and Royko's descriptions of Mayor Daley's leadership can be at least partially reconciled if one understands a critical principle that is a central feature of the machine politician's political understanding or, as we shall call it, his ideology.[22] Machine politicians can easily be characterized as unprincipled men exploiting the public for their own profit. In the past they did not attract scholars who could rationalize in sophisticated categories elaborate justifications for their actions. In fact early scholarly analyses as well as journalistic muckraking bitterly attacked the machine politicians' greed, selfishness, corruption, and general perversion of the democratic processes.[23] But this evaluation was too simplistic, too polemical, and could not account for the durability of this form of political organization. In the postwar period scholars have reexamined the machine and have reached more favorable conclusions. Although they admit the machine's private greed, they stress its public pragmatism.[24] From this perspective the machine politicians can be said to have an ideology which in certain significant ways is in accord with a basic principle of American politics—that policy be formed only after consultation with and in deference to the dominant interests within the existing social and political order.[25]

For convenience, the principle can be called *institutionalized bargaining* and the practitioners who serve this principle can be referred to as *pragmatists*. If this is a dominant principle of American politics, no group of politicians has served it better than the machine politicians. The breadth of their political constituency demonstrated the adeptness with which they could act as brokers among a plurality of interests. Business, labor, Irish, Poles, Germans, Jews, and blacks were among the disparate interests which were joined together within one organization. Conflict was diffused, as the machine leadership responded in turn to the most salient of the special interests of each element of its coalition.

At the same time, this commitment to an institutionalized bargaining process limited the machine politician's commitments to certain other principles that have been important for legitimating governmental action in the United States. As the country became increasingly industrialized, governmental operations became increasingly *rationalized*. Technically efficient administration, however, was inconsistent with the machine's desire to tie governmental outputs to the maintenance needs of their organization. The machine's criterion for distributing government resources was not whether the individual was deserving or fell within the category prescribed by the relevant law but whether the individual contributed to the political success of the organization. Both policy and personnel practices served to obliterate the distinction between party organizations and government bureaucracies, thereby inhibiting the latter's capacity to act in a rationalized manner. In fact the machine's defense of parochial and particularistic interests, perfectly consistent with its concern for institutionalized bargaining, was contrary to universalist, achievement-centered norms. If rationalization of administration meant one could not distinguish between black and white, Catholic and Jew, Pole and Italian, the machine's strength lay in its sensitivity to their parochial but nonetheless genuine concerns. In nominating candidates for office, machine politicians were usually more interested in obtaining the proper balance among these groups than in recruiting the most capable individuals for public office. Moreover, the very structure of their organization, which was ward- and neighborhood-centered, focused their attention on community problems and local concerns. Neighborhood clubs and organizations provided the infrastructure for the organization; politicians consequently defended neighborhood institutions against encroachment by those who insisted on public policies that could be defended on technically rationalized criteria.

Neither was the machine manifestly interested in increased public *participation* in political processes, a third important principle in American politics. Rather, the machine sought to concentrate power in its own hands. Material perquisites were carefully distributed among supporters so as to reinforce the power of the organization. The precinct captain distributed jobs, friendship, and "help" in order to gain his constituents' support on election day. Within the organization itself, dissension and conflict was actively opposed by party leaders. Since workers were paid for their services, they were not expected to criticize the decisions of the "company." As Boss Flynn stated it, "It is essential that no one successfully challenge the decisions of the organization. Every challenge must be met head-on and beaten, if the organization itself is to survive."[26] Thus, uncontrolled participation in elections and public airing of controversial issues were not regarded by machine politicians as inherently desirable political ends.

Machine practices could be defended, therefore, primarily on the grounds that they could manage conflict by bargaining successfully among disparate interests. Partisan ward elections, control of both policy and administration by like-minded politicians, recruitment of partisans to civil service positions, even corruption and graft were all defended as ways of maintaining a viable urban order. Machine politicians were not prone to conceptualize the significance of their activities at a high level of abstraction, but many of them recognized that personal gain was not the only basis for defending their actions. They talked in terms of friendship, loyalty, helpfulness, cooperation, standing up for one's own, harmony: such a defense, however, stated only more concretely that parochial institutions have their validity and that bargaining among these institutions is consistent with basic patterns in American political life.

The regime established by Chicago's pragmatic politicians required mayoral responsiveness to a broad set of legitimate interests. Downtown businessmen, neighborhood groups, established bureaucratic agencies, and labor unions all could make claims on city government. The compromising style of Mayor Daley (noted by Edward Banfield) was thus not only good politics but in accord with fundamental principles shaping political relationships in the city.

Daley's Chicago was not a closed political order. Many interests had been defined as legitimate participants in the institutionalized processes through which decisions were made. Yet some interests were excluded and some types of political expression were abhored. Broad "ideological" demands for peace and racial brotherhood made little sense to the Chicago politician. Street demonstrations, sit-ins, boycotts, and civil disobedience were poorly understood in a city where backroom deals, logrolling, and payoffs had been the standard mechanisms for settling disputes. Above all, the needs and hopes of an ever-expanding black community were only dimly recognized by an Irish political elite that had managed to raise itself from the poverty endured by its ancestors. These new currents in Chicago politics were outside the bounds of pluralist politics as it had been practiced in the forties and fifties. Daley's pragmatic ideology did not always include mechanisms for handling these new forces in the traditional way. Instead, he at times treated them as challenges to the political institutions of Chicago, responding to them aggressively and harshly, as Royko described. The mayor's own cultural and psychological background may have helped shape his response to these new forces. Yet the response was not inconsistent with the pragmatism of machine politicians generally, for this pragmatism required only consultation among the "brothers" within the bargaining order, not deference to any outcast crying in the streets.[27]

The Machine and the Schools

The "brothers" within the bargaining order appointed to the school board included representatives of diverse elements of the machine's constituency. Besides the labor representatives discussed earlier, members serving on the board in the late sixties and early seventies with close ties to Mayor Daley and the Democratic party included Frank Whiston, president of the school board, Marge Wild, Edward Scheffler, Gerald Sbarboro, and Mrs. Wendell Green. Although all five came from families with strong, enduring ties to the Democratic organization, each represented a different aspect of its constituency. The school board president, Frank Whiston, managed real estate in the central business district. Because his business affairs made him vulnerable to craft union pressures, he was sensitive not only to property tax issues but also the needs of unionized school employees. The other members reflected the diversity of ethnic Chicago. Mrs. Green was black, Scheffler was Polish, Sbarboro was Italian, and Wild was Irish. Since Whiston and Murray were also of Irish descent, Chicago's most politically predominant ethnic group was particularly well represented on the board.

Chicago schools themselves were regarded as institutions important to the welfare of the city. Although many of the city's political leaders were educated in Catholic schools, it was recognized that minimally adequate public schools were essential for maintaining the social fabric and economic prosperity of the city. As a result, the mayor on numerous occasions used his great political strength on behalf of the schools. Not only did he steadily promote increased state and federal aid for urban schools, but he backed increases in local property taxes for school purposes in each of the three years 1966 to 1968. In the third of these elections, white opposition in many neighborhoods provoked by a school busing plan nearly defeated the needed tax increase. But with the support of the black, Jewish, and reform-oriented voters living along the lake shore, who characteristically favored increased public school expenditures, machine backing proved decisive even in the face of organized resistance.[28] Moreover, in subsequent years, Daley helped the schools sidestep voter review of capital expansion policies by floating bonds to build schools through the Public Building Commission, the one agency in Chicago that could build new structures without voter approval. On the other hand, the school interests vested within the bargaining order were defined in narrowly institutional terms. At no time did prominent leaders of the Democratic organization actively promote the interests of black and Spanish-speaking pupils who comprised a majority of the public school population. Even though Chicago schools, like those in most big cities, seemed unable to minister to their educational needs, Chicago's powerful political elite made little, if any, effort to modify school practices. These pupils remained among the outcasts beyond the institutionalized bargaining order.

THE REFORM MOVEMENT

Although the political machine dominated Chicago politics, it was challenged in small but significant ways by a durable reform movement whose own posture was in many ways a function of machine power. Reformers were not a tightly knit political organization comparable to the machine but a melange of groups, organizations, and individual civic activists who were united by a common distaste for the Democrats in city hall. If the social base for the machine included low-income blacks and upper-class businessmen, reformers had the backing of middle-class professionals, often from Jewish and Protestant backgrounds. Whereas the geographical locus of the political machine's strength lay in the center of the city, the reformers lived primarily in the sophisticated, cosmopolitan lake shore communities both north and south of the central business district, including the Gold Coast, Lincoln Park, Rogers Park, Hyde Park, and South Shore. If the machine mobilized support through patronage and other material benefits, reformers achieved similar results by appealing to public concern about such controversial public issues as corruption, racist government policies, police brutality, and the Vietnam war.

The explicitly political arm of the reform movement had for years been limited to the Independent Voters of Illinois, who regarded themselves as liberal members of the national Democratic party but who supported local Republicans on occasion with the hope of either moderating or defeating the machine. They elected one alderman to the city council, one state senator, a state representative, and in 1968 succeeded in forcing the Democratic organization to slate one of their candidates for the U.S. House of Representatives. That same year another reform organization, the Independent Precinct Organization, was formed in the Lincoln Park area, where some of the bloodiest confrontations between police and demonstrators had recently taken place. Some members of the community, incensed at police brutality, decided to organize against the machine. And in the next couple of years they elected two independent aldermen.

From time to time the reformers could claim more spectacular political successes, though these were usually due more to shrewd alliance formation or accidental factors than their own organizational resources. Although reformers replaced regular Democrats as the Illinois delegates to the 1972 Democratic convention, this decision reflected power relations within the national Democratic party in the summer of 1972, not the balance of power in Chicago. In fact the reformers who were seated had been soundly defeated in the primary contest the preceding spring. Earlier reform successes were equally ambiguous. For example, although they successfully supported Governor Ogilvie in his campaign in 1968, Republicans did well generally that year. They also backed Adlai Stevenson III for senator at a time when the Democratic organization seemed reluctant to slate a Vietnam dove who had criticized Daley's handling of the 1968 Democratic convention. Even though the reformers took credit for forcing a good man on the party, the magic of the Stevenson name and Daley's own debt to the Stevenson family were also factors in the mayor's decision. Still, reform support lent respectability to a candidate's campaign. It was useful in securing newspaper backing, independent volunteers in the suburbs, and a measure of independence from the traditional party organization. Reformers were a small but not entirely negligible factor in Chicago electoral politics.

The reform movement included more than these electoral organizations, however. A variety of civic associations that promoted "good government" and other causes also found access to city hall difficult. They never endorsed candidates, often tried to maintain good relations with city officials, were more interested in their individual cause than a broader political movement, and would frequently sacrifice reformers for an approving nod from the mayor. Yet the difficulties these cause-oriented, idealistic professionals had in building contacts with the tough-minded, pragmatic politicians in city government generally drove them into the politically oriented part of the reform camp. The Housing and Planning Council, Welfare Council of Greater Chicago, League of Women Voters, Better Government Association, Church Federation of Greater Chicago, and National Conference of Christians and Jews were among the reform-minded organizations that found machine politics uncomfortable and governmental policies rather inhospitable to their objectives. The Civic Federation, too, was critical of the Daley regime and often found it useful to work with reformers. But their natural allies were Chicago's conservative Republicans, for the Civic Federation's major focus was a lower (or at least no higher) property tax.

Reformers and the Schools

The reform-oriented interest group directly involved in school politics was the Citizens Schools Committee (CSC). The organization had been founded by teacher leaders in the 1930s at a time when the Democratic machine and the business community had joined hands to cut local government costs to the bare minimum in order to keep expenditures in line with drastically declining tax resources. The teachers suffered severely from the cuts made in education, for not only were they paid less, they were paid in "scrip," which local merchants accepted at substantially less than face value. In this fight for more money and less patronage in the schools, CSC was the teacher's major front organization. In 1946 CSC led a campaign to reform the school board, an effort so successful that the CSC not only "cleaned the Augean stables"[29] that the schools had become but also forced the party organization to nominate a local businessman, Martin Kennelly, rather than one of the party faithful as its candidate for mayor in 1947. In subsequent years CSC established itself as a friendly watchdog of the school system, eager to support its demands for money from the city and state but ready to attack any hint of political influence in education.

CSC suffered from many of the weaknesses of the reform movement as a whole. It recruited parents, exteachers, and a variety of professionals, but its membership was never very large or very prestigious. Admittedly, it often had good relations with the news media, obtaining ample news coverage for its more significant press releases. But because it could not attract prominent businessmen to serve on its board of directors, it had severely limited financial and political resources. Still, CSC and the reformers managed to recruit from their ranks a considerable number of school board members, a phenomenon explored in chapter 4. Friedman and Oliver, together with Jack Witkowsky, a Jewish real estate broker, were the most faithful of the white reformers on the board. Louise Malis was a less reliable ally but voted with them on many of the key votes. Even as the reformers challenged the machine on a host of issues in city electoral politics, these reformers regularly came into conflict with the machine-oriented faction on the school board. The source of the conflict was not just personality or simple political aggrandizement on either side, but two quite contrasting ideological conceptions of the way in which schools should be governed. If the machine-oriented pragmatists believed in deference to established interests, the reformers had quite another set of principles that guided their behavior.

Reform Ideology

A generation ago two of the most eminent of the University of Chicago's political scientists—Charles Merriam and Harold Gosnell—contributed intellectually and practically to the efforts of reformers in Chicago politics.[30] In more recent years, reformers have been treated with greater skepticism by the academic community. Stressing the upper-middle-class, Protestant and Jewish social background of the reformers, scholars have suggested that many of their electoral innovations in city politics were designed to foster the return of middle-class rule. In nonpartisan elections, a favorite reform device, lower-class voters, lacking a middle-class sense of civic duty, stayed at home, because no organization stirred them to participate. At-large elections, another reform innovation, favored candidates with large and independent sources of income who could secure the backing of citywide interest groups and daily newspapers. In such an electoral arena the small businessman or neighborhood lawyer of ethnic background had little chance of success.[31]

Other, nonelectoral innovations are said to have had a similar effect. If reformers felt that nominees for appointed positions should be approved by blue-ribbon committees, this was only because upper-middle-class businessmen and professionals dominated the blue-ribbon committee. Recruitment of administrators from professional backgrounds shifted power away from working-class politicians. Establishment of autonomous governmental departments helped insure that public policies would be suited to the maintenance needs of a white, middle-class bureaucracy rather than responsive to working-class clients of the organization. In sum, it was often said, the reform movement seemed nothing more than a bid for power by the middle classes.

As powerful as these critiques of reform movement goals have been, they do the reformers no more justice than did the attacks by muckrakers on political machines. In focusing on the relationship between the policies favored by the reformers and their presumed class interests, these critiques ignored, as did early critiques of the machine, the reformers' own ideology, their own view of the goals they were seeking for American society. The reformers, too, had an ideology, and they were far more sophisticated than the machine politicians in developing and rationalizing it. Their behavior cannot be fully understood without reference to this ideology, which was based on a recognition that certain important principles of American politics were being ignored by urban machines.

First of all, the reformers sought wider participation in a democratic society. They abhorred the vote buying, vote stealing, and sheer organizational strength of the machine. In order to secure a more democratic political order, the reformers studiously tried to separate the electoral processes from the influences of administrative departments. By eliminating patronage, exposing graft and corruption, and rigorously adhering to the letter of the law, they made political criteria irrelevant to the quality of governmental services citizens received. The citizen was then expected to be free to participate in the political processes in accord with his own good judgment. Yet reform emphasis on participation was coupled with a not entirely compatible interest in rationalizing governmental policy. At a time when principles of scientific management were being widely discussed in the business world, reformers sought to implement them in the political world. Efficiency and honesty were the watchwords that guided their policy proposals. They favored hiring professionals trained in a field of specialization that qualified them for the governmental post to which they were appointed. City managers, school superintendents, and police chiefs were expected to have specialized educations that would enable them to perform their functions at a high level of technical proficiency. Partisan political connections were felt to be not only irrelevant but downright harmful—because they would inhibit the application of rational criteria to policy decisions.

At the same time, reformers did not particularly favor pluralist bargaining among disparate interests. They believed the interests of the city as a whole should take precedence over the demands and concerns of special interests. Electoral tickets should be determined by selecting the most suitable candidate available for each position, not by considerations of ethnic, racial, or religious balance. Administrative implementation of public policies should be in accord with the criteria specified in the law itself rather than with special-interest demands.

Reformers seemed to share with Thomas Jefferson and John Stuart Mill an optimistic view of human nature. Through education and elimination of corrupt influences, citizens could participate freely and wisely in politics, choosing leaders whose concern for the general welfare and technical expertise would enable them to design and implement rational policies. In urban political life, however, voters did not always share the interests of the reformers, choosing candidates for racial, ethnic, or some other self-interested reasons. And urban bureaucracies, far from designing rational policies, became "islands of functional power,"[32] acting in accord with their own interests, parochial values, and familiar routines of operation, rather than responding efficiently to the changing needs of society. In fact in many cities the issue in the sixties often became one of participation versus rationalization rather than the combined realization of both. When this occurred, reformers divided into more conservative "mugwumps," who defended expertise, professionalism, and bureaucracy, and more liberal "neopopulists," who called for citizen participation, direct democracy, and advocate planning. But both could appeal to the reform tradition, and in Chicago, where the machine was still so powerful, the contradictions within the reform movement, though apparent, did not tear it asunder.[33]

Potential Allies of the Reformers

Reformers would have been immeasurably strengthened if they could have formed stable and enduring alliances with four potential partners. The limited reform penetration of the black community is considered below. But reformers had equal difficulty in establishing close ties with the business community, with the Republicans, and with the press. The problem in all three cases was Daley's success in establishing amicable, if never exactly intimate, relations with the business community.

When Daley was first elected in 1955, he achieved victory without much help from leading members of the central business district, who distrusted an organizational stalwart who had "dumped" ex-businessman Kennelly. By the time Banfield finished his study of Chicago politics in the late fifties, however, Daley had shown that he not only had great power but a commitment to preserve the vitality of the central business district at a time when centrifugal social forces threatened to destroy it. Daley built superhighways, rapid transit systems, and enormous parking lots to attract consumers into the city. Urban renewal and special property tax policies enhanced the attractiveness of the city center for high-rise apartments and office complexes. The mayor used his influence to forestall economically costly strikes in both the public and the private sectors—though not necessarily to the disadvantage of the union man. A university was built at the edge of the city center, halting urban "decay" in that area. An exhibition hall was built on the lake shore to attract conventioneers to the city. Above all, in contrast to chaotic, strife-ridden New York, Daley provided order and predictability.

Of course, most businessmen would have preferred all this and clean, honest government as well. In other cities, such as Philadelphia, St. Louis, and Baltimore, they had provided the financial, organizational, and social resources necessary to sustain a rather effective reform effort. But Chicago businessmen were either too con- servative, too intimately connected with the organization, or, most probably, too convinced that machine politics were in Chicago a necessary evil to lend much support to the reform cause. Daley thus won substantial business support in every one of his reelection efforts, including not only financial contributions but newspaper advertise- ments and proudly displayed campaign buttons as well.

If Chicago schools had been ridden with patronage, this, in com- bination with the racial troubles the schools suffered, might have sparked business support of a reform drive. But since the schools had been "cleaned up" in 1947, businessmen gave them little orga- nized support. In the thirties a group of leading businessmen even recommended drastic cuts in educational expenditures to reduce city debts. In later years, however, businessmen came to see that a pros- perous city needs good schools. For example, in 1968, a Better Schools Committee, consisting mostly of businessmen, supported a tax referendum in the face of strong opposition in parts of the white community. This same committee also sponsored a proposal adopted by the school board that enabled a Public Building Commission to finance and build new schools, which were then leased to the board of education. The plan, designed to eliminate the need to secure voter approval of school building projects, was again proof of steady business support for improved educational facilities.

Businessmen showed public, organized interest in the schools on two other critical occasions. In the midst of racial controversy, Super- intendent Benjamin Willis resigned in 1963, insisting that the school board had interfered in administrative matters. As many white organ- izations rushed to the superintendent's defense, a group of prominent businessmen publicly urged the school board "to meet with Dr. Willis and reconcile your differences." Subsequently, the board urged the superintendent to remain, reversed the previous decision that had antagonized him, and voted against accepting his resignation. In the summer of 1965, after the board had signed another contract with Superintendent Willis with the understanding he would retire by December 1966, the board received a second message from another group of forty-eight businessmen. In this letter the businessmen urged that the "choice of Willis's successor be completed promptly," im- plying that one way of retiring Willis quickly would be to have his replacement waiting at the door. Significantly, even though the two groups of businessmen overlapped hardly at all, they were organized by the same president of a large downtown firm. The two public messages indicated how Willis's onetime popularity in the business community had eroded badly by 1965.[34]

These two actions provide a clue to what businessmen expect of the public schools, its board, and its superintendent. They do not particularly demand racial integration, for even by 1963 it was obvious that this goal was low on Willis's list of priorities. They do expect civic order, however, and Willis's contentiousness vis-à-vis blacks and other groups had seriously undermined that. This very concern with "order," which had soldified their backing for Daley, had eventually provoked them to demand Willis's retirement. Controversy and conflict had so plagued the school board, in fact, that prominent businessmen were no longer willing to serve on it. In the fifties, many well-known civic leaders had served on the board, but by the time James Redmond became superintendent in 1966 only one, Cyrus Adams III, vice-president of Carson Pirie Scott and Company, continued to provide a direct link between the school board and the central economic institutions of the city. As long as he was on the board, Adams's support for educational expansion, his animosity toward labor unions within the school system, and his desire for stability, harmony, and compromise represented well the interests and concerns of his associates. But he retired shortly thereafter, not to be replaced by a businessman of comparable stature. To be sure, Bacon, Oliver, and Witkowsky were all businessmen. But none of them were connected with a downtown business firm that had a great stake in Chicago's economic prosperity. President Whiston did have such ties, but he was a Catholic and too closely connected to the Democratic party, the labor unions, and the mayor himself to be a representative of the central business district.

If reformers could scarcely dent business's support of Daley, they found it even more difficult to develop a close alliance with Republicans. Ordinarily, Republicans could be expected to join with reformers to defeat a dominant Democratic organization, a pattern that has occurred in both New York and Philadelphia. And even in Chicago the Republicans at times made efforts to secure reform backing for statewide and county elections. But Chicago Republicans seemed not particularly eager to challenge Democratic control of the central city. First of all, chances of success were slim, though this could become a self-fulfilling prophecy. Secondly, aside from Senator Charles Percy, who has hardly been the darling of Republican regulars, Illinois Republicans were midwestern conservatives, who found it much more difficult to form alliances with liberal reformers than did their fellow Republicans in the East. Thirdly, segments of the Republican party, particularly on Chicago's West Side, were dependent on the machine for patronage, in return for which they limited their partisan fervor.[35] Above all, prominent businessmen that contributed to the Republican party nationally were opposed to challenging Daley in Chicago. As a result, each time Daley sought reelection he was confronted by a weak candidate. The first two Republican challengers were not suitable to the reformers—one was too conservative and the other had dubious political connections. When in 1971 the Republicans finally ran a reform Democrat as their candidate for mayor, he ran a very low-budget campaign and his liberal stance cost him much of the traditional Republican vote.

If Republicans gave reformers little help, something more can be said for Chicago's press, which provides as lively and interesting coverage of local politics as the press of any city in the country. In contrast to many cities, Chicago had vigorously competitive papers in both the morning and the afternoon. The *Chicago Tribune* has for decades been known as America's foremost conservative paper. The McCormick family, which during this period sponsored the Tribune's afternoon companion, *Chicago Today* (earlier known as the *Chicago American*), found the newspaper an effective weapon against Communism, the United Nations, Eisenhower Republicanism, and a host of "socialistic" experiments in the United States. The *Tribune,* which circulates widely in downstate Illinois, has been a major prop of conservative Republicanism in the state, using its prestige and power to hinder more moderate Republicans. Senator Charles Percy, in particular, has never found the *Tribune* especially friendly to his campaign efforts. The *Tribune*'s stance in local politics is rather more complicated. It regularly condemns patronage and corruption in the city, using its reporters to uncover scandals that make excellent headlines. On the other hand, it characterizes liberal reformers as wild-eyed fanatics who do not understand urban realities. In the end, it refrains from criticizing the mayor personally and has generally endorsed his reelection.

The Marshall Field family, long associated with the prestigious Marshall Field and Company department store, own the other pair of citywide newspapers, the *Sun-Times* and the *Daily News.* They have distinguished themselves from the McCormick press by their progressive Republicanism and, in the *Daily News,* some downright liberal sentiments. Although less influential within the Republican party, they successfully defeated the *Tribune* in 1966, when Charles Percy won the Republican primary and went on to become U.S. senator. In local politics they have been equally vigorous at uncovering corruption, have given reformers warm and expansive press coverage, and have taken a more liberal line on race issues. For example, when the states attorney's office sent policemen on an early morning raid of Black Panther headquarters, killing two leaders in the process, the Field press revealed information suggesting that the police had opened fire without provocation. The *Tribune,* on the other hand, obtained exclusive reports (which later proved false) from the states attorney's office, purporting to show that police had been fired upon. The war between the papers soon became as heated as that between the principals in the case. Although the Field press has limited its attacks on Mayor Daley himself, and in fact endorsed him for reelection three of the four times he ran, reformers have had better success with the Field press than with other potential allies. Without it they would have great difficulty in communicating their message to constituents scattered throughout the metropolis.

On school matters, the press reflects the perspective of the downtown business district. All four newspapers have regularly endorsed bond and tax referenda but have treated critically demands of teachers for higher salaries. On racial matters, the *Tribune* has tended to be more critical than the Field press of integration schemes, community participation in the selection of principals, and school boycotts by black students. And this difference between the competing newspapers was significant, for race issues—the product of enormous changes in Chicago's black community—have increasingly dominated Chicago politics.

THE BLACK COMMUNITY
Demographic Change

The machine has been powerful since the early thirties, and the reformers have struggled to provide a weak opposition since World War II. The changing component of Chicago politics has been the size and political potential of the city's black community. Chicago's total population actually declined from 3,397,000 in 1940 to 3,367,000 in 1970. The entire metropolitan area expanded rapidly, of course, but the great growth occurred in the surrounding suburbs of Cook, DuPage, and Lake counties.[36] The nonwhite population of Chicago itself, on the other hand, increased nearly fourfold during this period (see table 1), growing from 8.4 to 34.4 percent of the total population (in the suburbs, blacks comprised less than 2 percent of the population). When the Democratic machine solidified its hold on Chicago politics, the city was an ethnic, Catholic, working-class city. By 1970 it was still a city of the working man and the poor, but its ethnic and racial composition had undergone an enormous transformation. That the machine survived this dramatic demographic change testifies not only to its political flexibility but also to the vast array of its political resources.

TABLE 1

Growth of Nonwhite Population in Chicago, 1940–70

Year	Number of Nonwhites	Percentage of Total Population
1940	282,000	8.4
1950	509,000	14.1
1960	838,000	23.6
1970	1,115,000	34.4

As can be seen in figure 3, the in-migration of blacks was far from evenly spread throughout the city. Before 1940 blacks were concentrated in a long, narrow belt running on either side of State Street south of the Loop (the downtown area). A smaller, secondary community existed on the West Side. As the numbers of blacks rapidly increased, they spread out from these two geographical bases and penetrated a section of the Near North Side of the city as well. The elongated shape of the black belt rather than the formation of a ring around the central business district has been attributed to its spreading

> from original 'ports of entry' along the paths of least resistance: the middle status sectors containing white residents with sufficient means to move in the face of Negro influx and housing within the reach of Negro incomes.[37]

The concentration of a one-third racial minority, uprooted from rural southern poverty, into a highly restricted land area gave rise to enormous social problems and increasing political conflict. Since white property owners, real estate dealers, insurance companies, and bankers had in the past limited black sales and rentals to housing within the existing black community, blacks were segregated and found the cost of housing within black areas to be high relative to the cost in white areas.[38] As numbers continued to pour in from the South, the black community spread. But the spread was painful, occurring block at a time, and it involved panic selling, racial bitterness, and at times violence. Moreover, owing to their physical concentration, all elements of the black community suffered from the misdeeds of criminals, dope addicts, and the violent, which, among a geographically mobile but economically subjected people, were all too many.

Civil Rights and Chicago Politics

Under the circumstances, governmental intervention seemed necessary, and the black community, increasing in numbers, organization,
and political leadership, began to press for alleviation of their condition. To their demands, the machine responded, at least partially,
by providing some of the services needed by the poor and the outcast. Welfare services were provided more generously than in most
large cities. Many employment opportunities were made available to
blacks in the park district and sanitation bureau, as well as in the
police department and public schools.[39] Moreover, as the black population increased in the sixties, a larger number of blacks were appointed to high governmental positions, especially in such new agencies as the Commission on Human Relations, the Chicago Committee
on Urban Opportunity, and the model cities program. In electoral
politics, the power of the black community was recognized in 1971
with the selection of Cecil Partee as the leader of the Democratic
minority in the Illinois House of Representatives and again that year
when a black was elected for the first time to a major citywide office
(City Treasurer). But one should not exaggerate the extent to which
blacks had won a position of strength within the Chicago machine's
patronage structure; as of 1965, when blacks "comprised about 20
percent of [Cook County's] population, . . . 'out of a total of 1088
policy-making positions, Negroes held just 58,' about 5 percent."[40]

The total impact of government policies on the black condition
may in fact have been more negative than positive, especially in the
area of housing. Federal Housing Authority and Veterans Administration loans were generally withheld from blacks, particularly those
seeking to move into white communities. This program, together with
a tax deduction for interest on mortgages, helped finance the white
migration to the suburbs and left blacks compacted together in the
central city. At the same time housing in the city, especially in black
areas, was torn down to make way for urban expressways and to
"renew" blighted areas adjacent to the city center, the northern lake
shore, the University of Chicago and other places where valuable
land had fallen into the hands of poor minority groups.[41] The enormous housing projects that were built as replacements not only reinforced segregation of the poor black but left him in the most isolated,
anomic, impersonal institutions the city could devise.

This segregation of the black community gave rise to the racial
controversies that rocked Chicago politics in the sixties. The integration issue focused initially and most vigorously on Chicago schools.
The conflict began when a school board member and the Urban
League both questioned whether or not schools in white areas were

being underutilized while schools in black areas were overcrowded. When the board responded with no more than a token transfer plan, a number of community organizations—both black and white—formed the Coordinating Council of Community Organizations, which complained to the United States Civil Rights Commission that Chicago schools received federal funds without complying with federal Constitutional requirements prohibiting segregation. A number of law suits were also filed, and one was settled out of court in August 1963 with the understanding that the board of education would appoint a committee of experts "to analyze and study the school system, in particular in regard to schools attended entirely or predominantly by Negroes, . . . and formulate . . . a plan by which . . . inequities in the school system . . . may best be eliminated."[42]

In that same month, the board also approved a desegregation plan allowing honor students to transfer from overcrowded to under-used high schools. When Willis balked at implementing the plan in full, a court ordered that the superintendent comply with the board's directive. Willis resigned as general superintendent, and civil rights groups rejoiced. But within days the board of education both refused to accept the superintendent's resignation and reconciled itself to his wishes with regard to the permissive transfer plan.

From this point on, the dismissal of the superintendent became the overriding civil rights demand in Chicago. Demonstrations, boycotts, law suits, and complaints sent to the U.S. Office of Education sought to achieve this goal. But the school board retained his services not only until the end of his contract in 1965 but, after renewal, until Willis reached the age of retirement in December 1966. In the spring of 1966, however, when James Redmond was recruited to become the new superintendent, Willis announced that he would retire that summer.

In the meantime the committee of experts, headed by Philip Hauser, a demographer at the University of Chicago, had reported (in March 1964) that there was indeed a high degree of pupil segregation in the Chicago school system. Its recommendations for rectifying this situation were accepted by the board "in principle" but never implemented. Moreover, a second major report was submitted to the Board of Education that year. Over the resistance of the superintendent, the board had asked Robert Havighurst, an educator at the University of Chicago, to undertake a major survey of Chicago schools. When completed, the survey not only stressed the need for integrating Chicago schools but further recommended that its administrative apparatus be decentralized. Willis ignored both recommendations.

At times it appeared as if the civil rights controversy over school affairs would severely damage Mayor Daley and his Democratic organization's attempts to maintain biracial political support. As Samuel Lubell observed in the early sixties,

> Negro militancy seems to be transforming the civil rights struggle from what has been a North-South conflict into what could become a conflict of whites against Negroes across the whole nation. . . .
> The full effects of this change may take years to register, but they clearly will add to the stresses and strains within the Democratic party. To keep the Democratic coalition from splitting will require strenuous political exertions. . . .
> For some years to come the likely pattern of political conflict promises to be much stormier at the local and state levels than at the presidential level.[43]

Such a prediction seemed particularly appropriate for Chicago politics, where controversy over school policy received widespread media coverage and where civil rights groups attended board meetings en masse, flooded the streets with their demonstrators, filed court suits, complained to federal agencies, and held two widely honored school boycotts. And within the school board itself, racial conflict became increasingly apparent. To be sure, Mayor Daley's initial black appointment, Mrs. Wendell Green, the widow of a loyal Democratic judge, appointed to the board in 1958, remained supportive of Benjamin Willis throughout his stormy tenure in office. But when Warren Bacon was appointed in 1963, he became a strong proponent of integration, an antagonist of Willis, and a contributor to antimachine candidates in the black community. Mrs. Carey Preston, who had gained prominence for her civil rights work with the Urban League, became the third black board member in 1968; she, too, represented new, change-oriented forces among black leaders. And when Alvin Boutte replaced Mrs. Green in 1969, the three blacks at times found themselves voting with Mrs. David Cerda, a Spanish-speaking board member, against a white majority.[44]

Reform-leaning politicians seemed interested in capitalizing on this disaffection within the black community for the segregationist policies of the Daley-appointed school board. Reform-oriented groups and organizations supported the anti-Willis campaign, and such reform aldermen as Leon Despres were among the school system's severest critics. Reformers also backed a number of independent blacks who contested the regular Democratic organization for seats in the city council and state legislature. Finally, in the 1971 mayoral election, the reform-Republican candidate seemed to be more concerned about civil rights than any previous major candidate for a citywide office. In the end, these reform efforts made only the most marginal inroads into black politics. Like Mrs. Green, nearly all black politicians remained as faithful to the machine and as uncritical of the city's segregated institutions as they had in previous decades.[45] At the same time reformers had difficulty mobilizing organizational resources behind black candidates.[46] Although Mayor Daley's electoral support in black wards dropped by almost 10 percentage points from 1963 to 1971, table 2 shows that he was still able to appeal successfully in that year to nearly three-fourths of the black voters. Even in the 1975 Democratic primary, where the vote was divided four ways among a "law-and-order" candidate, a reformer with civil rights backing, and a well-known black legislator challenging the mayor, he received nearly half the black vote. Two months later he swamped

TABLE 2

Daley's Percentage of Vote in Chicago Mayoral Elections

	Black Wards[1]	Nonreform White Wards[2]	All Wards (= 50)
1955[3]	...	...	54.9
1959[3]	...	...	71.4
1963	84.1	44.0	55.7
1967[5]	83.8	68.6	73.1
1971	74.8	72.1	70.1
1975 (primary)	49.7	65.8	57.8
1975 (general)	88.5	78.6	79.5

SOURCES: Electoral data was provided by the Chicago Board of Election Commissioners. Racial composition of wards for the 1960s was determined by J. David Hood for the 1970s by the staff of the Chicago Municipal Reference Library. For procedures, see Hood's "Issues and Response: A Causal Analysis of Voting on Chicago School Finance Referenda in the 1960's," (unpublished M.A. paper, Department of Political Science, University of Chicago, June 1972).

[1]These wards (eight in the 1960s, eleven in the 1970s) were at least 86 percent black.

[2]These wards (twenty-four in the 1960s, twenty-one in the 1970s) were at least 88 percent white. Wards along the lake shore were excluded from the analysis even when they met racial criteria in order to exclude concentrations of reform strength.

[3]Racial composition of wards not calculated for this year.

[4]For all but one general election, Daley's percentage of the two-party vote was calculated. In 1967 Dick Gregory, a black comedian and civil rights leader, ran as an independent. Since in black areas the vote for Gregory was large enough to reduce the percentage of votes cast for the Democrats by a significant amount, the Daley percentage of all votes cast is reported for this election. The percentage for Daley of the 1975 Democratic primary race was earned in a four-candidate contest.

the conservative Republican generally throughout the city, but particularly in all-black wards.

If it seemed on the surface that civil rights issues would undermine the machine, they had exactly the opposite effect. When Banfield analyzed Chicago politics in the late fifties, he saw the overriding issue as good government versus organizational need for patronage in the inner city. As long as politics turned on that issue, the fate of the machine was, as Banfield argued, highly problematic.[47] But in the sixties corruption was no longer an issue of primary concern to white residents in fringe areas; the racial homogeneity of their neighborhoods, schools, and unions was a more pressing matter. Mayor Daley succeeded by taking cognizance of the racial concerns of his white constituents. Although he never adopted the "backlash" style of a Louise Day Hicks in Boston or a Frank J. Rizzo in Philadelphia, he resisted most demands for integration. In the face of intense pressure for Willis's dismissal, Daley appointed a school board that kept him in office until his retirement in 1966. When in that same year Martin Luther King launched a major open-housing campaign in the city, King achieved only the vaguest commitment from leading businessmen and government officials in a document given great publicity when signed but which, lacking any means of enforcement, was never implemented. When Jesse Jackson, the Southern Christian Leadership Council's dynamic Chicago leader, campaigned for more employment opportunities in the building and trades industries, a special program for training blacks paid for by the United States Department of Labor was established in an agreement union leaders helped draft. Yet the numbers involved were too small to have any more than a marginal impact on the industry, and in any case the program collapsed when its director purloined its funds to pay gambling debts.

Whites in Chicago were not unaware of the patronage, graft, and corruption in city politics; the newspapers would not let them forget it. But even those who themselves had no personal ties to the machine seemed to realize that it performed a valuable function. The large number of blacks hired by the park district, the sanitation bureau, the police department, the poverty program, and even the school system enabled the organization to moderate black demands for integration, a matter more vital to white residents than patronage and corruption. And when blacks turned to more violent tactics, Mayor Daley used language that whites in working-class, ethnic communities felt appropriate to the situation.

Daley's increasing popularity among whites can be seen in the electoral support he received after 1963. As can be seen in table 2, the mayor's percentage of the two-party vote in general elections increased from 56 percent in 1963 to 73 percent in 1967, and to 80 percent in 1975. The trend in nonreform, all-white wards was even more dramatic. In 1963, when civil rights agitation was intensifying, Mayor Daley received only 44 percent of the general-election vote in the all-white, nonreform wards; in 1967, after his position on integration became clear, his percentage increased to 69 percent, in 1971 it increased again to 72 percent, and in 1975 it reached a peak of 79 percent. Even in the more competitive 1975 primary, Daley gained nearly two-thirds of the vote in all-white wards not adjacent to the lake shore.

On the other side, the machine remained strong in all but middle-class areas of the black community. Table 3 shows that support for Daley in 1971 fell to 60 percent of the vote in two middle-class black wards—10 percent below his citywide average. In the 1975 Democratic primary he received only 40 percent of this area's vote—17 percent below his citywide average. The table also indicates that black voters in these wards discriminated among other machine candidates. The white machine candidate for city clerk in 1971 received 8.9 percent fewer votes than did the black machine candidate for city treasurer. And it was in these middle-class black areas that independent black candidates for aldermanic and state legislative positions were most successful. In other, less affluent parts of the black community, Daley and his Democratic machine did much better. As can be seen in table 3, Daley himself received 79 percent of the

TABLE 3

Daley and Democratic Percentage for Citywide Offices
in Selected Wards

	Middle Class Black Wards (N = 2)	Other Black Wards (N = 9)	White Wards (N = 21)
Mayor Daley (1971 general)	60.0	78.7	72.1
(1975 primary)	40.5	52.7	65.8
Black Democratic candidate for city treasurer (1971)	82.7	87.9	68.8
White Democratic candidate for city clerk (1971)	73.8	84.5	72.6

SOURCES: See notes to table 2 for sources and procedures used to construct this table.

Note that the falloff from the black candidate for city treasurer to the white candidate for city clerk in 1971 was 8.9 percent in black middle-class wards and only 3.4 percent in other black wards.

black vote in these areas in 1971, and 53 percent in the four-way Democratic primary in 1975. The white candidate for city clerk ran only 3.4 percent behind the black candidate for city treasurer. (Note also in this table that the machine was just as successful in obtaining white votes for its black candidates as it was in mobilizing votes for white candidates in working-class black areas.)

The success of the machine in poor black areas is striking when civil rights leaders had won few but symbolic concessions from city officials. One should not conclude too quickly that black civil rights leaders had no support among their own people. Integration meant equality, and, as an ideal, few in the black community were opposed —at least in the early and mid-sixties. Yet its immediate impact on poor residents in the heart of the black community was not obvious. They did not have the money to buy beautiful homes in white suburbs, they did not particularly want to "bus" their children long distances to attend schools in a hostile community, and they did not have the skills to gain admission to the building industry. The local precinct captain, on the other hand, could help them obtain a welfare check or perhaps find a job in any one of many federal programs that a Democratic administration in Washington had financed. Very likely, the masses of the black community were quite "rational" (in terms, at least, of their immediate self-interest) in choosing the machine over the reformers. The material benefits provided by the Daley regime were more valuable than the grand designs of white liberal reformers, civil rights leaders, and independent black politicians. Integration was a poor issue for destroying Chicago's political machine; in fact it may have saved it.

THE GENERAL SUPERINTENDENT

When Superintendent Benjamin Willis retired in 1966, primary responsibility for mediating these conflicting, changing political influences was charged to James F. Redmond, the new general superintendent. Redmond was born in Kansas City, Missouri, in 1915, and received his B.A. degree from Kansas City Teachers College in 1937 while serving as a teacher in the local public schools.[48] After wartime experience he earned his Ed.D. degree from Columbia Teachers College. At the same time he held increasingly important administrative positions in the Kansas City school system, which was superintended by Herold Hunt. When Hunt was asked in 1947 to become Chicago's school superintendent, he brought Redmond with him to serve as his assistant. In 1953, shortly before Hunt retired and Benjamin Willis was recruited to replace him, Redmond left Chicago to become superintendent of the New Orleans school system. In 1960 he supervised the initial, court-ordered integration of that city's school system. The event was marked by state intervention in the city's schools, with the legislature passing some twenty-nine laws designed to prevent integration, each of them being declared unconstitutional by the federal district judge.[49] Worse yet, the black elementary school children finally sent to the newly integrated schools were subjected to intense, prolonged verbal abuse. The following year Redmond left News Orleans to become a management consultant for the firm of Booz, Allen and Hamilton. In 1963 he assumed the superintendency of the small, prestige suburb of Syosset, New York, where he remained until in 1966 the Chicago school board asked him to become their superintendent.

Whatever difficulties Redmond might have encountered in the midst of racial crisis elsewhere, he seemed an excellent choice for Chicago. His former experience in Chicago was also appreciated by board members, including President Frank Whiston, the one member of the 1966 board whose tenure had extended that far back. At the same time Redmond had had no association with Benjamin Willis, whose controversial reign the board now wished to place firmly behind it. He was thus both an insider and an outsider. He was also Catholic. Above all, he was patient, tolerant and friendly. If he might have been more cautious than some would like, he was willing to listen carefully to all points of view. He was a refreshing change for Chicago. In contrast to Willis's tight reign, one could expect that under Redmond a wider array of political forces would help shape educational policy. As Redmond himself said to a group of principals,

> Our predecessors drew a circle and tried to close out politics. They also closed out society. Within the circle they established their programs of education, lived and worked and shared experiences with each other. . . .
> As individuals we now have to live with and in society. . . . Capitalize or lower case the word, but it will still mean political involvement in the community. The element missing from the challenge of years ago is the individual politician. . . . The successful politicians . . . will be those who, like us, are participating in finding solutions to society's problems and involved with all facets of the community in solving them.[50]

SUMMARY

In sum, school politics, Chicago style, was shaped by the political actions of the machine, the reform movement, and the changing politics in the black community. The machine played the dominant role, but in school matters the reformers have had a substantial sphere of influence, perhaps more than their electoral power would warrant. The clash between the machine and the reformers was not simply a struggle for power or a conflict among social classes. Although these aspects cannot be ignored, the two factions, above all, divided ideologically over issues that the school system had to resolve, the most controversial perhaps being the matter of school policy affecting race relationships. The internal politics of the black community thus was a potentially dynamic factor affecting the machine-reform struggle. On the one hand, an emerging reform-allied, civil rights leadership challenged the traditional neighborhood-school structure of the Chicago system. On the other hand, black voters and politicians remained loyal to the Democratic organization, limiting the impact of the civil rights movement on power relations in the city.

Two

PLURALIST AND IDEOLOGICAL
BARGAINING MODELS

Chicago's school board consisted of eleven individuals, each with his or her own interests, beliefs, perceptions, and capabilities. Some had past associations with the Democratic organization; others were known as independents who had little time for Democratic party politics. Members included businessmen, labor leaders, housewives, and professionals. Their ethnic origins varied from Anglo-Saxon to Polish, Irish to Puerto Rican, Italian to black. In publicly stated, widely read comments, board members seriously divided over important policy questions. Only by building coalitions, compromising differences, and reaching agreement could policy be formulated. Quite clearly, the Chicago school board was an arena for political bargaining.

Classifying their discusions and negotiations as bargaining, however, merges in one category patterns of political interaction that differ greatly in quality.[1] To take the example cited in chapter 1, Daley bargained with two types of community groups that, according to Mike Royko, visited his mayoral suite. In the first case the discussions were satisfying to all parties, whereas in the second both the mayor and community leaders parted frustrated and angry. A compromise was reached in the first instance, but in the second the bargain concluded was a reaffirmation of the status quo, clearly not acceptable to the groups who called on the mayor. Rather than characterize all such activities simply as bargaining games, we shall distinguish between *pluralist* and *ideological* bargaining. Although numerous differences between these two types of bargaining, including variations in conflict levels, can often be identified, the varying interests perceived to be of relevance—the stakes for which games are played—seem particularly crucial. Pluralist bargaining occurs when the dominant policy makers combine (1) an interest in maximizing votes with (2) an interest in compromising among group demands; ideological bargaining occurs when the dominant policy makers perceive the issue to raise large questions involving class, race, or regime interests.[2] From these varying perceptions of the stakes at issue, many other things flow.

BARGAINING MODEL A: PLURALIST BARGAINING
Vote Maximizing

To the extent that a political leader seeks to maximize votes in his forthcoming election, he pursues policies he believes are preferred by the majority of the electorate. In fact it is the desire of leaders for reelection which Anthony Downs and other analysts have identified as the mechanism by which democratic government can be realized in a large, complex industrial society.[3] The democracy of a New England town meeting, at which each citizen supposedly speaks his mind and the majority decides, is impossible in all but the smallest and most homogeneous of communities. Yet political leaders can implement what the majority prefer (or would prefer if they gave the matter consideration) as long as leaders are subject to popular control in free, competitive elections. Although imperfect information about voter opinions limits responsiveness, the politician, ambitious to remain in office, will anticipate as best he can what the public wants and will pursue appropriate policies so as to be rewarded with reelection.

Of course, such processes will not take place unless policy makers are subject to the control of the electorate. Public officials are not invariably beholden to the voting electorate even within a formally democratic polity. The Chicago school board was hardly at all responsible to Chicago voters, and therefore assumptions about vote maximization are of doubtful utility. Board members were appointed by the mayor to a five-year term of office (with the terms of office of two or three members expiring each year). If the voters were dissatisfied with board decisions, they theoretically could have elected a new mayor pledged to appoont board members with another point of view. But mayors were likely to be elected for reasons other than their appointments to the school board. And since a new mayor cannot appoint a board majority in less than three years (and mayors themselves hold office for four years), seven years could elapse between a shift in public opinion and an altered school policy. Moreover, in Chicago the mayor appoints board members upon the nomination of an advisory commission, which is in no way responsible to the electorate. If these considerations suggest that policy makers do more than simply maximize votes, urban scholars have taken them into account by further assuming that decision makers are interested in political compromise.

Compromise

The compromising decision maker is the political leader who responds sympathetically to the legitimate interests of all groups participating in the political process.[4] The compromiser is not interested solely in reelection, and therefore he does not hinge his decisions simply on what the majority wants. Rather, he feels that there are a variety of groups in the city with an interest in the character of the school system, and that each group may appropriately seek to protect or enhance its interests. Since he is realistic about the need for cooperation among a wide range of interests in order to keep a complex system a viable functioning entity, the compromiser will search for ways of satisfying—at least minimally—the various competing interests with a claim to be heard. He waits patiently in order to give all points of view an opportunity to express themselves, takes into account the intensity with which various interests feel about the issue, and mediates a reasonable compromise. Some combination of these two interests of policy makers has been the preferred explanation for their behavior in urban politics.

Combining Vote Maximization with Compromising Politics

Robert Dahl's classic volume on New Haven stressed the political leaders' interest in reelection.[5] He argued that even though mayors and other public officials made many of the decisions, the fact that political leaders sought reelection constrained them to pursue policies preferred by the majority. As long as a competitive, two-party system continued in the city, no elite could depart radically from popular preferences. Dahl nonetheless also noted the special deference given to the preferences of minorities, when held intensely. Political leaders seemed unwilling to antagonize specific interest groups with even a limited popular base. As a result, political influence varied from one issue area to another. Groups active and concerned about urban renewal were unlikely to be influential in educational politics or in the selection of party leaders (and vice versa). Power was fragmented, dispersed, multicentered, fractionated; influence depended upon the topic under discussion. One could not exercise power unless one actively sought to influence policy; since different people were concerned about different issues, the degrees of influence and the persons wielding it varied with the policy area. Dahl was none-

theless able to interrelate the politicians' ambitions for office and the
deference they gave to minority interests. He did so by emphasizing
that majorities consist of a coalition of minorities:

> To build an effective political coalition, rewards must be con-
> ferred upon (or at least promised to) individuals, groups, and
> various categories of citizens. . . .
> In devising strategies for building coalitions and allocating
> rewards, one must take into account a large number of different
> categories of citizens. . . . A successful political coalition neces-
> sarily rests upon a multiplicity of groups and categories.[6]

Dahl made the same point more concretely a hundred pages later
in summarizing his interpretation of influence patterns under New
Haven's Mayor Lee: "The preference of any group that could swing
its weight at election time—teachers, citizens of the Hill, Negroes on
Dixwell Avenue, or Notables—would weigh heavily in the calculation of the Mayor."[7] In other words, the attention that political leaders paid to the expressed interests of various groups and categories
of voters is an integral part of an intelligent political strategy designed to win forthcoming elections.

Perhaps partly because Chicago politics have not been as competitive as New Haven's, Banfield's analysis of Chicago's mayor did not
focus simply on the mayoral need to win future elections.[8] The interpretation instead depends more heavily on the politician's interest in
compromise. The mayor is concerned about the welfare of the city,
but the only way he can determine how to advance the city's welfare
is to listen to the specific claims of particular welfares within the city.
In developing this view, Banfield begins by noting that issues are the
product of the maintenance and enhancement needs of large, formal
organizations, not necessarily the articulated preferences of sizable
minorities. He then argues that political leaders move slowly before
reaching decisions so as to provide all the variety of special interests
relevant to the issue at hand an opportunity to articulate their view-
points. The intensity with which various organizations agitate on
behalf of their position gives the political leader some idea of the
importance of that interest to the community. "The 'representative-
ness' of a position is judged in part by the number and character of
the civic associations supporting it." And this is a reasonable way
of determining the interest of the community as a whole because
"each association has created for itself a corporate personality and
aura. It has made itself both the custodian and the symbol, as well
as the spokesman, of certain values which are widely held in the
community."[9]

Banfield emphasized that the mayor considered interests as well as power in making his decision. In the cases Banfield studied, the mayor had to consider, among other things, interests the city had in its downtown business district, conservation of its park land, an urban university, its rapid transit system, and its hospital and medical facilities. What seemed as important as the political power of any of these interests was the importance of that interest to the welfare of the city as a whole and the seriousness with which specific proposals affected these interests. Policy outcomes were "therefore both a 'resultant' (from the standpoint of the interested parties) and a 'solution' (from the standpoint of the mayor), who decided which interested parties should be allowed to enter the process, how their ends should be weighted, and what importance should be accorded to 'public values.' "[10]

Banfield nonetheless implied that such a concern was consistent with a politician's desire for reelection. A careful balancing of interests in a city would lead to a reasonable level of satisfaction with the mayor's performance among most people in the city. According to Banfield, members of the political community have a variety of particular interests: an interest in hospital care, conservation, maintenance of the center city, economic growth, a rapid transit system, and so on. Not everyone has an identical interest in each of these matters, but directly or indirectly the great majority of citizens have some interest in all of them. Formal organizations, voluntary associations, and individual experts specialize in articulating the general community's concern in particular areas of public policy. By giving weight to the opinions of experts and organizations and by balancing among their conflicting opinions, the mayor reaches decisions that are acceptable to the majority of voters needed to sustain his position of power.

Clearly, Dahl and Banfield both attempt to combine politicians' interests in reelection and in compromise in presenting their total interpretation or model of urban decision-making processes. Dahl combines the two ideas by arguing that majorities are formed by building coalitions among minority groups. Banfield sees minorities as specialized articulators of interests more generally shared throughout the community. We shall therefore treat this view as a single model of policy making, which we shall refer to as bargaining model A, or the pluralist bargaining model.

Characteristics of Pluralist Bargaining

Significantly, Dahl, Banfield and other writers within this tradition have not only developed a model of the bases upon which elected officials make their decisions but a model of the processes of policy formation taken as a whole. Since political leaders shape policy by compromising articulated interests in order to pursue more effectively their own reelection, groups, organizations, competing elites, and other political participants adopt strategies appropriate to the situation. Specifically, the model expects that politically active groups (and groups are typically the basic unit of analysis in studies utilizing the pluralist bargaining model) will: (1) concentrate their energies on those issues having the greatest immediate impact on their interests; (2) develop new alliances as the issues and tactical situation change; (3) migrate from one political faction to another as political leaders' positions on matters of group concern are modified; and (4) compromise their differences within a system tending toward equilibrium. Each of these characteristics of group activity is worthy of some elaboration.

From the pluralist bargaining perspective, groups, first of all, concentrate on issues in which they have the greatest immediate stake. Just as the politician is interested in his own immediate political future, groups define their interests narrowly, seeking to maximize those very specific objectives that have a large material payoff to themselves. As a result, the groups of greatest significance in the political process are those that have relatively small, homogeneous memberships and which concentrate on a specific area of public policy.[11] Groups with broad objectives, which attempt to appeal to widely diffused sentiments, are infrequent, ineffective political participants. Not only do they find it difficult to mobilize potential adherents to their cause, but they have difficulty legitimizing their claims in the bargaining process. To the extent that decision makers are pluralist bargainers, they seek to compromise issues through decomposing, disaggregating demands. Groups generating highly specific demands on a limited range of policy questions can be and will be the more easily accommodated.

All groups, to be sure, seek to demonstrate that their demands, while of great concern to themselves, are not seriously contrary to the interests of the public at large. Teachers claim their demands are in the "best interest of the children," neighborhood groups only want for their schools "what other communities already enjoy," and taxpayer organizations claim they are defending "the interests of the average homeowner." In order to promote their cause, groups are thus at times willing to publicize their demands and accentuate the diffuse benefits they are expected to produce. But, significantly, groups focus more on winning public acquiescence than building a broad coalition of active supporters. Specific demands by narrow-based organizations are the normal components of the policy-making process.

Secondly, the pluralist bargaining model expects that as issues change, the participating groups and the alliances among them will change. Simply because most groups have narrowly defined objectives, their interest in policy questions is highly variable. The movement in and out of the bargaining arena is rapid and continuous. And even when a group remains to contest several matters under dispute, it discovers that its allies have changed. Opponents on one issue may be neutral on a second and allies on a third. From above the field of battle, the analyst can see numerous cross-cutting cleavages which divide the bargainers in a myraid of variegated patterns.[12] "To overstate the point," Dahl says, "every ally is sometimes an enemy and every enemy is sometimes an ally."[13]

Thirdly, the bargaining process, according to this model, is characterized by transient relationships between broad social groups and political factions. The model does not assert that such inclusive social categories as class, race, and ethnicity are without political significance. Issues do arise that are at times meaningful to large blocs within the population. However, this seldom leads to massive, continuing support by any single social group for any one set of political elites. Specifically, major political parties do not depend heavily on the overwhelming support of any one or two well-defined social groups. On the contrary, whenever a group migrates heavily toward one partisan faction, the other develops a strategy to win a goodly portion of the group back to its side. As a result, religious, class, ethnic, and racial groups have typically divided in their political support. To be sure, Democrats may be more popular among skilled workers than among businessmen, and more successful in appealing to Catholics than Protestants. Republicans, on the other hand, do particularly well in small towns and among northerners of Anglo-Saxon descent. But the relationships between these social categories and political parties vary over time and are never very strong. If the Democrats under Kennedy do well in attracting Catholics, then the Republicans try to win back some of this group by promoting such policies as aid to parochial schools and abortion control. In brief, "polarization of politics along social, economic, or regional lines is inhibited."[14]

Finally, to the extent that the pluralist bargaining model accurately portrays the character of American politics, it provides an important explanation for its stability. If groups limit their demands to narrow policy questions in which they have an immediate interest, political leaders can respond to the concerns of one group without unduly antagonizing others. If the alliances among groups constantly change, groups will restrain their attacks on opponents for fear of jeopardizing the possibility of future political alliances. As Aaron Wildavsky has observed, the "opponent of today may be the indispensable ally of tomorrow, and . . . it is most unwise to alienate other leaders for the sake of one policy to the extent that agreement on other policies is precluded."[15] Finally, the tenuous connection between social divisions and political cleavages facilitates compromise, limits the rate of change, keeps the system at least partially open to all groups, protects the most critical concerns of each, and, in the end, preserves system stability and persistence. In short, the pluralist bargaining model provides an explanation for elite decision making, group interaction, and system stability. Even more, the model suggests that American political practice is roughly in accord with two of its basic principles: rule by the majority and respect for the rights of minorities.

These considerations alone make the pluralist bargaining model a tempting framework for the analysis of Chicago school politics—especially when Chicago's political bargaining processes were so brilliantly analyzed from this perspective more than a decade ago. And a cursory glance at the composition of the Chicago Board of Education in 1968 would seem to confirm the continued relevance of the interpretation Banfield reached in his classic study, *Political Influence*. Three businessmen, two union officials, a representative of the PTA, two (and later three) blacks, a Pole, two Jews, five Catholics, and four Protestants: these were the interests directly represented on the board of education. If Banfield himself did not study school affairs, does not this array of interests on the board by itself indicate that the pluralist model is as appropriate a framework for analyzing this policy area as it is for so many others?

Limits on the Pluralist Bargaining Model

Although a definitive answer to this question remains one of the major foci of the ensuing study, certain elements in Chicago's school politics do not fit easily within the pluralist bargaining model that has been elaborated. The bitter controversy over Benjamin Willis, the enduring social base of the political machine and the reform movement, and the competing ideologies of machine and reform politicians all suggest the need for an alternative framework for analyzing Chicago school politics.

In addition, there are more general reasons for not relying exclusively on the pluralist bargaining model. As convincing a portrayal of American politics as the pluralist bargaining model has proved to be, only the most tentative connection between public opinion and elite behavior has been established by analysts working within this tradition.[16] Certainly, public opinion on some issues can powerfully constrain elite behavior. A mayor in the 1960s could not pursue distinctly unpopular policies on matters touching race relations, "law and order," economic prosperity, and property taxes without endangering his political coalition. But on other matters (or even with respect to significant aspects of policy on these salient issues), political leaders have considerable flexibility in the decisions they reach. Bargaining model A, as developed by Dahl and Banfield, exaggerates citizen interest in, and awareness of, political issues.

The analyst cannot resolve the problem by speaking of coalitions of minorities, each of which has specialized interests. The citizens particularly interested in educational policy, those intensely concerned about parks and conservation policies, those vitally concerned about the details of urban renewal policy, even together with a multitude of other special interest groups, do not add up to a significant portion of the electorate. Nor do these special interests speak for a broad segment of opinion, as Banfield would have us believe. Most people in the city do not *really* care if the city has a convention hall, if welfare agencies merge or remain separate, if the rapid transit system gets an additional subsidy from the state, or if a big state university is built in the Chicago area. Most of the time political leaders can ignore special interest groups in making decisions, which is one reason that mayors and other political leaders are approached deferentially by those pleading on behalf of a special cause. A political leader knows that if he acts appropriately on a few major issues, he can make decisions with great flexibility on other, less crucial matters. Certain well-known southern senators have learned this lesson well. Provided they voted properly on race-related issues, Senators William Fulbright and Sam Ervin knew that they could take stands on foreign policy and civil liberties issues that differed from the positions of a majority of their constituents. In the quiet, covert, less newsworthy arena of city government, leader flexibility is even greater.[17]

If politicians have a considerable degree of latitude in policy formation, it would seem that an adequate account of this process would have to consider their goals and policy objectives. This is one advantage of bargaining model B, the ideological bargaining model, to which we now turn.

BARGAINING MODEL B: IDEOLOGICAL BARGAINING

Few studies of urban politics have found the concept of ideology useful for interpreting the policy-making process or the workings of urban institutions. Even Agger, Goldrich, and Swanson, in their path-breaking work on urban ideologies, applied the concept only in small and medium-sized communities and suggested that it would have more limited applicability in the study of big-city politics.[18] In large measure, this is due to use of the concept of ideology by scholars in a host of diverse ways to convey significantly different meanings.[19] I believe, nonetheless, that one definition of the term useful for the analysis of policy formation, yet consistent with many of the connotations and implications that the concept has in ordinary usage, can facilitate the study of politics in even the largest American cities.[20]

Definition of Ideology

The concept of ideology has been used to characterize two dimensions of political thought: its internal consistency, cohesion, and comprehensiveness, and its extremist nature within a given cultural context. Many uses of the term confuse these two dimensions, and it is easy to understand why. Those who suggest major departures from the status quo, either in a revolutionary or reactionary direction, usually defend their proposals with a more or less comprehensive statement on the interdependencies among social, economic, and political institutions and the consequent need to restructure many, if not all, of them, simultaneously. Defense of the status quo or modest reform proposals need not be defended in such sweeping categories. Nonetheless, a set of political ideas which defend existing institutions or call for only moderate changes in their character can be systematically elaborated, can cover as comprehensive a set of topics, and can be as coherent as a revolutionary program. And it is these characteristics —coherence, consistency, and comprehensiveness—of a set of political beliefs that permit an analyst to label them appropriately an ideology.

Politically significant ideologies express the interests of inclusive social roles within a society. Most familiarly, socialism is an ideological formulation of desired social and political changes expected to serve worker interests, whereas conservative defenses of capitalism are espoused by, and used to protect the interests of, business entrepeneurs and corporate executives or, more generally, those in dominant positions in a society's economic structures. More recently, ideological formulations of the interests of blacks and whites in their racial roles have become a significant aspect of American politics.

Of course, there is no perfect correspondence between role interests and ideological formulations. There exists no warrant for such socio-logical determinism. The same interests can generate different ideologies in varying cultural contexts, and in many instances the interests of significant social roles will not be articulated ideologically in a given milieu. Ideologies are nonetheless more than free-floating statements unrelated to the structured relationships among groups and segments of a society. Ideologies in fact often champion in a straight-forward manner the interests of those in particular social roles. In other cases, the implications of an ideological viewpoint for various social roles, though not clearly spelled out, can be easily detected through both consideration of the consequences of proposed policies and analysis of their social base of support.

For the most part, ideological formulations are expressions of the interests of inclusive rather than exclusive social roles. By inclusive social roles, I refer to roles played by many members of the society, which have a significant impact on those individuals' lives. Ideologies are constructed around such inclusive social roles as those defined by race and class, because the welfare of those playing the roles is necessarily affected by a broad range of economic and social policies. As the number of policies relevant to a role increases, the need for comprehensive, coherent, consistent—that is, ideological—formulation of policy positions increases.

The concept of ideology is less appropriate when used to discuss the political beliefs of those seeking changes, no matter how drastic, affecting the welfare of those in more exclusive social roles—roles encompassing small numbers of people or roles affecting only a limited aspect of the lives of role incumbents. An organization of air-control personnel, for example, may demand that their pay be doubled, their working hours cut in half, and their fringe benefits drastically augmented. Although they might defend such demands in terms of the arduous and critical task they perform, few would either accuse or praise the organization for taking an ideological stance.

Regime Ideologies

If ideologies articulate the interests of broad social roles, this does not necessarily mean that only race and class roles have been the bases for ideological formulation in American politics. Indeed, it is just such an assumption (however implicitly it has been made) which has led many analysts to conclude that ideologies are of little relevance to the study of American urban politics. As Robert Dahl has observed, most politicians have taken "the existing socio-economic structure . . . as given, except for minor details."[21] But American politicians have quarreled at great length over the political structure of American cities; as Dahl observes in the same context, "local reform movements have concentrated on defects in the political system."[22] And these conflicts over the political structure have been guided by divergent emphases on the several authority structures that shape and control role relationships between urban citizens and their authorities. Just as class and race roles are rooted in a society's social structure, so the citizen's role is a function of its authority structures. In the United States four distinctive authority structures can be readily identified: democratic participation, rationalization of governmental policy, constitutionalism, or the protection of individual rights, and institutionalized bargaining, that is, the introduction of social change incrementally and only after deferring to existing vested interests.[23] The existence of these structures is marked by widespread verbal commitment to these principles and by roughly corresponding behavioral practices—although, as with any other structural relationship, substantial deviations always exist. Citizens have what may be called a regime interest in maintaining and enhancing these authority structures, although citizen recognition of these interests may vary over time and from place to place. Significantly, certain political groups have a highly manifest awareness of certain of these regime interests and, indeed, develop ideologies which give important guidelines for their orientations toward urban public policies.

As we saw in chapter 1, the two most significant ideological factions in Chicago were concerned with one or another regime interest. The machine politicians, I argued, were most concerned with the maintenance of the institutionalized bargaining authority structure, while the reformers were more concerned with maintaining democratic participation and rationalized government policies. As Wilson observes in his study of reformers in Chicago and other cities, "the concern for goals displayed by amateur political clubs not only tends to thrust them in the direction of extreme statement of these goals, it also imparts a quest for goals of general or national significance."[24] Machine politicians, too, have an ideological commitment to the principles and practices of institutionalized bargaining. Indeed, at times even these master politicos will place the preservation of this bargaining structure above any immediate electoral gain. In Banfield's analysis, institutionalized bargaining and the pursuit of power are treated as synonymous. But if the overlap is considerable, it is nonetheless useful to understand that the Chicago machine, though it bargained with diverse groups and interests, responded differently to demands from interests outside the institutionalized bargaining order. With these "illegitimate" interests, pluralist bargaining could not proceed without violating a basic component of the ideology that supported and legitimated the structure of power that the Chicago machine had constructed.

The same point can be made analytically. A clear relationship exists between the institutionalized bargaining authority structure and the utility of the pluralist bargaining model. The utility of the model is obviously enhanced in the American context by the existence of this structural relationship that has endured since the beginning of the republic and has been explicated and defended theoretically by such thinkers as James Madison, John Calhoun, Pendleton Herring, Herbert Agar, and, most recently, Robert Dahl and Edward Banfield. The pluralist bargaining model, however, implies responsiveness to all the significant interests in the society so as to insure both majority rule and minority rights. The institutionalized bargaining structure, as it works in practice, requires deference only to already vested interests; indeed, the very protection of these interests demands resistance to the "vesting" of interests whose political strength is only emerging. One example illustrates the point. Since the New Deal, policies affecting most labor unions have been formulated only after the unions have been consulted; but before the transformation in the structures of authority, American constitutional theory and political practice permitted, even required, that unions be excluded from the bargaining system.

Characteristics of Ideological Bargaining

The ideological bargaining model can also be used to characterize the policy-making process taken as a whole. In contrast to the pluralist bargaining model, it anticipates that: (1) participants in the policy-making process will include groups committed to broad-gauge objectives who become involved in a range of policy questions; (2) such groups will find similar allies and similar enemies across a range of policy questions; (3) enduring and significant linkages between inclusive social groups and important political factions will occur; and (4) groups will find defeat of opposition preferable to "reasonable" compromise. The points deserve some amplification.

From the perspective of the ideological bargaining model, policy-making processes involve groups and individuals other than those with an immediate and vested interest in a particular issue. At least some important participants will view many urban controversies over proposed policies from a broader perspective, examining the effects of proposed policies on more inclusive social relationships. Thus, Agger, Goldrich, and Swanson in their study of ideological politics in four smaller American cities, write of "inner cliques" who:

were regarded by others as in some sense central political figures who stood for or embodied political programs, perspectives, or preferences of some importance in community politics. . . . The inner cliques did three things more consistently than most other political leaders: first, they propounded general doctrines of their political ideologies; second, they applied those doctrines to decisional questions and announced the "proper" decisional preferences and outcomes to others; third, they acted as the chiefs of staff, the planners of the broad strategies to be followed by members of their groups, in the making of the political decisions.[25]

In other words, some set of participants—they need not be formally organized interest groups—will view prominent issues from a longer-range, broader, more ideological perspective, and these views will not be of trivial significance to the outcome. Agger et al. imply that the role of such participants tends to be covert, but this may not always be the case. At times some of those identifying the broadest repercussions of a policy may be generating the most political conflict. More on that below.

Secondly, the ideological bargaining model expects to find enduring cleavages in the political life of the community. Coalitions on one issue tend to be similar to coalitions on second, third, and forth issues deliberated in a community. The consistency of the belief system of ideologues produces reasonably consistent actions over time and across a range of issues. Ideologically motivated participants see a variety of problems from a consistent perspective; they see interrelationships among the various policy questions with which they must deal; and they establish a consistent orientation with respect to most of them. Liberals concerned about the welfare of workers can be expected to oppose conservative, business-oriented interests on a range of policies affecting such varied matters as health insurance, social security, tax policy, mechanisms for allocating scarce energy resources, and aid to education. Lowi's discussion of redistributive politics makes this point succinctly:

> Owing to . . . the impasse (or equilibrium) in relations among broad social classes of the entire society, the political structure of the redistributive arena seems to be highly stabilized, virtually institutionalized. . . . Shared interests are sufficiently stable and clear and consistent to provide the foundation for ideologies.[26]

Thirdly, from the ideological bargaining perspective, the conflicts between competing political factions in American politics involve ideologically significant issues that affect the welfare of broad social groups. Leaders of political parties or other significant political movements are committed to certain ideological objectives that have motivated them to participate in politics. As much as political realism forces them to consider the electoral situation, their own ideology not only colors their view of the best way to maximize votes but indicates policy goals to be pursued independently of electoral considerations.[27] Whenever voter interest is not apparent, an issue is likely to be treated by political elites in ways consistent with their ideology. And even when a policy may be politically costly, an ideologically motivated leadership will nonetheless pursue it. But since ideologies are not neutral with respect to the interests of broad social groups, one expects to find enduring alliances between certain political factions and specific social groups. To cite just one example, David Greenstone, in his analysis of the relationship between labor unions and the Democratic party, found a link so close and so enduring— at least since the beginning of the New Deal—that he has characterized labor as a "valued and integral part of the Democrats' normal campaign apparatus."[28] And it is quite clear from his analysis that the link is strengthened as much by ideological rapport as by any immediate calculations of group interest.

Finally, one can expect that political decision making will involve considerable political controversy and, in the end, political victories and defeats, if the ideological bargaining model is applicable. An ideologically committed policy maker does not alter his position easily. He is generally unpersuaded by group pressures, noisy demonstrations, lengthy public hearings, detailed private communiqués. His political position is likely to be shaken only if (1) expert testimony indicates that the goal he is pursuing will not be achieved by the means that he intended to employ, or (2) individuals or groups with a known ideological preference that is similar to his have taken a contrary position on the issue at hand. The ideologue is not interested in compromise for its own sake; he will only compromise if forced to do so by the political power of the opposition. The ideologue sees the issues as conflicts over principles rather than as competition among specific interests. Convinced of the correctness of his position, the ideologue is not likely to stray from it when subjected to the traditional tactics and strategies of group politics. Rather, he will become angry with the "pressure" being placed upon him, and will feel it is his duty to stand up against these pressures.

Consequently, a crucial group strategy will be to place ideologically allied actors in strategically placed positions. Groups seek to elect or to have appointed favorably predisposed ideologues to positions of authority. In fact advantaged groups prefer ideological to pluralist decision makers, because the ideological decision maker will try on his own to protect the group's interest rather than simply responding to mobilized group influence. On the other hand, if the decision maker is ideologically opposed to a group's position, the group is at a severe disadvantage. Whereas in the pluralist bargaining process groups could win victories simply by demonstrating that they *could* defeat decision makers, in ideological bargaining, groups *must* defeat ideological opponents (that is, remove them from office) in order to win policy victories.

Decisional outcomes in an ideological bargaining game will be determined by the ideologically dominant perspective among those in authoritative positions; an ideologically cohesive majority can administer regular and repeated defeats to the minority. Change can occur quickly, but this is most likely to happen when decision makers change.

To the extent that the ideological bargaining model is applicable, the stability of the political order seems less assured. Whereas pluralist bargaining insures stability as a byproduct of conflict and compromise over particular issues, the pattern of cleavage identified by the ideological bargaining model points to the sources of social and political change in a community. If conflicts reinforce one another, involve broad social categories, place ideologically committed elites in confrontation with one another, are not amenable to compromise, the wounds in the social order are rubbed repeatedly. Of course, ideological conflict may not necessarily lead to system change. Urban ideologies included strong commitments to some of the existing authority structures of the policy. But the maintenance of the regime depended not on the accidents of the bargaining process but on the durability of the support by leaders and public for the principles upon which the regime was founded.

CONCLUSIONS: COMPARING THE TWO BARGAINING MODELS

Determining whether the ideological or the pluralist model applies in any particular bargaining instance is complicated by the difficulty, if not the impossibility, of interpreting motives of political actors. Did a board member act for reasons of political ambition, out of a desire for compromise, or out of a conviction that his decision was the only option in accord with his principles? Any attempt to suggest the "real" reasons for the decision involves the imputation of motives to individuals with whom one may not be personally acquainted, a risky undertaking. Undoubtedly, any single assumption will oversimplify the cognitive processes actually taking place. On the other hand, some assumptions about the bases of political action are more useful than others. Some assumptions can explain a wide range of actions over an extended period of time. They are more consistent with the totality of available data on decision making. They may even have predictive value. Although these assumptions cannot be shown conclusively to correspond with the "real" reasons for the decision, they may nonetheless be extremely useful for understanding, interpreting, and even predicting political action.

Perhaps because motives are hard to detect, even careful observers of Chicago politics have disagreed over the character of its bargaining processes. On the one hand, Edward Banfield found a more or less consensual decision-making process, in which the policy makers took into account the whole range of interests articulated by groups and organizations. Royko's more journalistic account, on the other hand, perceived the dominant political leadership as unyielding, arrogant, and unresponsive to the concerns of all but a few vested interests. As we shall see, both views could be presented persuasively, because Chicago politics in the late sixties was marked by both pluralist and ideological patterns of policy formation.

Three

IDEOLOGICAL BARGAINING ON THE
SCHOOL BOARD

Many school board decision-making processes are marked by an appearance of consensus. At times the consensus is genuine, as school boards depend heavily on their superintendent for information and guidance.[1] In other cases the consensus is only apparent, as boards attempt to keep public involvement in their internal disputes as minimal as possible.[2] In such circumstances one might find it difficult to apply either pluralist or ideological models of political bargaining. But the Chicago school board in the late sixties was so marked by public disagreement, even acrimony, that the pattern of bargaining among board members could be relatively easily observed. Indeed, at almost every meeting during these years, the verbal divisions within the board translated into at least a few roll call votes on which the board members publicly divided. This fact permits us to analyze some of the patterns of conflict within the board. The data will help us determine whether the type of political bargaining on the board can best be characterized by the pluralist or the ideological bargaining model.

Analysis of roll call data, of course, cannot provide information on all aspects of the policy-making process. It cannot identify the groups initiating proposals, the role of the board's administrative staff, or the consequences of the decisions for various segments of the community. But the votes have the advantages of being publicly available, "hard" data about concrete behaviors of some consequence, which are relatively easy to collect over a fairly long period of time (thereby providing a historical perspective on school policy formation), and are amenable to manipulation by certain statistical techniques that permit efficient statement of a great deal of information. Although such analysis is no substitute for the case study material presented later, it may suggest the extent to which conclusions from

56

those case studies may be generalized to Chicago school politics as a whole.

The data permit us to test at least in a partial way the relative adequacy of the pluralist and ideological bargaining models in three respects. (1) Through statistical analysis one can determine whether or not the conflicts on the Chicago school board are multiple and cross-cutting or whether they have a unitary dimension which leads allies and enemies to square off against one another repeatedly over a range of policy questions. (2) By examining the substantive content of the issues, it may be possible to identify whether or not there is any ideological stance that could account for the pattern of conflict. (3) If there is a dominant cleavage on the board, analysis of the social background of board members can permit some assessment of the extent to which these are rooted in conflicts among social groups.

CONFLICT PATTERNS: UNITARY OR CROSS-CUTTING?

In testing whether or not conflicts are multiple and cross-cutting (as the pluralist model suggests) or repetitive and reinforcing (as is predicted by the ideological model), we confronted certain limitations posed by our roll call data. In the first place, analysis of the roll calls of the Chicago school board does not permit examination of the groups and organizations participating in school policy issues. But it does facilitate examination of the cross-cutting or reinforcing character of conflicts among board members themselves. If the members continually divide in new ways, one could reasonably account for such a pattern in terms of changing pressures directed at the board. If the members divide along the same lines on most roll calls, this can most reasonably be explained in terms of board member ideologies that interrelate a variety of issues from a consistent perspective.

Secondly, the analysis examines only the nonunanimous roll calls cast by the school board. The methodology obviously cannot examine the bases of board cleavages when they do not become evident in the public record. And it must be said at the outset that split votes are cast on only a small percentage of the total number of items of business coming before the board—even in the most controversial periods of the board's history. While some of the most important matters may never reach the school board for a decision,[3] many items of business are technical matters that are decided by the board only because state law requires it. For example, purchases of supplies account for a large number of the specific decisions the board takes. Other items are approved unanimously by a board dependent on the judgment of the superintendent and his administrative staff. In still other cases, specific items only implement generally accepted school policy. Indeed, it is just such instances that will turn our attention later to the two unitary policy-making models. Yet examination of matters so divisive that they publicly pitted board members against one another at least directs our analytical attention to those questions which school policy elites believed to be important issues.[4]

Changing Levels of Conflict

That the conflict within the Chicago Board of Education varied significantly over time is evident from changes in the number of nonunanimous roll calls from year to year.[5] As can be seen in figure 1, the number of divided votes was never higher than twenty in the late forties and fifties. At times the number dropped to three or four split votes during the course of an entire school year. It is hard to believe that this reflects the true state of opinion within the board; it is more likely that during this period board members acted according to a norm that frowned upon public displays of conflict. After completing his service on the board during this period, one member wrote of

> the unity which the Board frequently adopts in responding to criticism and pressures by employees, civic groups, and the press. . . . The individual member ordinarily hesitates to venture into stormy areas by himself or to disassociate himself from the stand taken by the Board, on a particularly delicate or controversial matter.[6]

Beginning about 1960, board members became less hesitant about openly disagreeing with their colleagues. The number of nonunanimous roll calls increased markedly, running between 30 and as high as 112 split votes in 1965. The greater level of public controversy in the sixties reflects the extent to which school policy had become "politicized," that is, had become a point of discussion in the community at large. The debates over school integration, Benjamin Willis's resistance to civil rights demands, and the achievement of collective bargaining rights by the Chicago Teachers Union opened up the processes of policy formation in Chicago just as similar developments had comparable consequences in many other northern cities.[7]

Consistency of Conflict

The political bargaining among board members was becoming more public in the sixties. But what was its character? Were the issues coming before the board dividing it along similar lines again and

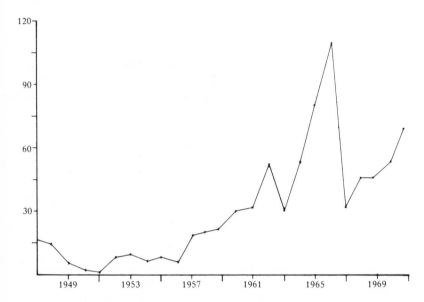

FIG. 1. Number of nonunanimous roll calls per year, Chicago Board of Education, 1946–71. Information was coded by school year, not the calendar year; 1947 figures, for example, are for the period September 1946 to September 1947.

again? Or did the board respond differently to the various matters on its agenda? In order to investigate this question, we performed a cluster analysis of all nonunanimous roll calls. We first divided the postwar era into seventeen distinct time periods, each coinciding with the life of a single board. This was necessary because the Chicago Board of Education, unlike the U. S. Congress, does not have a major change in its composition at specific points in time. Instead, as members resign or their terms expire, new appointments are made by the mayor. As a result, the composition of the board at some times has remained unchanged for over two years and at other times has changed twice within the course of a single year. Each time one or more new members were added to the board, we have treated it as a "new" school board for the purposes of the cluster analysis.

The cluster analysis for each of these seventeen analytically defined school boards was performed by intercorrelating every roll call of a board with every other roll call.[8] This undertaking generated a matrix of correlations which was then visually inspected. Whenever a cluster of intercorrelations, each with a value of .7 or higher, was found, it was determined that a significant cleavage existed. We then

calculated the percentage of all nonunanimous roll calls falling within
the largest and second largest clusters of interrelated roll calls for
each school board. The results of this analysis are reported in table 4.

These procedures, which have been used in the study of legislative
voting behavior,[9] are a useful beginning toward systematically identifying the degree to which conflicts are multidimensional and cross-
cutting as opposed to unidimensional and reinforcing.[10] If nonunani-

TABLE 4

Nonunanimous Roll Call Votes on Board of Education

	Number of Nonunanimous Roll Calls	Percent in One Conflict Dimension	Percent in Two Conflict Dimensions
1946–47	10	70%	80%
1947–48	16	62	93
1948–52	24	33	54
1952–54	11	36	73
1954–55	6	. . .[1]	. . .
1955–56	3	. . .	. . .
1956	1	. . .	. . .
1956–57	17	70	70
1957–58	11	54	54
1958–61	70	37	60
1961	5	. . .	. . .
1961–62	36	89	97
1962–63	34	73	91
1963–64	37	90	90
1964	18	84	84
1964–66	174	50	65
1966–68	95	56	77
1968–69	51	43	72
1969–70	28	75	89
1970	37	43	81
1971 (Jan.-June)	36	44	72
1971 (July-Sept.)	19	63%	84%
Averages			
1946–61	12 per yr.	52%	69%
1961–66	51 per yr.	79	85
1966–71	53 per yr.	54%	79%

NOTE: The definition of a single board was one in which the membership
did not change. Boards could thus have a term of one meeting or several
years. Dates given are approximate. The exact date at which a "new" board
came into being depended on the arrival of a new board member, which could
occur at any time during the year.

[1]If a board had no more than six split roll calls, intercorrelations were not
computed.

mous roll calls within the life of a single school board were totally unrelated to one another, new coalitions would have formed around each division. Allies on one matter would be enemies on others. The pattern of alliance formation would be so variegated that it would not make sense to speak of factions, coalitions, or the like. The pluralist bargaining model would be the obvious vantage point from which to explain the policy-making process. At the other extreme, if all nonunanimous roll calls were perfectly correlated with one another, if the board divided along a single dimension of cleavage with one polar group always contesting the same opposing group and with the same moderates always holding the balance of power in the middle, then the ideological bargaining model would seem to be more relevant. One could then usefully speak of the board dividing into opposing factions and inquire into the substance of the issues over which they disagreed.

Neither of these extremes obtained, of course. But inspection of table 4 reveals that a high percentage of the nonunanimous roll calls did fall within only one or two dimensions of cleavage. While the reader should examine the overall pattern for himself, the significance of the table can be illustrated by presenting one example in detail. The school board which sat from the period 1958 to 1961 divided seventy times. Thirty-seven percent of these roll calls fell within only one dimension of cleavage, and 60 percent fell within two dimensions. In other words 37 percent of the votes intercorrelated at a .7 level or better (indeed, most were perfect correlations). Similarly, another 23 percent of the votes clustered together within a second dimension of cleavage. In other words, over a majority of the divisions on the board divided the group in one of two ways.

This finding for the 1958–61 school board is in a sense ambiguous. Is the glass half-empty or is it half-full? Not all the votes fall neatly into any one or two dimensions. Yet over one-third of the votes divided the board in a consistent fashion, and nearly two-thirds of the votes fell within just two conflict dimensions. The splits were regular enough so that one can identify factions analytically that were in all probability meaningful to the actors participating in the controversy.

What can be said about the 1958–61 board can also be said of the boards of the late forties and fifties taken as a whole. Although there is some variation from year to year, in the average year 52 percent of the roll calls fell within a single conflict dimension, and 69 percent of the roll calls fell within two dimensions. Although conflict during this period was to some extent multiple and cross-cutting, at a minimum it can be asserted that certain cleavages occurred regularly enough so that the board can be said to have identifiable factions.

This level of conflict consistency held even in the late forties and fifties when controversy was minimal and muted. In the sixties, the patterning of controversy within the school board was much more apparent. Whereas only 52 percent of the votes fell within one conflict dimension in the earlier period, in the sixties this increased to 79 percent of all divided roll calls. The proportion of votes falling within the two largest dimensions increased from 69 percent in the forties and fifties to 85 percent in the sixties. As the number of divided votes in the sixties increased, the consistency of the division on the board also increased. Board members found it necessary to disagree publicly more frequently, and they found that, more often than not, their allies on the board tended to be the same individuals. Cleavages occurred more frequently, and they were more consistent when they did occur. However, with Willis' departure, conflicts on the board receded, though not to their pre-civil rights levels. Although the number of split votes remained at an average of more than fifty per year even after Redmond arrived, the proportion of votes falling within one conflict dimension fell to an average of 54 percent. Those within just two such dimensions of conflict dropped to 79 percent. The ideological quality of the civil rights struggle slowly began to abate. As the demands of civil rights groups were articulated more sharply and clearly, the pluralist bargaining model became less applicable.

Conflict Consistency over Time

Especially at the height of the civil rights controversy, the same patterning of conflict regularly occurred. Board members discovered themselves voting with similar allies and against similar enemies with some regularity. But did this conflict dimension reproduce itself from year to year, or did each "new" (in the analytical sense mentioned earlier) school board divide along completely new lines? To examine this possibility, we compared the cleavage dimensions on earlier boards with later boards of slightly differing composition.

Certain rather obvious methodological problems had to be taken into account. Since the membership of the board continually changed, there were eventually no members left of the board with which the analysis began. There was thus no direct way of examining the relationship of a conflict dimension on a wholly new board with the entirely different board of an earlier period. Yet the total transformation of the Chicago board took a number of years, and in the meantime we could analyze the relations among the conflict dimensions on one board with those on subsequent boards at least for those members who served on both boards. This comparison over time was undertaken as long as six of the eleven board members remained the same on any two boards.

For this analysis, we divided the postwar era into three time periods: 1946–54, the time of the Hunt superintendency, when reformers cleaned the schools of patronage and corruption; 1954–62, the early years of the Willis administration, a period of peace and physical expansion until the civil rights controversy began to emerge; and 1962–68, the period of confrontation between the school system and civil rights organizations. During the initial period, 1946–54, the composition of the school board changed so slowly that we were able to compare the cleavages among all four of the school boards that sat during this period. We examined for comparison among boards the cleavages within which the most nonunanimous roll calls fell. As can be seen in table 5, the same pattern of conflict persisted rather clearly throughout the Hunt administration. All interrelationships correlated at least at the .4 level and four of the six correlations were better than .7, the level identifying a conflict cluster within each of the single boards.[11]

TABLE 5

Relationships among Board Conflict Dimensions, 1946–54

	1946–47	1947–48	1948–52
1947–48	.41[1]	. . .	. . .
1948–52	.75	.88	. . .
1952–54	1.00	.53	1.00

[1]Coefficient of association is gamma.

The cleavage formed under Hunt's administration persisted in a modified, reduced form into the early years of the Willis administration. To show this, we constructed an overall summary measure for the entire 1946–54 period.[12] We then compared the distribution of board members on this index with the major dimensions of cleavage during the second time period, the early Willis era. Table 6 suggests a somewhat lower level of consistency in the pattern of conflict during this period. Not only were nonunanimous roll calls so infrequent in the first two years of the Willis administration that cluster analysis was pointless, but even when some conflict did develop in subsequent years, conflict continuity from one board to the next was

TABLE 6

Relationships among Board Conflict Dimensions, 1946–52

	1946–54 (Summary Measure)	1956–57	1957–58	1958–61
1956–57	**1.00**[1]	. . .		
1957–58	. . .[2]	.29	. . .	
1958–61	. . .[2]	**1.00**	.40	. . .
1961–62	. . .[2]	. . .[2]	.80	.50

[1]Coefficient of association is gamma.
[2]Insufficient cases (fewer than six) were available to relate one variable reliably to the other.

lower than in earlier years. One correlation in the table is only .29, and two more are no greater than .50.

Within this generally pluralist framework, certain continuities with the machine-reform cleavage of the Hunt era stand out in table 6. The summary measure is perfectly correlated with the pattern of conflict on the 1956–57 board, and that conflict pattern is in turn perfectly correlated with the conflict dimension on the 1958–1961 board. These unusually strong relationships, set in boldface type in table 6, suggest that the dominant pattern of cleavage established in the immediate postwar period persisted until 1961, even as the board changed in composition, superintendencies changed, and the school system expanded to meet the needs of a growing school-age population. As we shall see later, inspection of the issues on which the school board divided during these early Willis years also suggests a continuation of the earlier machine-reform conflict.

If this machine-reform conflict seemed to pluralize somewhat in the mid-fifties, events moved rapidly in the opposite direction as civil rights controversy increased in the sixties. Earlier we noted an increase in nonunanimous roll calls and an increase in the percentage falling within a single dimension of conflict in each of the school boards. These indicators of polarization are further substantiated by the high consistency in the cleavage from one board to the next reported in table 7. Specifically, the table shows that correlation coefficients in all but three cases achieved a level of at least .5 and the median value of all twenty-one coefficients was higher than .7, the point established for identifying issue dimensions within single boards. Quite clearly, the factional commitments of board members were even sharper and more persistent in the sixties than in the earlier period. Whatever applicability the pluralist bargaining model might have had during the less conflict-ridden school politics of the fifties, its relevance to the internal politics of the sixties seems, from these data, to have dramatically declined. The factions on the board became more clearly delineated, involved a larger number of issues, and continued from year to year throughout this tumultuous decade. As we shall see, this highly structured conflict divided those who wanted racial integration from those who wanted to preserve the neighborhood school.

TABLE 7

Relationships among Board Conflict Dimensions, 1961–70

	1962–63	1963–64	1964	1964–66	1966–68	1968–69	1969–70	1970
1961–62	.53[1]	1.00	...[2]	...[2]	...[2]	...[2]	...[2]	...[2]
1962–63	...	.78	.75	.57	...[2]	...[2]	...[2]	...[2]
1963–64		...	1.00	.83	.50	...[2]	...[2]	...[2]
1964			...	1.00	1.00	.33	...[2]	...[2]
1964–66				...	.82	.65	.46	.86
1966–68					...	.43	.57	.73
1968–69						...	.85	.91
1969–70							...	.80

[1]Coefficient of association is gamma.
[2]Insufficient cases (fewer than six) were available to relate one variable reliably to the other.

In sum, neither the pluralist nor the ideological bargaining models perfectly characterized the pattern of cleavage on the Chicago school board during the postwar period. During the years of the Hunt administration, a fairly consistent cleavage indicating an element of ideological conflict was identified. In the mid- to late fifties, this cleavage, though still persistent, organized relationships among board members less clearly. The consensus which marked national politics under Dwight Eisenhower seems also to have prevailed locally.[13] In the sixties conflict increased on the school board, and the pattern of cleavage became more firmly delineated than ever before. Thus far, we have only intimated the nature of the issues that divided the school board during these years. Now that the pattern of cleavage has been established, we can examine in more detail its substantive content.

IDEOLOGIES AND ISSUES IN CHICAGO SCHOOL POLITICS

A consistent cleavage on a school board does not necessarily mean that the members were committed to opposing ideological perspectives.[14] Enduring coalitions may be built around very narrow organizational or electoral objectives. But it is more likely that any set of competing coalitions dividing regularly on policy questions are reflecting differing conceptions of the relationships of schools to the social and political order. At the very least, shared ideological attachments help to ease the strain that personal ambitions and idiosyncracies always place upon any political grouping. Indeed, one might suspect that ideological perspectives are likely to be considerably more important. School board members called upon to make hundreds of decisions each year need simplifying devices to guide their actions. The administrative staff supplies many of these, to be sure. But when the board divides, at least one faction is no longer taking guidance from the school superintendent. Board members are therefore called upon to calculate swiftly the costs and benefits of alternative policy options. If they do not have an ideological perspective upon joining the board, they may well be tempted to develop one quickly. Through constant discussion of issues with other board members and educationally knowledgeable members of the city, a member begins to define his own position. Once that has been achieved, quick decision making becomes possible. One learns which other members of the policy elite, including other board members, have views closest to one's own, and cues from them help in selecting options. The source of support for a particular policy provides a critical hint as to its probable consequence. For this reason, policy elites are likely to develop ideologically sophisticated systems of thought more quickly than ordinary citizens.[15] If they do not, they are left as confused and bewildered as Mrs. Wendell Green proved to have been in the trophy case controversy.[16]

In the Chicago school board, the basis of cleavage was quite clearly rooted in differing ideological perspectives. On the one side, reformers were committed to taking schools out of politics, rationalizing the administration of education, establishing universalist and achievement norms as the criteria by which policy should be formulated, and providing greater opportunities for citizen participation. Although the reform faction had its more conservative and more liberal components, it was held together by a common distaste for the political machine's apparent violation of two basic authority principles: rationalized administration and democratic participation in selection of rulers. On the other side, representatives of the dominant political coalition in Chicago politics, the Democratic machine, sought to protect the legitimating principle of pluralist bargaining that preserved institutional arrangements which they treasured.[17]

The Hunt Administration

The conflict between the machine- and reform-oriented board members crystallized during a crucial period immediately after World War II. Our analysis of nonunanimous voting on the Chicago school board begins in 1946 when six reform-minded board members were appointed to clean corruption from Chicago schools. Their appointment, to which Mayor Kelly acquiesced after great political controversy, made possible the selection of a professional superintendent, Herold Hunt, who was given authority over all aspects of school policy, including contracts and purchases, and who relied heavily on his reform allies on the board to remove from the school system patronage practices characteristic of Chicago politics.

Machine-oriented members accepted this transformation passively, for the most part. But enough divisions occurred within the 1946–54 school boards to indicate what questions were of greatest importance to board members. These nonunanimous roll calls dealt, for the most part, with such typically reform-machine issues as patronage, economy in government, and support for the professional administrator. Perhaps the key issue was patronage, for several board votes during the 1946–54 period related to the removal of political influence from hiring and contract practices. The most important of these was the conflict over the establishment of a superintendent in charge of personnel, an organizational reform designed to eliminate the Democratic party's influence over principal appointments. Similar considerations led reformers to oppose enlarging a particular school, which would have rewarded with an increased salary a principal suspected of having been chosen by the previous administration because of her political connections. Also, reformers refused to award a contract to the brother of one of the machine-oriented members.

Public honesty in school operations was a second, closely related issue. Reformers sought to defer automatically all real estate proposals coming to the board. Through deferral they gained time necessary to determine the need for the land, assess the value of the property, and determine its ownership. By so doing, they hoped to eliminate corruption from real estate sales. In the early fifties a board employee was dismissed, after a rather lengthy board trial, over the objections of machine-oriented members, because his signature had appeared on an unauthorized order form leasing a fleet of cars from an automobile agency. It was alleged that the employee was aiding the establishment of a taxi service.

Reformers were also opposed to what they believed to be irresponsible wage increments and, in general, were concerned about economy in the schools. Thus, they voted in favor of postponing extra vacation allowances for blue collar personnel and favored charging tuition to nonresidents attending the Chicago Teachers College.

Finally, reformers gave strong support to the professional superintendent, who had taken on the responsibility of removing the schools from political influence—even when on technical grounds it appeared the superintendent was not following proper procedures. If there were professional reasons for accepting only one bid on an item or accepting a bid other than the lowest one or permitting a contractor to charge more than the amount stated in the original contract, the reformers supported the superintendent in these decisions. Machine-oriented members, on the other hand, enjoyed embarrassing the superintendent and his supporters whenever they could identify technical (but presumably not genuine) deviations from proper procedures.

These issues were the traditional issues which have divided the machine from the reform movement in urban politics. At first glance, they do not appear to be matters of great ideological significance. At least at the overt level, there was little evidence of a great class struggle or intense racial conflict. Yet the two sides did have alternative conceptions of the proper functioning of the political order. Reformers insisted on rationalizing educational services; they wanted efficiency, honesty, and professional integrity as predominant values in the operation of the schools. Machine-oriented members sought to use school resources to sustain particularistic ties among loyal partisans, watched out for the special concerns of blue collar employees of the system, and, in general, tried to sustain the structures that had facilitated the system of pluralist bargaining which dominated Chicago politics. Two competing understandings of politics, each with its own internal logic, provided the basis for a fairly consistent pattern of conflict on the board of education.

The Early Willis Years

With the arrival of a new but still very professional superintendent, the lines of cleavage "pluralized" to some extent. For one thing, the frequency of conflict declined; on only ten roll calls were dissenting votes cast during the years 1954 to 1956. And the conflict which developed in 1957 was largely a function of a new member's disenchantment with the difficulty of obtaining information from Superintendent Willis. To some extent these concerns of Raymond Pasnick, a labor union official, divided the old reform coalition. Although most felt that support for the professional superintendent was fundamental to keeping schools out of politics, some felt they needed more information to make "rational" decisions. Even so, the conflict on the 1958–61 board still was associated with the old machine-reform division. By this time Pasnick's criticisms of the superintendent met greater resistance from the reform coalition, which also opposed increased salaries and improved working conditions for employees which they believed the system could not afford. On the other hand, consistent with their concern for fiscal responsibility, they supported tax increases broadening the system's financial base.

Although nonunanimous roll calls during the Hunt and early Willis years involved traditional issues that divided the machine from reformers, it might be argued that members' public voting record may be at some variance with their private, but perhaps more crucial, activities. To check whether board members had systematically attempted to disguise their political beliefs and affiliations from the general public, sixteen individuals who were well informed about school politics during this period, either through serving on the board or observing it closely, were interviewed by Fred Muskal.[18] Each informant was asked the strength of each board member's interest in public education and the degree to which the member was responsive to political pressure from the mayor's office. Board members were scored as high, medium, or low on a reform-machine scale according to the overall assessment of informants. They were rated as proreform if they were regarded as having a high interest in education and were free of pressure from the machine-controlled mayor's office. Although the informants represented a broad spectrum of political opinion, the sample was biased somewhat in a reform direction. This does not negate but in fact strengthens the validity of the findings, for we were not interested in the quality of each member's performance but the extent to which the board members had a general reputation for being oriented toward the machine or the reform movement. Presumably, these informed individuals would take into account activities other than their public voting record—particularly if that record systematically disguised important patterns of action.

These assessments of the board members were compared with the member's voting behavior. The member's average score for all boards on which he had served was used as an indicator of his position in comparison with other members.[19] Board members were then dichotomized into two groups with twelve members ranked near the reform end of the distribution distinguished from the fourteen members whose votes placed them toward the machine end.[20] It is noteworthy how congruent were the assessments of the informants and the results of the voting analysis. As can be seen in table 8, none of the members voting with the machine faction were given a high rating on the reform scale; only two of twelve of the reform-voting members were

TABLE 8
Voting Behavior and Informed Assessments of Board Members,
1946–61

Informants' Evaluation of Reform Orientation of Members	Voting Behavior of Board Members	
	Reform	Machine
High	6	0
Medium	4	4
Low	2	2
Total	12	9

evaluated as low by informants. The overall .8 correlation between
voting behavior and informants' evaluations suggests that the differences in voting record reflected less formal board behaviors as well.

The Civil Rights Controversy

With the rise of the civil rights movement, the issues which divided
the board changed rather abruptly. As the level of conflict and degree of polarization increased, racial issues replaced questions of
patronage, honesty, and efficiency as the focal point of dispute.
Nearly two-thirds of the votes falling within the largest cleavage on
the 1961–62 board were in some way related to the racial controversy that had developed in the community. Late in 1960, and
throughout 1961, charges of de facto segregation were directed at
the Chicago school system. A large number of schools, nearly all of
which were in black neighborhoods, were on double shift, a problem
which Superintendent Willis had been attempting to relieve through
his building program, and, beginning at this time, through the use of
mobile classroom units. Civil rights groups complained that a large
number of classrooms in predominantly white schools were empty,
and that black students were forced to attend double-shift schools
when space was available in adjacent communities. Willis denied
this contention, and truth squads of civil rights activists sought to
determine the exact utilization of classroom space.

This civil rights controversy provoked an increasing number of
divisions and an increasingly tense atmosphere within the board itself. In 1962–63 the board had to choose between building more
segregated mobile units and altering attendance areas so that more
desegregation would occur. The integrationist faction proposed that
a permissive transfer plan be adopted, and they opposed the board's
legal fight against a court suit, which had been brought against the

schools by civil rights organizations. Other proposals for desegregation came before the 1963–64, 1964, and 1964–66 boards, as attention shifted from one part of the city to another. As the superintendent opposed every major plan to increase integration, the conflict became more personal and bitter. At one point Willis resigned, but the board begged him to return to his position (over the objections of the integrationist faction). The integrationists also struggled for a racial headcount of all students in all schools, so that the degree of segregation could be accurately assessed. Since Willis resisted these and other demands for information, procedural questions became involved in the racial dispute.

Even in 1967, after Willis had retired in a carefully arranged compromise, the divisions within the board still revolved around racial questions. The new superintendent, James Redmond, offered a "bold and imaginative" plan, as it was described by Mayor Daley, for integrating the schools. But his attempt to initiate the implementation of the plan through busing children in two communities met strong resistance from white parents, and the board divided in ways consistent with the divisions during the Willis era.

Although most roll calls within this dimension of conflict related to these racial controversies, a number of other issues similarly divided the board, suggesting that a broader range of policies were viewed from the same ideological frameworks. For example, a shared-time proposal, which involved cooperation between public and parochial schools, was among the roll calls that clustered together in the 1963 conflict dimension. Also, union issues, particularly those after 1965 that involved collective bargaining for teachers, fell within this same dimension of cleavage. Those who supported the neighborhood school prefered shared-time arrangements and responsiveness to union demands; integrationists opposed both aid to parochial schools and the establishment of collective bargaining procedures. In short, organized working-class, Catholic, neighborhood-school-oriented interests, traditionally associated with the machine, continued to oppose reformers concerned about integrating blacks into a rationalized, achievement-based social order.

Once again, interview data is consistent with the results of the roll call analysis. According to information collected by Muskal on board members serving during the 1961–68 period, informants rated the members who voted for integration and other reform policies as much more concerned about education and independent of political influences (in our categories, therefore, more reform-oriented) than were the members who voted to keep the neighborhood school and service other interests important to the Democratic machine (see table 9).[21] The gamma coefficient of association was almost as high (.71) for this period as it was for the earlier one. Interview data thus show that reform support for integration and machine support for neighborhood schools included more than just the public stance taken on roll call votes.

TABLE 9

Voting Behavior and Informed Assessments of Board Members, 1961–68

Informants' Evaluation of Reform Orientation of Members	Voting Behavior of Board Members	
	Reform (Integration)	Machine (Neighborhood School)
High	4	2
Medium	4	2
Low	0	5
Total	8	9

This differential response of the machine and reform factions to the civil rights issues of the 1960s can best be understood by considering the relationship of their respective regime ideologies, as discussed in chapter 1, to the integration controversy. Reformers on the school board had traditionally sought to separate schools from politics so that school board policies and recruitment practices would be determined by professional criteria, that is, by universalist and achievement standards. Indeed, they became so supportive of Superintendent Willis that even when he seemed to be discriminating against black pupils, they continued to try to protect him from political pressures.[22] However, as new reform-oriented board members joined the board, this faction began to oppose ever more vigorously the superintendent's blockage of integration proposals. On the other hand, the machine faction became staunch defenders of the neighborhood school policy as civil rights demands became increasingly intense, as demands were articulated outside normal bargaining channels, and as they threatened other pluralist interests the machine had traditionally protected. When the machine members realized that Benjamin Willis, the professional superintendent, about whom they had not previously been very enthusiastic, was also committed to the neighborhood school, they gave him strong backing.

The machine has always emphasized the ward, the precinct, and neighborhood institutions; ward rather than citywide elections have been their preferred method for selecting public officials. The alderman was expected to defend his ward, not seek to make policy for the city as a whole. Consistent with this orientation, the school was seen as an institution for community integration rather than as an avenue for social mobility. Athletics were a significant, not a peripheral, part of the school program. Busing students, changing attendance boundaries, or otherwise changing the composition of a school so that it did not reflect the composition of the community as defined by the residents of the area were perceived as threats to a pluralist urban society. Integration was not perceived as a means by which equal opportunity for all children could be achieved but as a slogan which threatened important community institutions. The machine's commitment to institutionalized bargaining placed the protection of pluralist interests above blind adherence to such vague ideals as equal educational opportunity.

In sum, taking the postwar period as a whole, the board of education divided in ways more consistent with the ideological than the pluralist bargaining model. Although voting patterns varied from issue to issue and over time, especially during the early Willis years, enough consistency occurred so that two rather stable factions could be identified. In the late forties and fifties, this reform-machine cleavage revolved around issues of patronage, efficiency, and professionalism. In the sixties, the two ideological factions divided primarily over civil rights questions. Significantly, these divisions did not simply reflect the transient views of a few specific board members but were deeply rooted in sociocultural differences in the larger political community.

SOCIAL SOURCES OF IDEOLOGICAL CONFLICT

According to the pluralist bargaining model, urban conflict is so transitory that no single political faction can be expected to win enduring backing from significant social groups. Until recently, this proposition, consistent with pluralist theory, was not applied to the machine-reform conflict in urban politics, because it confronted a contrary argument that saw machines and reformers as representative of distinctive social, economic, and cultural interests.[23] In fact Banfield and Wilson have characterized reform rather straight forwardly as the "Anglo-Saxon Protestant middle-class style of politics."[24] In so doing, they only apply to contemporary politics Hofstadter's interpretation of the earliest reformers, active in the Progressive movement, as individuals whose perspectives were founded upon "Yankee-Protestant political traditions, and upon middle class life."[25] Apparently, the reformer's social base has been notably consistent over time, as true at the turn of the century as in reform drives that developed after World War II, including the reform club movement, which, in the words of its most careful analyst, was "with few exceptions, a middle class phenomenon."[26] The only exception to the "WASPish" character of the reform movement in the postwar period was its special attraction to Jewish urbanites.[27]

If the reformers have been identified as predominantly middle-class, Anglo-Saxon Protestants, the machine is said to be dependent on working-class ethnic groups who have recently migrated to the city. Hofstadter spoke of the "system of values . . . of the immigrant," upon which "the urban machine was based."[28] Cornwell has flatly stated that "the classic machine would probably not have been possible, and certainly would not have been so prominent a feature of the American political landscape, without the immigrant."[29] The immigrants were poor and needy, and the machine politicians gave them "help" that no other urban institutions were able or willing to provide. In return the machine coopted within its organization first the Irish and later the Italians, Germans, Poles, and other east European groups. What is frequently not stated, but is nonetheless implied, is that in most cases these immigrants shared one important sociopolitical characteristic in addition to poverty—the Roman Catholic faith. Although religious diversity does not necessarily preclude political cooperation, the common Catholic faith, which contrasted sharply with the Protestant and, later, the Jewish, faiths of the reformers, was important for welding disparate groups together. That Catholicism was a minority religion despised by many Protestants only cemented the alliance among Catholic ethnic interests within the machine. Today, they still seem to share a similar value structure identified as "private-regarding" by Banfield and Wilson.[30]

Inasmuch as it established a close relationship between social groups and political factions, this view of the conflict between machine and reformers was a well-established exception to the pluralist argument. Recently, however, Wolfinger and Field have presented data which indicate that even in this case the pluralist argument that political conflict is not a simple reflection of social cleavages holds true.[31] In an analysis of American cities over 50,000, they show that, if one examines relationships within each of the country's four regions, ethnicity and class variables do not account for the incidence of such reform panaceas as nonpartisan elections, council-manager form of government, at-large electoral districts, civil service coverage, or city planning expenditures. Consistent with a pluralist perspective, they argue that variation in the incidence of reform institutions is due more to historical accidents than to the presence or absence of particular social groups. Banfield and Wilson, they suggest, were overgenerous to the bulk of the Anglo-Saxon population. "While professors and account executives are not particularly interested in patronage, ticket fixing, and the like, these and other elements of the private-regarding style may be quite congenial to people who have little in common with college faculties but nonmembership in the Catholic Church."[32]

Among urbanists, the matter has since become an issue of some controversy.[33] To help resolve it, Banfield and Wilson have suggested that analysts "look at the [social background of] activists who supported and opposed the [reform] measures in question."[34] Accordingly, we examined the social composition of the machine and reform factions of the school board.

As can be seen in table 10, cultural differences between machine and reform elites were significant and consistent with Banfield and Wilson's expectations. To be sure, class differences were insignificant; members of both factions tended to come from higher status occupational categories.[35] The only occupation-related differences on the Chicago board were the ties between the machine and trade unions, and the tendency of women (who, because we lacked data on their husband's occupations, were treated as a separate occupation category) to favor the reform side. This was only to be expected. In Chicago, craft unions, from which the three machine-leaning members came, have been little more than appendages of the machine.[36] Female community activists were likely to be particularly indignant about attempts to mix politics and education. Religious, ethnic, and educational differences, on the other hand, were sharply drawn. Machine members were more likely to have come from an immigrant group, tended to have less education (or, if they had received one or more degrees, did not leave Chicago to obtain them), and were more likely to be Catholic. The reformers were more likely to have come from native stock, were far more likely to have had a more cosmopolitan educational experience, and were more likely to be Protestant or Jewish. Even though the universe of board members on one school board of eleven members over a fifteen-year period is necessarily small, the social differences between the machine and reform factions were large and systematic. The ideological cleavage was nourished by an underlying value conflict between native-born Protestants and Jews, on the one side, and the descendents of immigrant Catholics, on the other.

The socially differentiated basis of support for the early machine-reform cleavage was also characteristic of divisions in the sixties, as can be seen by the relationship between social and cultural back-

TABLE 10
Social Background of Factions on Chicago Board of Education,
1946–61

	Machine Faction	Reform Faction
Occupation		
Businessmen	5	4
Professionals	4	4
Labor officials	4	1
Women	1	3
Total	14	12
Education		
High school	6	1
Some college	2	0
Higher education all at local institution	3	0
Higher education at nonlocal institution	3	11
Total	14	12
Member of recently migrated ethnic group		
Yes	8	4
No	2	8
Total	10	12
Religious Affiliation		
Catholic	10	2
Protestant	3	8
Jew	1	2
Total	14	12

ground and voting behavior presented in table 11.[37] As in the early
years, civic-minded women were an important minority of the reform-
oriented integrationists. Although occupational and especially educational differences between the two factions were less significant than
in earlier years, there remained notable continuities in ethnic and
religious characteristics. The integrationists in the sixties, like the
earlier reformers, came from a native background and shared a Protestant or Jewish religious heritage. The machine members who
formed the neighborhood school faction in the sixties, like the earlier
machine faction, consisted of Catholics who came from ethnic groups
that had more recently migrated to the United States.

CONCLUSIONS
According to the ideological bargaining model, one would expect to
find stable, reinforcing cleavages over issues importantly affecting the

TABLE 11

Social Background of Factions on the Chicago Board of Education, 1961–68

	Machine Faction (Neighborhood School)	Reform Faction (Integrationist)
Occupation		
Businessmen	5	3
Professionals	2	2
Labor Officials	1	1
Women	1	3
Total	9	9
Education		
High school	2	1
Some college	1	1
Higher education all at local institution	3	3
Higher education at nonlocal institution	3	4
Total	9	9
Member of Recently Migrated Ethnic Group		
Yes	5	3
No	4	6
Total	9	9
Religious Affiliation		
Catholic	5	1
Protestant	4	6
Jew	0	2
Total	9	9

welfare of broad social categories. Although conflicts within the Chicago school board were more plural than that, especially during the 1950s, such an ideological interpretation characterizes fairly well the pattern of conflict throughout the postwar period, and particularly during the bitter confrontations of the sixties. Board members divided increasingly frequently, ever more consistently, and in a manner consonant with the conflicting interests of broad social groups represented on the school board.

Of course, the particular groups seeking to shape board behavior changed from one policy question to another. Teachers' organizations were above all interested in salary and working conditions, Catholics were interested in shared-time proposals, civil rights organizations were interested in attendance boundaries and pupil assignment policies, businessmen were interested in financial policies, and neighborhood groups were interested in decentralization proposals. In brief, consistency in board voting behavior was not produced by identical mobilization of political forces in the city on each item of business.

Although board members were certainly cognizant of these varying political contexts within which they were making decisions, they were more than billiard balls pushed in one direction or another by the forces of the moment. Votes on any particularly issue did not necessarily "represent the composition of strength, i. e., the balance of power, among the contending groups at the moment of voting."[38] In interviews board members indicated that most groups and individuals seeking to influence them knew less about the school system than they did. As their tenure on the board lengthened, they realized that outsiders were naive in their recommendations and that they as board members had to make their own judgments on policy questions. More than outsiders, they understood that most policies were interrelated if for no other reason than that each had important financial implications. As a result, board members were particularly concerned with the implications of one decision for their other policies, and they tended to develop coherent perspectives on what the system should and could do. Forced to consider school policy as a whole, they developed one or another "philosophy" or, in our categories, "ideology" about the relationship between schools and society, and they sought by their votes to promote policies that would realize these ideological goals. Because two distinct ideological perspectives were well represented on the board, the members tended to polarize into two groups and found themselves voting with the same allies on a large number of issues.

This ideological conflict was perpetuated by a comparable cleavage in the city as a whole. The division on the school board was the product of different, politically significant subcultures in the larger political community, as indicated by the contrasting social backgrounds of the machine-oriented and reform factions on the board.

By examining the processes of recruitment to the school board we shall see how social cleavages in the larger community became relevant for school board decisions. But at no time should it be thought that there is ever any perfect correlation between the political forces operating in the urban polity as a whole and the behavior of the school board. The board member's own ideological perspectives form a distorting lens through which group pressures pass.

Four

MAYOR AS PLURALIST BARGAINER

The conflict between machine and reformers on Chicago's school board did not occur in a social or political vacuum. The board is appointed by the mayor, who in turn is elected by the voters of the city. The politics in the city as a whole thus inevitably affected the internal conflicts on the board of education. As obvious as these facts are, they do not account for a pattern of school board appointments that perpetuates prolonged conflict among its membership. Given the fact that since 1955 all board members were appointed by the same mayor, it is strange that they divided so clearly and consistently. A mayor, to be sure, cannot be expected to predict with perfect accuracy the future behavior of his appointees. Just as presidents of the United States have not always anticipated correctly the legal positions of their Supreme Court appointees, so one might expect similar errors on the part of urban mayors. For example, after Mayor Daley made a special effort to appoint Raymond Pasnick to the school board, Pasnick, by attacking school desegregation, ignited one of the most troublesome issues that Daley confronted. But mayoral error is most useful for explaining peculiar, deviant cases; appointment and *reappointment* of a divided board cannot be similarly explained.

Neither the ideological nor the pluralist bargaining model account for this pattern in a completely satisfactory way, but we shall in the end lean more heavily on the latter. The very fact that the ideological bargaining model proved so persuasive in accounting for the behavior of school board members themselves limits its capacity for interpreting mayoral behavior. If the mayor is committed to a particular ideological perspective, one would expect him to appoint similarly committed individuals to his school board. Instead, the mayor, in addition to choosing friends and allies to the board, appointed several members who opposed his views on important issues.

79

By emphasizing electoral considerations, the pluralist bargaining model provides the beginning of a more satisfactory explanation. According to this model, the mayor suppresses whatever policy preferences he himself may have in favor of at least partially satisfying the various groups and interests in the city. A diverse group of board members are appointed to the school board in the expectation that the compromises they thrash out will correspond roughly to the balance of interests in the city and the balance of power in the electorate. Even though a good deal of ideologically tainted conflict occurs, the final result is acceptable to a mayor operating according to the pluralist bargaining model.

This interpretation is essentially correct, but it has one major difficulty that must be explored in some detail: reform strength on the Chicago school board is by no means proportionate to reform power in Chicago electoral politics. Most other decision-making groups for the city are consensual, cohesive, machine-directed entities. The Democratic delegation to the state legislature, Democratic representatives on the Cook County Board, the vast majority of the City Council, the directors of the Chicago Housing Authority, and the directors of the Chicago Sanitary District are all under the clear, almost undisputed leadership of loyal Daley partisans. Daley, the pluralist bargainer, recruits to these positions loyalists who contribute little to political dissent in the city. Indeed, the unity which most Daley-appointed or machine-selected bodies operate led Edward Banfield to claim that a machine is a vital informal mechanism for overcoming decentralization of formal authority among fragmented governmental institutions.[1] Diversity of opinion on Chicago's school board thus cannot be attributed in any simple and direct way to pluralist bargaining.

At one time in fact the school board consisted almost entirely of machine-oriented members. During the thirties and early forties, the board consisted of politicians from immigrant backgrounds who directed the schools with little internal controversy. Since there was no general superintendency, administrative responsibilities were divided among three separate departments. In the process of coordinating the three administrators who reported to them, the board intervened regularly in their affairs. Board members had friends and relatives sprinkled throughout the school system. Charges of patronage, corruption, and nonprofessional conduct in the schools were rife, widely believed, and not entirely unfounded. During that period the mayor never appointed more than one reformer to the board at a time. In the postwar period, on the other hand, the reform movement succeeded in winning an important position of influence in the formulation of school policy making—even while the machine continued to dominate city politics more generally.

Most liberals and reformers in Chicago do not understand the problem in this way. For them, mayoral domination of the school board is taken as the essential fact to be explained. For example, one newspaper reporter, writing in a liberal periodical, unqualifiedly asserted in 1970 that

James F. Redmond has been Chicago's superintendent of schools for just four years now, and in each of those years, Mayor Daley has tightened the grip of direct political control of the schools. The school board, with the pretense of independence, performs a puppet show for public consumption. Redmond does what he is told.[2]

Similarly, one reform board member, Harry Oliver, explained his resignation from the school board in the following terms:

It became clear to me—I suppose a year and a half ago—that the board is controlled by a combination of organized labor and City Hall in Chicago.

This wouldn't necessarily be bad under some sets of circumstances, but when the combination acts in concert to put money into salaries, for example, when I think it should go into educational programs; when it acts in concert to keep very rigid labor contract provisions which in my opinion are not serving the best interests of the schools and the children of the city, then I'm opposed to any one or any combination of entities that can control. I don't believe a school board should be controlled by any one person, or any one faction, and certainly not by any outside individuals or organizations. I feel that the board majority has been subordinated to interests that are outside the school system, and I resent it.[3]

And in Mike Royko's tightly controlled, machine-directed image of Mayor Daley's Chicago, Daley "had his own, obedient board running the school system, helping maintain its reputation as being among the very worst in the nation."[4] Even Mary Herrick could assert in 1970 at the close of her massive historical account of the development of the Chicago schools that "the present situation gives the mayor of Chicago open control of the policies of the Board of Education."[5]

As these comments suggest, the mayor did not ignore his political allies altogether in the process of making board appointments. One could hardly expect otherwise. On the other hand, the presence of a sizable bloc of reformers on Chicago's school board is contrary to the mayor's normal manner of allocating governmental positions. And the number of reform-appointed board members in no way diminished as the mayor's electoral strength increased in the sixties. This curious pattern, not immediately explained by even the pluralist bargaining model, is best approached by considering certain peculiar features of the politics of education.

BASES OF REFORM STRENGTH IN SCHOOL POLITICS

The success of urban reform, as we have seen, was rooted in widespread, if not always clearly articulated, recognition that governmental legitimacy depended in part upon rationalized formulation and implementation of public policy. In many cities, police departments were professionalized, park districts were placed in the hands of self-perpetuating trustees, transportation policy was delegated to independent authorities, welfare services were contracted out to private agencies, and even garbagemen were incorporated into the civil service. But if the tendency to atomize decision making in the name of honesty, efficiency, and professionalism was pervasive, nowhere was its effect more swift and enduring than in school politics.

If politics were dirty, the schools were sacred.[6] Because the United States lacked an established church, schools became the citadel of American democracy. If children did not learn a common faith in school, they would not have one at all. As with all churches, their practical import reinforced their sacrosanct position. As much as Americans rejected social change through collective action, they assiduously sought social mobility for themselves and their children. And schools were the one most visible institution providing opportunities for the future. Only the central role they were expected to play in a liberal democracy can account for the rapid growth—both outward and upward—of American schools.[7] But this central, vital, sacred role required that petty politics be removed from the educational process.

Although Chicago is, and for decades has been, a machine city, reform appeals touch a more responsive chord in the public than might be imagined. And if Americans in general have been concerned that politics be kept out of the schools, Chicagoans, though perhaps somewhat more tolerant, had similar beliefs. No random sampling of the attitudes of Chicago voters on these matters has ever been conducted, and so conclusive evidence can never be obtained. Yet the widespread insistence in public discussions that politics be kept separate from education is an important indicator of a cultural norm of some political significance. Schoolmen and reformers regularly reaffirm the need to keep schools out of Chicago politics, of course.

It is in their political and professional interests to limit the influence of Democratic machine politicians. But even loyal Republicans and regular Democrats espouse a similar belief. When Mayor Daley was pressured to remove Superintendent Willis from office, for example, he insisted "I have adhered strictly to the principle that there should be no interference of any kind with the policies and administration of the board of education."[8] And when a Republican alderman opposed two black candidates for the school board, he accused them of "playing politics, and the school board is supposed to be outside of politics."[9] The day another alderman admitted that a school board nominee was "doing something in my campaign" Mayor Daley, appearing incensed, declared about one of his own nominess: "This is a serious matter. If there is someone on this list [of nominees] who is injecting that kind of politics into the schools, I will withdraw him."[10] On another occasion, Daley defended a position he had taken by asking rhetorically, "Would you want to put the school board in politics? I'm a politician and proud of it, but putting the board of education in politics, you wouldn't want."[11]

Separating schools from politics has in fact been a major theme in Chicago political history—at least since World War I.[12] During the raucous, chaotic days of Prohibition, Al Capone and Mayor William ("Big Bill") Thompson, the schools were a political football. Even though it would eventually cost them five days in jail, Thompson's school board recklessly fired a school superintendent, sold valuable central business district property owned by the schools to political pals, and took school furniture to their summer homes.[13] When Chicagoans, in an unusual burst of reform, elected William Dever mayor in 1923, he promptly appointed a reform-minded board who hired a superintendent from New York to "clean" the schools and institute principles of scientific management. But Dever's' attempt to reform Chicago during the Prohibition era proved impossible, and Thompson came back to power in 1927. Once again, the schools were a major issue, as Thompson accused the superintendent of "destroying the love of America in the hearts of children by encouraging teachers to attend special classes at 'Chicago University' at which a text was used which pictured George Washington as a rebel and a great disloyalist."[14] When Thompson was elected, his board placed the superintendent on trial, at which the prosecutor screamed, "And you left out of the schools the name of that great hero, Ethan Allen, who said he had only one life to give for his country."[15] For his part, the mayor insisted that "specific Polish, German, and other ethnic heroes be 'taught' in the schools."[16] At the same time, school positions once again nourished the Thompson machine.

When Thompson and the Republicans were discredited by the depression, the Democrats, first under Cermak's leadership and then under Kelly and Nash, reshuffled the school system. Still another superintendent was fired, and Republican workers were removed from the schools—to be replaced with Democrats. As Roosevelt's popularity increased nationally, Democratic control within the city and over the schools solidified. During the depression years school system patronage at both the administrative and custodial levels was an important source of succor for a new and better-oiled machine.

The power relations between machine and reform in the postwar period are directly related to this depression experience. In the face of financial pressures, the machine, in cooperation with downtown businessmen, cut back on teachers' salaries while continuing to pay civil service employees their previous wages. Incensed by this placement of "political" ahead of "educational" concerns, teacher groups organized the Citizens Schools Committee (CSC) to fight for the restoration of teacher salaries and remove political corruption from the schools. In seeking support from outside their own ranks, teachers naturally turned to social groups who could be counted on to support reform drives. According to Hazlett:

> Most of the [CSC] members were Protestant, though there was a significant Jewish element in the group and the committee co-operated with Jewish organizations. . . . Catholic affiliation seems to have been quite small even though Catholicism was powerful in the Chicago community. There were Negroes on the committee . . . but contact with ethnic minority groups . . . was inconsequential. Organizations representing Poles, Germans, Lithuanians, Italians, Russians, Czechs, and so on, did not figure in the work of the committee.[17]

Throughout the thirties and the war years the reform groups repeatedly charged the school board, school superintendent, and, by inference, Mayor Kelly, with improper, illegal, and unprofessional behavior.[18] But they were unable to transform their allegations into serious threats to Kelly's control. The Democratic machine had only recently defeated the Republican machine and was enjoying locally the benefits of Franklin Roosevelt's national popularity. The voters, during the depression, were more concerned about their material welfare than about the appeals to good government made by the reformers. The war years, too, dampened civic controversy; attacks on the "ins" were regularly interpreted as unpatriotic attacks on the war effort.

But with renewed prosperity reducing dependence on the machine's largess, and with the end of the war in sight, CSC was able in 1945 to turn the people's attention once again to civil problems. The same allegations which had been unsuccessful in challenging the machine's power in the thirties became the focus of a major controversy. After investigating the Chicago schools, the National Educational Association condemned the corrupt practices they said they had found. The press, particularly the *Sun-Times* and finally even the *Chicago Tribune,* aired the charges and called for the resignation of board and superintendent. When the North Central Association of Colleges and Secondary Schools finally threatened to withdraw its accreditation of the Chicago school system, parents became concerned that their children would have difficulty entering college.

Facing an aroused community, the mayor capitulated, asking the presidents of universities in the city to advise him on needed reforms. In their report, they called for the superintendent's resignation and the implementation of a new procedure for selecting board members: Selection by the mayor from a list of nominees recommended by representatives of prestigious community organizations. Shortly after the report was submitted, the superintendent and a majority of the board members resigned, and the forces of reform, which had closely coordinated the entire campaign against the schools, gained the ascendancy in school politics. Soon thereafter, party leaders convinced Mayor Kelly that he could not run for re-election, and the school scandals threatened to set off a major reform drive in Chicago politics.

As the pluralist bargaining model would predict, Chicago mayors, eager to maintain their position of power, have never reasserted full machine control over the school system since that time. Citizens seemed to want honesty and efficiency in their children's schools, if not elsewhere. In the words of one board member, "The experience left Chicago's citizenry with a hypersensitivity to possible injection of political influence or considerations into the school system and accentuated the separation . . . between public schools and city government proper."[19] Capitalizing on these sentiments, reformers managed to secure for themselves a relatively strong power position within the educational decision-making system. Their influence seems to have been due to continued recognition by Chicago mayors that reform appeals have particular potency when they touch upon school policy. Not only had school reform driven Mayor Kelly from office, but it forced the machine to nominate (and elect) as mayor from 1947 to 1955 an honest but weak businessman, Martin C. Kennelly. Although Kennelly was eventually dumped as the machine's mayoral candidate in 1955, even Mayor Daley continued to respect reform power in the arena of school politics.

INSTITUTIONALIZING REFORM POWER

While cultural norms can have important behavioral consequences, the belief that politics should be kept separate from education did not automatically translate into power for the reformers. When mobilized, such citizen concerns can be a potent force. But citizen arousal occurs rarely and uncertainly; it can be deflated with symbolic gestures and delay tactics.[20] Only if organized and institutionalized can these sentiments become the basis for significant and enduring influence.

In a skillful analysis of American trade union politics, Greenstone analyzes the way in which organizational structures mediate between diffuse public sentiments and the formulation of governmental policy.[21] Borrowing heavily from both Weber and Michels, Greenstone argues that organizational structures both modify and magnify public sentiment. In partially accepting Michel's argument, Greenstone notes that the channeling of worker unrest into bureaucratic structures made workers more manageable in the thirties, thereby reducing their revolutionary potential. The United Auto Workers, which achieved power through militant sit-down strikes, eventually became just a left-wing component of the Michigan Democratic party. But Greenstone also asserts the Weberian argument that organization "magnifies, clarifies, and rationalizes" tendencies that might otherwise remain inchoate, formless, or ambiguous.[22] If trade unions did not sustain the peak of militancy achieved by workers in the depression years, the unions have acted with more class consciousness than their own members during most of the succeeding decades. Were it not for the organizational structure of the trade union movement, the labor connection with the Democratic party would very likely have been a casualty of postwar affluence.

What the trade unions did for working-class interests, reformers needed to do to enhance citizens' interest in efficiency, honesty, and "fair play" in school affairs. Reformers have always had difficulty sustaining citizens' outrage against patronage and corruption, which is why George Plunkitt, the Tammany Hall politician, could observe that reformers "were mornin' glories—looked lovely in the mornin' and withered up in a short time, while the regular machines went on flourishin' forever like fine old oaks."[23] Since the reformers' own ideology precluded excessive dependence on patronage, they sought to provide structures within the governmental apparatus that could protect the reform base of power. Elsewhere, these included the city manager system, professionalization of bureaucracies, elimination of elections for minor offices, establishment of regulatory commissions, and removal of partisan considerations from the appointment process. In the case of Chicago schools, reformers in 1946 succeeded in establishing two new institutions, a professional superintendent recruited from the outside and an advisory commission on school board nominations, which both magnified and modified citizen concern about keeping schools separate from politics.

Recruitment of the Superintendent

Selznick has observed that "decisions regarding *recruitment of personnel* may become part of [an organization's] critical experience."[24] If this is correct, then there is no single mechanism for changing organizations available to nonmembers as direct and efficient as introducing new personnel from outside the structure at its apex. In this context, Carlson's distinction between superintendents who are place-bound "insiders" and career-bound "outsiders" is of particular relevance. He makes a convincing case that the "insider, because of his history in the organization, appears to be so bound by the internal and external 'political' structure that if appointed at a time when changes are desired he will be unable or unwilling to make the needed moves."[25] When a school board selects an outsider, on the other hand, "it signals a desire for a break with old ways."[26] Carlson discovered that the larger the school system, the greater the tendency to recruit from within the system.[27] And when school boards have turned to outsiders, organizational subordinates have proved capable of destroying the effectiveness of big-city superintendents. In recent years Calvin Gross in New York City, Mark Shedd in Philadelphia, and Barbara Sizemore in Washington, D.C. suffered the fate that insiders enjoy inflicting on a reformer imposed upon them.[28]

If big-city school systems generally prefer insiders, we could expect this pattern to be particularly typical of Chicago. Recruitment to positions of political leadership—whether in party or government— usually is achieved either through long-time service to the Democratic party or faithful contributions over many years to one or another local government agency—or both.[29] And, indeed, this pattern of insider recruitment was the dominant mode of filling the school superintendency in Chicago before 1946. For more than forty-one of the first forty-six years of this century, "insiders" superintended the system. The circumstances under which "outsiders" were appointed are no less revealing. In 1919 Charles Chadsey was hired from Detroit by a reform board to protect schools from the manipulations of the Thompson machine, but Thompson succeeded in keeping Chadsey from ever occupying office.[30] In 1924, William McAndrew, the only outsider who assumed direction of the city's schools before the war, was hired by Mayor Dever's reform-minded school board. Moreover, it was McAndrew whom Thompson attacked in his comeback campagin of 1927. Significantly, Thompson's outrageous attacks on McAndrew's patriotism did not quell teacher and other "inside" support for his effort to dump the superintendent.

In 1946 reformers, in proposing the recruitment of an "outside" professional superintendent to clean up the schools, opted for a familiar but controversial institutional device. When Superintendent William Johnson, an "insider" who had served as superintendent under the Kelly-appointed school board since 1936, resigned in disgrace, the new reform-dominated school board looked outside the city for his successor. Herold Hunt, who had been superintendent in Kansas City and would become a professor of educational administration at Harvard, instituted a program of school reform during his tenure in Chicago from 1946 to 1953. At the time he was recruited, a major new structural change within the administrative structure of the schools took place. Formal authority, which by state law had been divided among three individuals, was concentrated in the hands of the general superintendent. Hunt also reorganized the personnel office and excluded the board from participating in what he felt were administrative matters.

Hunt's selection, however, occurred only after "a rear action fight" led by board members who wanted a local man to head the system.[31] Although the public record does not indicate the extent of support for the local man, there are indications that at least some of this support came from the machine faction on the board. Bernard Majewski, the most machine-oriented (in his voting behavior) of all the board members, made a statement supported by John Doherty[32] in which Majewski said that his first choice for superintendent was:

> Mr. George F. Cassell, who has rendered outstanding service to the Chicago Public Schools as Acting Superintendent of Schools during a trying and difficult period and for thirty-four years prior thereto. . . .
> With other members of the Board I believe in promoting to higher positions in the system of meritorious persons from within the system.[33]

When Hunt retired in 1953, the machine and reform factions on the board again split on the selection of a new superintendent. Six board members favored Benjamin Willis, who had developed a reputation as a strong, professional superintendent during his tenure in Buffalo, New York. Five members favored Thaddeus J. Lubera, an insider, who had faithfully served the school system for over thirty years.[34] Of the five votes cast for Lubera, four came from members voting with the machine faction. All but one of the reformers plus two members who were identified with the machine faction provided the six member majority for Willis.[35] This relationship between the fight over the superintendent and the machine-reform conflict was recognized by informed individuals at the time. The *Chicago Daily News* editorialized that

> the faction of the board which is primarily concerned with a better educational system for Chicago was engaged in a bitter struggle with the politically minded faction headed by Bernard Majewski. The people of Chicago naturally should be grateful that the better schools element, led by Board President William B. Traynor, won the battle.[36]

Significantly, Majewski defended himself against newspaper criticism in the following manner:

> I had the privilege of casting the first vote for Dr. Lubera . . . not because of his nationality, . . . although I believe he is an outstanding American of Polish descent, if you please. . . . Not because of his religion, although, like me, he is a sincere, practical Catholic. . . . Not because he is a "politician," because I know of no one in the system who has had less acquaintance with men and women in the political arena. Passage of time has only strengthened my belief that we ought to encourage our own personnel and let them know unequivocally that they can aspire to the top post in their profession.[37]

The superintendency did not go to an outsider by default; machine support for an insider was sustained and came close to victory. Nonetheless, the reformers still succeeded in maintaining the practice of recruiting from the outside.

Twelve years later, when Willis retired amid great controversy, the board again looked to the outside for James Redmond who had been superintendent of schools in New Orleans from 1953 to 1961 and in a small but prestigious Long Island suburb from 1963 to 1966. Again, there was support for an insider, but the board eventually decided against him. In addition to the criticism from civil rights groups of anyone identified with the Willis administration, the lingering suspicion of insiders helped to perpetuate the pattern of recruiting superintendents from the outside. Redmond, to be sure, was not without experience in the Chicago school system; he had worked under Hunt and had at that time come to know a number of influential people who would participate in the selection of the superintendent in 1965.[38] Still, Redmond's absence from the system for thirteen years negated any claim that he came from inside the system.

Although recruitment from the outside was not a firmly established tradition—insiders were put forward as serious candidates each time a vacancy occurred—the balance of forces was nonetheless favorable to outside recruitment. That this pattern of recruitment could be sustained over two decades was particularly significant in a machine city where most leading administrative posts were given to long-time residents who had worked themselves up through the system. Although "outside" recruitment of school superintendents has not been successful in most big cities, it was a key pillar of the institutional arrangements which preserved reform influence within Chicago's educational system.

RECRUITMENT OF SCHOOL BOARD MEMBERS
The Advisory Commission on School Board Nominations

As important as the school superintendency was, school board recruitment was no less important for reformers. Since in the end superintendents depend on boards for their contracts, reform influence in education could not be achieved without insuring its influence over the way in which board members were selected. Prior to 1946 the mayor had almost always appointed close partisan allies. Although strong reform pressure might force the mayor to modify this appointment pattern, this pressure could not easily be sustained continuously. Reformers did not see an elected board as a viable alternative over the long run either, because in Chicago the voters could not be regularly counted on to support reform candidates to the school board. This point was conceded by the university presidents, in their 1946 committee report, when they observed that many talented individuals would not seek an electoral office. But if reformers felt mayoral appointment would have to continue to be the mechanism for recruiting members, they did not think the mayor could be trusted to make the proper selection by himself. The university presidents thus recommended that appointees be made from a list nominated by a commission "consisting of no more than fifteen members elected or appointed by community organizations which together reflected the interests of 'business, education, the home, labor, the professions, and welfare.' "[39]

Mayor Kelly, acting under reform pressure, agreed to this recommendation in 1946. As a result, mayoral appointment upon commission recommendation was the means by which board members were generally selected throughout the postwar period. Although a number of minor changes in the advisory commission's composition were made from time to time, an analysis of its membership in 1968, as presented in table 12, gives a fairly accurate account of machine and reform influences within the body over the entire two decades.

TABLE 12

Organizations Represented on Chicago's Advisory Commission on School Board Nominations, 1968

Business and Professional	Labor
Civic Federation	Chicago Federation of Labor
Association of Commerce	Teamsters Union
and Industry	Veterans
Chicago Bar Association	American Legion
Universities	Schools
Prestige	Citizens Schools Committee
Northwestern University	Parent Teachers Association
University of Chicago	Black
Local, liberal	Cook County Bar Association
Roosevelt University	Urban League
Catholic and locally oriented	
De Paul University	
Loyola University	
Illinois Institute of Technology	
University of Illinois	

The diversity within the advisory commission reflected the various forces at play in Chicago school politics. On the one side, two organizations that gave considerable attention to the nominating process—the CSC and PTA—were reform-minded. On the opposite side, the machine could count on the support of two labor representatives and one from the American Legion. Three organizations represented business and professional groups who were not closely associated with the Democratic organization but were not strongly pro-reform either. After civil rights issues began to arise, Daley appointed two black organizations: these were of moderate to conservative orientation but on a race-related issue were not dependable machine allies.

The large number of university representatives cannot be treated in an undifferentiated manner. The university presidents' committee, in suggesting groups to serve on the commission, had not mentioned themselves, but they did leave seven positions on their proposed fifteen-member committee vacant. If they were leaving room for university representatives, Kelly took the hint and named six universities to the list of organizations who would send representatives to the advisory commission. Once on the commission, university representatives reflected the variety of institutions from which they came.

Northwestern and Chicago were nationally oriented institutions that attracted students, faculty, and financial resources, from throughout the country. Although they needed to maintain friendly relations with important centers of local power, both public and private, they could act with a degree of independence and autonomy from city politics that sharply delineated them from the other universities. The other four universities—De Paul, Loyola, Illinois Institute of Technology, and the University of Illinois—were all more locally dependent. Financial resources, faculty, and students all came largely from either Chicago itself or the surrounding area. The University of Illinois was dependent on Chicago's state legislative representatives for financial support; De Paul and Loyola formed part of the Catholic constituency of the machine. Roosevelt University was also locally oriented in terms of staff, students, and financial resources, but as its name suggests, it was a liberally oriented institution formed after World War II. A relatively high proportion of its students were blacks, and a sizable amount of its support came from the Jewish community. Although dependent upon the Chicago community, it was associated more with the machine's opponents than with its friends. It was not appointed to the advisory commission until 1955, when it had proved that it was a reasonably viable and stable degree-granting institution.

The composition of the advisory commission was thus fairly diverse. It cannot be unequivocally identified either as a tool of the mayor, as some reformers have claimed, or as a hotbed of anti-machine activity. Machine-oriented mayors presumably could count on the support of veterans and labor organizations as well as Catholic and locally oriented universities. Reformers could presumably gain the support of school-oriented groups (inasmuch as the PTA was under the control of reform-leaning women),[40] prestigious and liberal universities, and, if integration issues were at stake, of black organizations. Significantly, the organizations representing the business and professional community held the balance of power; if the mayor could persuade the business community to support him, reformers would be left in the minority. If the mayor and business community ever split irrevocably, business might well provide the necessary support on the commission to challenge the mayor on school nominations.

Pluralist Bargaining over School Board Nominations

This analysis assumes open confrontations between machine and reform segments on the advisory commission. Such analysis is useful for understanding the political configuration within which political calculations are made, but prior to 1968 the advisory commission's internal politics did not involve such naked struggles for power between easily identifiable factions. As the pluralist bargaining model would anticipate, decision-making processes usually involved far more subtle, covert bargaining. Thus, in order to understand the bargaining game, one must examine not just the open conflicts but also the resources available to each side.

Because the advisory commission was extralegal and its nominations in no way binding on the mayor, he remained the dominant partner in the school selection process. The university presidents committee had recommended that the commission "should suggest at least twice the number of persons to be appointed in any one year and the mayor should then make his appointments from the list."[41] Since this recommendation, which was adopted by Mayor Kelly, was never written either into state law or as a Chicago ordinance, the advisory commission existed at the sufferance of the mayor. It could advise him on board nominations, but at any time the mayor could reject their advice and appoint any person he chose. If the mayor had been forced to accept the commission's nominees, the commission could have acted boldly, forthrightly challenging the mayor. As it was, the commission had to act in the knowledge that any time the mayor might reject all its nominees and appoint his own preferences instead.

The advisory commission's strength depended upon its prestige and the latent political threat that the mayor would be criticized for meddling in school affairs if he ignored the commission's advice. As long as the mayor could get his commission to make recommendations he himself wanted, he had nonpartisan sanction for his school appointments. And there is some evidence that Mayor Daley did attempt to influence the internal decision-making processes of the commission. Yet the reformers were not excluded from participation, as they were in so many areas of policy formation. At a minimum they were a significant, highly interested minority that could speak vigorously at commission meetings. Moreover, many organizations and institutions that might not be regarded as part of any reform movement, such as business groups, professional organizations, and universities, sent representatives who regarded the educational qualifications of a potential board member as more important than his political connections. Quite clearly, the mayor did not have a majority of close political allies who would nominate any personal friend of the mayor he wanted to reward. Within the commission, every nomination had to be justified in terms of the potential contribution the individual could make to Chicago schools. In this way, the mayor was constrained in his selection of board members.

The pattern of appointments during the postwar period reflects this rough balance of power between a machine mayor and his reform opponents. The advisory commission's impact on the recruitment process was most dramatic in the beginning. When several board members resigned under fire, the commission had its first opportunity to nominate candidates to the board. As can be seen in table 13, the orientation of these commission-nominated appointees contrasted sharply with the machine-oriented behavior of members appointed before the commission was formed. Whereas four out of the five members appointed by Kelly prior to the formation of the advisory commission voted with the machine faction on the board, four out of the five board members appointed after its formation voted with the reform faction. Kennelly's and Daley's appointments were divided rather evenly between the two factions. Although there is some suggestion in the table that Kennelly favored the reformers more in his later years as mayor, perhaps a reflection of the increasing distance between Kennelly and the Democratic organization in Kennelly's second term of office, the number of cases is too small to permit anything more than speculation. In general, the pattern of appointments by Kennelly and Daley indicates the accommodation between the mayor and his advisory commission that emerged as the 1946 crisis receded into the past.

TABLE 13

Recruitment of Members to Chicago School Board
and their Voting Behavior

Year of Appointment to Board	Voting Behavior	
	Machine	Reform
Pre-1946 (Kelly)	4	1
1946 (Kelly advised by commission)	1	4
1947–48 (early Kennelly)	5	1
1952 (late Kennelly)	0	2
1955–68 (Daley)	4	4
Total	14	12

In fact power relationships between mayor and advisory commission were so well understood by both parties that until 1968 there was, by and large, little public conflict between them. Significantly, the four instances where conflict did occur all involved mayoral support for a candidate who came from a segment of the machine's constituency. Kennelly in 1950 reappointed Majewski, the Polish board member who had been the most steadfast machine supporter on the board, even though the advisory commission voted against his renomination. Then in 1954 the commission refused to renominate

John Doherty, a CIO union official. When Mayor Kennelly felt constrained to abide by his commission's recommendation, he alienated part of a machine mayor's usual constituency, and his failure to maintain two labor representatives on the board became a major issue in the successful campaign of Daley supporters to dump Kennelly as the mayoral candidate of the Democratic organization.

Daley, too, had difficulties securing a labor nominee from his commission. When he tried to make his first appointment to the board from the ranks of labor, the commission refused to nominate a union man. The new mayor acquiesced in the commission's decision the first time around, but when a second appointment became available he appointed to the advisory commission a representative of the CIO and then encouraged him to push within the commission the name of William Pasnick, an official of the United Auto Workers. After strenuous, persuasive efforts by the mayor, the commission finally nominated Pasnick, who was promptly appointed to the board. Later, in 1960, the mayor again had to exert particularly strong pressure on the advisory commission in order to secure the nomination of Edward Scheffler, a Polish, Catholic judge.

These instances of conflict between mayor and commission revealed the reform orientation of the advisory commission as a whole. The conflict in each case involved the commission's reluctance to nominate a labor official or a man of Polish descent acceptable to the mayor. The mayor, who felt that the school board should represent a broad range of interests, was particularly concerned that groups and organizations that had supported him politically, such as the Polish community and the labor movement, be adequately represented. The advisory commission was more concerned about finding suitably qualified individuals who would help to maintain the separation of the school system from "political" considerations.

Although the commission had a reform orientation, reformers still were but one influence among many within the pluralist decision-making system. As the pluralist bargaining model suggests, the mayor must consider a variety of influences in appointing school board members. He cannot easily ignore ethnic and labor interests merely because advisory commissions find individuals with such backgrounds unsuitable for board membership. If the mayor followed his commission unerringly, he would lose support from other quarters within the city. As long as the commission remained extralegal, the mayor could perform the balancing act covertly. His friends on the commission could suggest that the mayor was very interested in a certain kind of appointment and the commission had to be realistic in the nominees it approved. Otherwise, the mayor might ignore the commission altogether. Reformers still played a junior role in the recruitment of board members.

A junior role was still greater than the role reformers played in most aspects of Chicago policy formation, and it is worth emphasizing the limits the commission placed on mayors. Although in three of the four cases just considered, the mayor finally made the appointment he wanted, there may well have been other occasions, not so easily detected, when the mayor abandoned a candidate rather than involve himself in internal advisory commission processes. The mayor in many cases simply had to accept his commission's biases, and, as a result, a sizable contingent of reformers served on the school board. Had the mayor manipulated the commission too openly or ignored its recommendations too frequently, it no longer would have served as a legitimizing body. Inasmuch as the commission certified that the mayor was appointing qualified public servants to the school board, it protected him from the charge of mixing politics and education. Whenever accused of interfering in board affairs through the appointment of board members, he could always claim that his appointees were approved by a disinterested and distinguished commission, which, in the words of the *Chicago Tribune,* had been "established in 1946 to keep bad political influences out of the schools." If the commission were regularly ignored, it would lose all prestige, organizations would resign, and it would fall into disuse. The mayor would then be vulnerable to the charge of mixing politics and education; another move to reform the schools and dump the mayor could gain steam.

A REFORM INSTITUTION UNDER PRESSURE

During the 1960s this pluralist bargaining game came under increasing pressure. As the civil rights controversy divided the board ever more clearly into two ideologically divided factions, the issue of board recruitment became increasingly salient in the community at large. Whereas in previous years, the mayor could quietly adjust interests with a stake in school policy, the significance of board appointments made this increasingly difficult in the sixties. Each time a vacancy appeared, reform groups and the city press gave it close attention. The whole matter finally came to a head in the spring of 1968, when the advisory commission on school board nominations almost collapsed as an institutional structure shaping school politics.

The conflict over board appointments derived directly from the desegregation controversy that had so bitterly divided the city a few months earlier. In that controversy Frank Whiston and Thomas Murray, the board's president and vice-president, respectively, had in a key vote cast their ballots against the desegregation plan, the last of many decisions which over the years had firmly identified them with the neighborhood-school faction on the board. Warren Bacon, a reform-minded black, was the most vigorous integrationist on the board. Since all three terms of office had expired along with two other vacancies that had been created, the advisory commission considered them for reappointment together with numerous other candidates.[42]

With the conflict so structured, the advisory commission's reform bias became unmistakably clear. It simply refused even to consider the candidacy of an energetic woman who had actively campaigned for the appointment on a neighborhood-school platform. More significantly, it nominated Warren Bacon along with ten other candidates but in a close nine-to-eight vote refused to recommend for reappointment either President Whiston or Vice-President Murray. Although the mayor was known to favor the reappointment of both, the age of the two men—both were over seventy—was said to militate against recommending their continued service.

Although commission deliberations were supposedly secret, the *Daily News* published the results of the voting presented in table 14, a report which was never denied by any member of the commission. Support for Whiston and Murray came from representatives of organizations associated with the machine, whereas the reform-oriented and black organizations opposed them. The machine-oriented Catholic, immigrant, working-class institutions and organizations that supported Whiston and Murray included two labor organizations, the American Legion, a Catholic university and two other locally oriented universities dependent upon established centers of power for their

TABLE 14

Support within Advisory Commission for Reappointment of
Two Neighborhood-School-Oriented Board Members

Organizations favoring neighborhood-school members:	Organizations opposed to neighborhood-school members:
Civic Federation	University of Chicago
Association of Commerce and Industry	Northwestern University
Loyola University	Roosevelt University
University of Illinois	Citizens Schools Committee
Illinois Institute of Technology	Parent-Teachers Association
American Legion	Urban League
Chicago Federation of Labor	Cook County Bar Association
Teamsters Union	Chicago Bar Association
	De Paul University

support.[43] Reform-oriented organizations and institutions opposed to the two board members included two prestige universities, CSC, the PTA, Roosevelt University (dependent upon the Jewish and black communities), and two black organizations. Significantly, the Civic Federation and Association of Commerce and Industry, the representatives of Chicago's business community, voted in favor of renominating Whiston and Murray. And the vote against the two men cast by the representative from the Chicago Bar Association reflected the views of a young member of the association's education committee, which was regarded by Chicago's leading lawyers as too unimportant to seek membership on. Once again, the characteristic conflict between machine and reform is evident. Labor, working-class, and Catholic organizations backed the mayor's candidates, while institutions opposed to them came from the educationally concerned, professional, cosmopolitan institutions, and from the black community.

The close division within the commission notwithstanding, reformers had demonstrated considerable power in an otherwise machine city. Not only had they been able to subtly influence the recruitment of board members over the entire postwar period, but in an open break with the mayor, they were able to organize a coalition which managed to defeat in the commission the nomination of two board members who had performed long and, from the perspective of their supporters, distinguished service on the board of education. Whiston and Murray had been selected by their fellow board members to serve as president and vice-president of the board. They faithfully performed their duties, as they saw them. Only their age—if experience of the elderly is a defect—could be held against them. Yet the reform coalition was strong enough to defeat their renomination by the advisory commission.

The mobilization of reform strength was impressive, but it nearly destroyed its institutional base. In the past, bargaining between mayor and commission had been polite and hidden from public view. Both sides realized that certain limits had to be recognized. Provided the mayor could appoint representatives of various constituent elements of the machine to the school board, reformers were to be allowed a fair but not controlling number of board members. When the commission at a stroke threatened to deny renomination to two Irish Catholics with intimate connections with the machine, the union movement, and the mayor himself, a tacit but nonetheless real mutual understanding was broken.[44] Citywide controversy was inevitable.

The breakdown of pluralist bargaining was evident in a number of ways. First of all, within the advisory commission itself, both sides were reluctant to compromise. As Dr. Eric Oldberg, professor at the University of Illinois Medical School, political ally of the mayor, and chairman of the advisory commission, observed, members of the commission had already made up their minds before the meeting. "Some members may have been conscientious, but few were conscientious enough to get the facts before making up their mind," he alleged.[45] As a result, the majority reform-black alliance insisted not only on denying Whiston and Murray renomination but on nominating only blacks and those white liberals clearly committed to racial integration. They refused even to interview a defender of the neighborhood school who had collected thousands of signatures on a petition advocating her appointment to the board. Moreover, at one meeting, when the Urban League wanted to add another liberal candidate and the Civic Federation another conservative one to the list of nominees, the reform-black alliance accepted the first but not the second. Dr. Oldberg charged, "It was a case of 'you take my man, but I'm not going to take yours'."[46] For his part, Oldberg asked the members of the commission to cast several ballots (rather than allowing the first ballot stand as a definitive action) in the hope that eventually a majority of the commission would vote for Whiston and Murray. When one reformer left the meeting, Oldberg even tried to declare eight votes (out of sixteen) a "majority." Later, reform members of the commission would publicly accuse him of having used "dictatorial tactics."[47]

Secondly, in contrast to previous disagreements over nominations, the conflict did not end with the division among commission members themselves. As the ideological bargaining model would expect, the defeated faction sought to overturn the commission's decision by magnifying the conflict. With the very announcement of the commission's decision, its chairman, Dr. Oldberg, forthrightly attacked his own organization. He called the members "jerks" and "morons," and said they were "stupider than I thought."[48] He then asserted that the commission "has lost its usefulness and should no longer be used."

Other groups and leaders then entered the fray. In an unusual public comment on local issues the president of the Chicago Federation of Labor asserted, "It was most unfair that the commission treated men of this caliber in such a shabby manner."[49] John Desmond, president of the Chicago Teachers Union, echoed:

> I don't think the recommendations of the commission were proper and just, by excluding them. . . . They are two valuable men with experience that cannot be duplicated. . . . If this is what dedicated and civic-minded people receive, then future recognition and rewards have gone out the window.[50]

Several days later, when Mayor Daley decided to reject the bad advice given him and reappoint the two men, the criticism from the other side was equally vigorous. Reform alderman Leon Despres opposed approval of the appointment by the City Council, saying that Whiston and Murray "professed lip service to the ideas" of Superintendent Redmond but in fact "acquiesced and supported and defended" inferior black schools.[51] Moreover, since Whiston's firm had the contract with the City of Chicago to manage the Civic Center, he had "a hopeless conflict of interest."[52] William Cousins, a black independent alderman, was equally critical: "This committee is on its deathbed. . . . No two men were more responsible for perpetuating politics of *de facto* segregation than these two."[53] Their reappointment was "a bad day for Chicago," commented the *Chicago Daily News*.[54]

In short, the selection of school board members had become embroiled in racial controversy and ideological politics. Compromise within the commission proved impossible, the rules of the game were disputed, the conflict escalated out of the commission into the news media—even to the point where the *Daily News* published the ballots cast in a supposedly secret vote, and numerous organizations and politicians publicly entered the fray. No wonder Mayor Daley said he was "stunned and shocked" by the commission report.[55]

After giving what the mayor declared to be his "most important appointments . . . long and solemn consideration," after giving the question "all my thought and effort,"[56] Daley responded with a brilliantly conceived solution that took into account the intensity of feelings among the contesting parties together with their potential electoral strength. Faced with competing demands from reformers, blacks, neighborhood-school groups and the business community, Daley mediated among them, arriving at a solution which achieved at least some of the primary objectives of each of these groups. Although the mayor might have responded ideologically by crushing this overt challenge from the reform-black alliance, he bargained in the familiar manner of pluralist politics.

Simple acquiescence to the commission's nominations would have angered neighborhood-school groups within the city. The president and vice-president of the school board had been for nearly a decade two of the most steadfast opponents of most integration plans. Had Mayor Daley rejected them, he would have provoked many local white homeowners throughout the city, which had only recently become highly agitated over Superintendent Redmond's desegregation plan. Moreover, Whiston and Murray had been faithful allies of the Democratic machine. When two loyal Irish Catholics are treated so rudely, the mayor can accept such an affront only at the cost of alienating powerful elements in his organization and generating a belief that he has lost his grip over the city's political life. Indeed, this challenge to the legitimacy of the existing political structures of the city was so basic it is surprising that the mayor, in return, did not simply destroy the institutional bases of reform power in school politics. In retrospect, it is clear that the least he could do was reappoint Whiston and Murray. And so he did.

Because business chose not to oppose Whiston and Murray, Daley's decision to reappoint them was made all the easier. Successful reform movements in urban politics almost always have had substantial backing from important segments of the business community.[57] Deprived of such backing, one officer of the CSC could only lament, "Our board of directors should consist of leading businessmen, not technicians and professional educationists." Support for Whiston and Murray from the two organizations on the advisory commission most closely connected to the business community was the most apparent indication of businessmen's preferences.

The mayor also had to take into account the views of the black community. By reappointing Whiston and Murray against the advice of the advisory commission, Daley signaled to blacks his continued opposition to civil rights demands. This dramatic act of reappointment, of both symbolic and substantive significance, could possibly renew civil rights agitation just when the Redmond superintendency had greatly reduced its intensity. It was in fact rumored that the reappointment of Whiston and Murray would so antagonize leading blacks that Warren Bacon, who had become an important figure among reform-minded blacks, would reject reappointment on the board and attack Whiston, Murray, the school board, the superintendent and the mayor himself. Citywide protests might follow.

The mayor, recognizing this possibility, entered into negotiations with the Urban League, which was militant enough to have the respect of a fairly broad spectrum of opinion among black activists but also reasonable and responsible enough—in the mayor's eyes—that he felt he could bargain with it.[58] The advisory commission had nominated two other blacks in addition to Bacon. The mayor proposed to the league's executive director that black representation on Chicago's school board be increased to three. If Bacon was willing to serve another term, the mayor was ready to appoint a third black member. When the Urban League acquiesced in this arrangement, civil rights protest over the reappointments was foreclosed.

Daley's response to the reformers had to take into account the special influence they had in school affairs. Indeed, before the mayor reached his decision, Alderman Leon Despres warned that failure to comply with the advisory commission's decision would "break a very solemn promise he made in 1955 to keep schools out of politics."[59] By gaining a majority on the advisory commission, reformers placed Daley in a politically difficult position. In defying the commission, the mayor revealed his own hand in the desegregation controversy more clearly than he would have liked and he exposed himself to criticism that he had mixed schools with politics. Indeed, the *Daily News* editorialized in exactly these terms:

> Mayor Daley . . . reasserted political control of the schools to a degree unmatched since the days of Boss Ed. Kelly. He couldn't have said more clearly that this is Dick Daley's town and what he says goes, from the City Council to the classroom. . . .
> Whatever crises arise now in the schools—and there are certain to be some—will come to roost on the mayor's doorstep.[60]

In order to take as much of this issue away from the reformers as possible, Daley proposed to the Urban League that the third black position be given to Mrs. Carey Preston, who had not been nominated by the advisory commission, rather than either of the two blacks the commission had recruited. Since Preston was a reform-minded, educationally well-informed Urban League activist, blacks could hardly object. But reformers could not criticize mayoral betrayal of his commission in the Whiston and Murray cases without at the same time faulting the way in which Daley increased black representation from two to three.

Reform influence in the Whiston and Murray controversy was thus effectively isolated, and the reformers apparently lost most of the battle. Even so, Daley did make one concession to them above and beyond the two reform-oriented black appointments of Bacon and Preston. The fifth vacany to fill a two-year term was given to one of the advisory commission nominess—Jack Witkowsky, a liberal Jewish real estate broker, who in the next two years would emerge as a leader of the reform forces on the school board. In time, this appointment would prove significant, though in the course of the controversy it seemed to reformers a small gain in comparison to the defeat represented by the mayor's successful defiance of the institutionalized structure reformers had created to protect their base of power in school politics.

Reformers lost the most because they had the fewest resources. Since they could not endanger the mayor's position without support from both business and blacks, the mayor could isolate them by bargaining directly with these other political forces. Because of the mayor's vast power and prestige, black leaders willingly bargained with the mayor to reach compromises that marginally improved their position. The ideological politics of reform was rapidly reduced to the politics of bargaining and compromise at which the mayor excelled. Even in the sector of educational policy, reform influence, though not negligible, had sharp limits.

REESTABLISHMENT OF A REFORM INSTITUTION

The aftermath of the Whiston and Murray appointments indicated that reformers would continue to play a significant role in Chicago school politics. Although the mayor had the capacity to ignore the advisory commission's recommendations in May 1968, he chose not to disturb the overall structure of power in school politics by abolishing the advisory commission altogether. During ensuing months, the problems of acting without such a commission's advice became increasingly evident. In the state legislature, bills affecting school board recruitment were being taken seriously. Some legislators, representing neighborhood-school enthusiasts, introduced bills requiring board elections. Other bills required an advisory commission which would legally constrain mayoral appointments to the school board. Although Daley had enough power in the legislature to prevent passage of a bill he detested, downstate Republicans, by supporting an elected-school-board bill, could call attention to Daley's direct interference in the educational process.

Although an institutional device was needed to protect the mayor against such charges, the advisory commission was so discredited that it could hardly be called back into service without alteration. A number of the reform-oriented representatives, including those chosen by the University of Chicago and Northwestern University, indicated they would probably no longer serve on the commission. The dean of Northwestern's school of education, for example, commented that the Whiston-Murray battle had "made a farce" out of the advisory commission.[61] Fully aware of these difficulties, Daley in the spring of 1969 asked the CSC for recommendations concerning the proper way by which board members might in the future be recruited. A decision would have to be made shortly, because two more vacancies on the board were about to occur. CSC suggested, and the mayor agreed, that the membership on the commission should be reduced to thirteen, including five permanent organizational representatives, five representatives chosen from groups of organizations and three appointees of the mayor.

As the CSC had probably anticipated, the reformers were actually stronger on the new advisory commission than they had been on the old one. Besides the CSC, the permanent representatives included the PTA, Urban League, Association of Commerce and Industry, and the Chicago Federation of Labor. The reform-black alliance, if it can be called that, thus gained three out of the five permanent places. Other organizations were grouped into five panels: education, human relations, welfare, public affairs, and professions.[62] In the initial election of representatives from these five panels held in 1969, the reform-black alliance captured all five of the panel positions on the advisory council. Although the mayor himself appointed three representatives to his advisory commision, the reform-black alliance had a larger, more stable, and more reliable majority than the one-vote margin by which they defeated recommendations for Whiston's and Murray's nominations.

The internal structure of the newly revised commission indicated the increasing power of reformers within it. The former chairman of the advisory commission, who had attacked the commission's rejection of Whiston and Murray, was replaced by Roald Campbell, dean of the School of Education at the University of Chicago, who had no close ties to the mayor. Under its new chairman, the committee established procedures designed to increase their strength and independence of pressures from the mayor's office. In contrast to a rather informal search for board members in the past, the new commission had clear guidelines for internal decision making. Any Chicago citizen between the ages of twenty-five and seventy could be nominated as a candidate by another citizen, provided the individual nominated stated his willingness to serve on the board. Each candidate was required to fill out a fairly detailed questionnaire. The commission reduced the list of candidates, then interviewed those remaining and finally selected the nominees from among those interviewed.

The strength of the reform element in the processes of recruiting board members was thus maintained, even slightly increased, after the 1968 crisis. CSC had hoped to alter power relations more substantially by writing into the law that the mayor must accept the advice of his commission. Daley said that if the new system worked out well, he was prepared to have it codified into a city ordinance. But the period of testing proved to be a prolonged one; seven years later no such ordinance had been enacted. Thus, the formal authority of the commission was no greater than it had been previously. On the other hand, the mayor could have ignored the commission's advice at least in the immediate future only at the great risk of utterly discrediting the whole procedure.

The pattern of appointments subsequent to the 1968 crisis reflects a restoration of the pluralist bargaining relationship between mayor and commission. Indeed, detailed analysis of the nominating and appointing process suggests that the mayor tolerated increased reform influence in order to preserve a system that had protected mayors from school-related political storms since the war. In 1969 the advisory commission did not recommend reappointment of Mrs. Wendell Green, the black, machine-oriented board member who had supported Willis, because she was beyond the age of seventy. Although Daley had never in the past failed to reappoint a board member willing to serve, he acquiesced in the replacement of Mrs. Green by another black whose ties with the Democratic organization were only marginal. For the second position that opened in 1969, Daley, selecting from the list of commission nominees, appointed Mrs. David Cerda, who gave the growing Spanish-speaking community its first major post in Chicago's governmental structure. Once again, however, the mayor, by following an increasingly reform-oriented commission, appointed a board member who was not closely allied with the Democratic organization.

Reform influence on the school board in fact became so strong that reformers planned to capture the board's executive offices from Frank Whiston and Thomas Murray in the spring of 1970. Jack Witkowsky, the recently appointed reformer, and Warren Bacon, the long-standing black opponent of the mayor, expected to become board president and vice-president, respectively. Besides themselves, they counted on the votes of Friedman, Preston, Cerda, and either Boutte or Malis.[63] Significantly, this coalition included all of the new board appointments Daley had made in the midst of and subsequent to the Whiston-Murray struggle. It appeared for a moment that reformers had lost the battle in 1968 but won the war.

Daley was too politically astute to be defeated by this relatively weak reform-minority group coalition, however.[64] Before the annual election of the board president in May 1970, Jack Witkowsky, who had been appointed to fill only a two-year vacancy, needed to be appointed to a full five-year term. This was regarded as a formality, since Daley had always reappointed board members willing to serve for another term (except, of course, for the special case of Mrs. Green). Under the circumstances, the commission, finding Witkowsky a worthy board member, routinely processed applications. Unaware of the secretly planned bid for power by the reform faction within the board, they did not treat the forthcoming appointment as particularly significant. Besides Witkowsky, they nominated a couple of other qualified applicants, including Gerald Sbarbaro, the scion of a prominent family who practiced law and already had had a distinguished governmental career. Given his qualifications, the commission, which had been criticized for its antiethnic, Lake Shore bias, felt it could hardly refuse Sbarbaro a nomination. Witkowsky was to be reappointed in any case. In a brilliant manipulation of the pluralist bargaining system that had been restored to Chicago's board recruitment processes, Daley appointed Sbarboro in Witkowsky's place. Although this broke the informal norm against reappointment, Daley had not ignored his commission's advice. When Whiston was reelected president with Sbarbaro's vote, reformers could scarcely complain.

The issue arose again within months, quite unexpectedly. Death removed both Whiston and Murray from the school board, and a new president and vice-president had to be selected in the fall of that same year. In deference to the expectation that labor be given two board seats, the advisory commission, still operating within a pluralist bargaining framework, nominated another labor leader to take Murray's place. The hope of the reformers lay in the capture of the vacancy caused by Whiston's death. Since the board presidency battle had by this time become public, the advisory commission examined its candidates with care. Although they thought none of their three nominees were politically connected, they misstepped a second time. Catherine Rohter, though a long-time member of the League of Women Voters, was picked by the mayor to serve on the board. She promptly chose John Carey, the labor leader, over Warren Bacon, as her preference for president. In recognition of the growing strength of the reform faction, however, Carey Preston was elected vice-president. This division of the two high offices between the machine and reform-minority group factions symbolized a return to pluralist bargaining within Chicago school politics.[65]

CONCLUSIONS

Reform influence within school policy formation was possible in a machine city, because Chicago mayors had learned that, within this policy sphere, open machine dominance could be electorally costly. Acting within the framework of the pluralist bargaining model, Chicago mayors accepted a relatively autonomous school system directed by a professional superintendent recruited from outside the city and bargained with a reform-oriented advisory commission so that a balanced school board emerged. In 1968 the integration issue so polarized Chicago school politics that the processes of pluralist bargaining nearly gave way to a more ideological style. The advisory commission openly challenged the mayor on a question of great importance not only to his electoral constituency but to the very structure of the existing regime. Ordinarily, one might have expected the mayor to have responded in kind. He could have appointed Whiston, Murray, and three other machine-allied board members, ignoring the advisory commission's recommendations altogether. At a stroke he could have removed much of the reform influence from the schools, though at the risk of provoking reformers and blacks alike.

If this response might not have been altogether politically astute, Daley had taken actions in other instances which did not seem to be carefully calculated in terms of electoral costs and benefits. Although we cannot state the "cause" of the mayor's response, the type of policy decision being made might have something to do with the nature of his decision. As compared to other issues, board and commission appointments tend to be distributive policies.[66] The dispenser of the patronage can give different positions on a board to different groups with a stake in the matter. Mayors, governors, and presidents have found such a practice a very useful means of moderating conflict, or at least deflecting it from themselves. In 1968 the advisory commission had tried to change board appointment policies from their distributive character to a redistributive one. By refusing to renominate Whiston and Murray, they made the appointment question a race-related issue, a redistributive issue affecting relations between blacks and whites. Fortunately for Mayor Daley, the very nature of the policy question made it possible for him to disaggregate the issue, thereby returning it to the arena of distributive politics. In this regard, the unusual coincidence of five positions opening up simultaneously was helpful. Had the mayor only the Whiston, Murray, and Bacon reappointments on his desk, disaggregation would have been more difficult. As it was, he was able to reappoint these men, give the reformers a new appointment, and reward blacks with an additional position on the board. An integration issue was turned into a question of black patronage. The processes of pluralist bargaining continued unabated.

Part Two

UNITARY MODELS
OF POLICY FORMATION

Five

SCHOOL SYSTEM AS AN ORGANIZATION

Chicago policy makers clearly bargained in the course of formulating school policy. The school board, recruited through structural mechanisms penetrated by both machine and reform forces, had factions so divergent in social background and political orientation that policy could be formulated only after considerable debate, conflict, and adjustment. Yet these bargaining games were constrained by factors which affected the ways in which policy questions were considered and which limited the alternatives either faction of the school board considered. If we concentrate exclusively on the differences between political machine and reform movement, we tend to overlook factors which unite them. Within a strictly bargaining framework—whether of the pluralist or ideological variety—we cannot appreciate the way in which membership on a school board with responsibilities for the direction of a school system in a major city imposes certain burdens on all board members that they cannot easily escape.

Accordingly, unitary models of policy formation also need to be constructed. As underdeveloped as such approaches have been in studies of domestic policy formation, theories about system behavior, which treat the system as a single unit, can be found in two analytical traditions. From the variegated body of ideas about organizational behavior developed by such distinguished contemporary social theorists as Parsons, Simon, March, Selznick, and Etzioni, one can fashion what Gouldner has called a "natural-system" model of organizational behavior.[1] From this perspective, it is critically important to realize that a school board, as most other policy-making entities in modern societies, depends on a large, complex organization for processing information, recommending among policy alternatives,

This chapter was written in collaboration with Thomas R. Williams.

and implementing its decisions. Even though organization is necessary for increasing the efficiency of a board's operations, the organization, as a "natural system," takes on a life of its own, that is, it develops its own goals and objectives quite distinct from those of the agent it is expected to serve. Specifically, organizations have their own sets of interests to which they become committed, they develop their own operating routines which they are willing to change only slowly and reluctantly, and organizational members often develop a set of shared values to which they are strongly committed. All these factors together importantly shape policy alternatives processed by the organization.

Generally speaking, organizational theorists construct their natural-system model as if the organization is an interdependent, unified whole. Although in some cases internal bargaining within organizations is explored, those using a natural-system model generally recognize that what makes a system an organization is the unity and interdependence among the parts.[2] As a result, the organization is typically seen as an autonomous, self-guiding, enclosed system which, for all its size and complexity, is motivated by a parochial concern for its own persistence.

As dominant as the natural-system approach to organizations has been in recent decades, an early tradition to which Weber made the most important contribution, treated modern organizations as highly rationalized systems of action.[3] Although this approach has not in recent years been dominant in the study of organizations,[4] a quite similar set of assumptions has been brilliantly exploited in the study of international relations. As Graham Allison has shown, much of the finest work in that discipline has been guided, either implicitly or explicitly, by the asssumption that nation-states are—or at least could be—purposive, efficient, value-maximizing entities that rationally pursue certain strategic objectives.[5] Although Allison himself finds this view of limited value in his own case-study research, we shall show in chapter 6 that this kind of unitary model also materially adds to our understanding of that process.

UNITARY MODEL A: SCHOOL BOARD AS HEAD OF A COMPLEX ORGANIZATION

A school board gathers information, considers alternative policies, and eventually implements policy by means of a large, complex, formal organization. The organization enormously increases the amount of information that can be collected for decision makers, provides an opportunity for the board to receive recommendations from experienced professionals, and increases the board's capability of implementing its policy decisions. An organization approximating the "ideal-typical" bureaucracy that Weber described is an efficient instrument for enlarging the scope of instrumentally rational action. Yet no organization's bureaucratic structure is a perfect instrument for the policy maker. However essential organizations may be for rationalizing social processes, what has impressed most contemporary theorists is the extent to which organizations are satisfied with less than full achievement of their ostensible objectives, how overt organizational objectives become displaced by maintenance needs, how organizations choose among alternatives as much by their familiarity as by their efficiency. In specifying the exact ways in which organizational characteristics have these consequences, it may help to distinguish among an organization's standard operating procedures, organizational interests, and the shared values of its members.

Organizational Routines

An administrative staff communicates to its board through channels which are structured by formal guidelines and informal norms and expectations. These channels of communication are patterned so as to facilitate the rapid conduct of routine affairs. In Allison's words: "Organizations perform their higher functions, such as attending to problem areas, monitoring information, and preparing relevant responses for likely contingencies, by doing 'lower' tasks, for example, preparing budgets, producing reports, and developing hardware."[6] These operating procedures, once established and standardized, place constraints on the problem-solving activities of an organization. They narrow the options actively considered. They bias the evaluation of options in directions consistent with organizational structures and routines. They limit the range of policies the organization is capable of implementing. Consequently, organizational behavior is prone to "error" in crisis situations, those times when almost by definition routines are inappropriate for dealing with problems the system faces. Rather than selecting the most appropriate alternative, the organization suggests one that conforms most closely to its standard operating procedures.

Organizational Interests

The structure which evolves to perform routine functions efficiently also gives rise to a variety of roles within the organization. Playing these roles implies that the players possess certain interests.[7] Although at times these various role interests provoke intraorganizational conflict, the organization, taken as a whole, forms a set of social interrelationships and interests that separate it from other elements of the society. Such organizational interests may be defined as those things which maintain or enhance the desirability of organizational membership in general. Policies in the interest of an organization include those which (1) increase salaries of organizational members, (2) increase the number of jobs within the organization (for an increase in jobs improves the promotion opportunities of incumbents of existing roles), (3) recruit higher-ranking personnel from lower-ranking positions within the organization (because this also improves promotion opportunities), (4) increase organizational autonomy from outside pressures (for by increasing the number of options available to role incumbents, it increases their power), (5) increase the prestige of the organization in the larger society or (6) increase the probable longevity of the system.

Organizational interests limit the options of those dependent upon the organization for information, policy recommendations, and implementation. Indeed, many studies emphasize the ways organizational maintenance needs interfere with maximization of organizational goals. To secure substantial private donations, hospitals may concentrate on glamorous public relations gimmicks at the expense of patient care.[8] Unions may concede pay increases and improved working conditions in exchange for "check-off" privileges.[9] Schools may emphasize flashy music programs and art shows at the expense of basic educational goals. In short, organizational interests place limits on the instrumentally rational character of policy formation.

Shared Values of Organizational Members

If organizations are reluctant to act contrary to their interests, neither do they eagerly promote alternatives inconsistent with the values of organizational members.[10] Members typically adhere to certain norms that distinguish them from other groups in society, particularly when they belong to a single profession, as do educational administrators. Such professionals tend to be recruited through similar channels, to have a similar educational background, to endure similar "periods of testing," to perceive in similar ways the heroes who pioneered in the field, to orient themselves toward similar career goals, to read and hear of "progress" in the profession from similar sources, to develop common images about clients and other outsiders who are relevant to the work of the profession, to understand professional problems in a similar way, and to evaluate the importance of particular professional endeavors similarly.[11] In short, the "sharedness" of the values of organizational members will usually increase when it is an organization of professionals. Alternatives considered by an organization's professionals are therefore limited by professional images and myths.

Organizational routines, organizational interests, and the shared values of organizational members have more than a random relationship to one another. The shared values of organizational members are usually consistent with their interests. Although at times professional values, by providing justification for action independent of office within the organization itself, can become a source of internal conflict, these values can as easily reinforce and justify interests. Standard operating procedures, too, are typically consistent with both organizational interests and professional values. They in turn become valued objects themselves. Procedures that are purely instrumental at the time of their inception may become sacred and revered patterns of operation as time passes.

Since organizational interests, shared values, and operating procedures dovetail to shape the decision-making process, the contribution that each of these factors makes independently is difficult to decipher. In a school system based on the concept of the neighborhood school, for example, all three elements seem to work together to perpetuate that system. Efforts to change that system may well be frustrated by the challenge they pose not only to organizational interests and values, but even to routine patterns of operation. In such a case it is difficult if not impossible to determine whether interests, values, or routine procedures are separately shaping organizational proposals. In this study the unitary model will be used only to demonstrate the way in which decision making is affected by the cumulative and interactive impact of all three factors.

Organizational Unity

In constructing this model, we are emphasizing the unifying aspects of the organization, even though internal conflict bedevils most large, complex bureaucracies. For example, within the Chicago school system, important differences could be easily detected between the central office and field administrators, between the old guard that Willis had established in power and the Young Turks whom Redmond promoted to higher levels of responsibility, between inner-city principals and those in outlying areas, and between bureaucrats with general line authority and staff members given functionally specific supervisory roles. Much of what passed among insiders as politically important involved competition and maneuvering for position within the bureaucratic structure. But if these bargaining relationships within the organization are considered to be the most significant facts, then a school system can hardly be considered an organization at all. It is simply another arena within which pluralist or ideological bargaining occurred.

What makes a system an organization is that bargaining and conflict within the structure are secondary and subordinate to dominant unifying factors. Especially from the outside, what is more impressive than organizational infighting is the way in which an organization constructs mechanisms that protect its autonomy, that is, its common interests, values, and routines. As much as organizational members vie for internal power and position, all members are dependent upon the survival of the organization, taken as a whole. Since any major threat to the power, prestige, or material resources of the organization may damage the functioning of most component parts, mutual interdependence places important bounds on internal conflict. And it is in this sense that a natural-system understanding of organizational behavior quite properly treats such structures as unified wholes.

ORGANIZATION OF CHICAGO'S SCHOOL SYSTEM

Chicago schools, like schools throughout the country,[12] had developed structures, values, and patterns of operation that helped isolate them from the external political world. Although the political machine, the reform movement, and the changing politics of the black community were three external political forces impinging on school politics, the school system itself was hardly a neutral entity pushed and pulled by outside pressures. Both formal structures and informal norms reinforced tendencies toward organizational autonomy.

Legal Arrangements

In the first place, legal relationships separated the Chicago Board of Education from the operation of other governmental agencies. To be sure, responsibility for providing education rested with the state of Illinois, which had the authority to create and destroy school systems, city governments, and any other governmental entity within its jurisdiction. Thus much of the structure of the Chicago Board of Education was specified in the Illinois School Code, some of whose sections contained provisions that dealt specifically with Chicago, by far the largest school district in the state.[13] For example, as early as 1839, the state legislature, while requiring that school trustees be elected in all other districts, made them appointees of the mayor in Chicago, a tradition that still persists. But the state's constitutional powers, for the most part, were delegated to local school boards.

Significantly, the state left the bulk of the financial burden of public education to its local school districts.[14] In 1966–67, for example, it provided only 32 percent of the Chicago school district's budget.[15] Consistent with these low expenditures, the state exercised little supervision over local boards. The State Superintendent for Public Instruction was an elected official better known for his political connections than his professional qualifications. In 1971, for example, newspaper reports alleged that Ray Page, who had been the previous superintendent, had allocated federal funds passing through his office to a private school that contributed to his political campaign. That the accusations hardly surprised informed observers suggests the low reputation of the office in the eyes of school professionals.[16] It lacked the prestige to supervise carefully educational instruction throughout the state and it certainly made little attempt to do so.

Within the state legislature an informal norm further protected the city's schools from statewide pressures. In matters affecting Chicago only, preferences of Chicago legislators were crucial. If they disagreed among themselves, other legislators usually abstained from action until a compromise could be arranged. If they sought a change that did not affect state financial resources, it was routinely approved.[17] For example, when Chicago legislators in 1961 wanted an increase in the allowable property tax rate, it was granted. And when Chicago in 1946 wanted to bring all administrative positions under the supervision of the general superintendent, the necessary state legislation was passed.[18]

State politics did affect Chicago schools in one particularly significant way. Each year educators sought additional funds from the state treasury, and state officials had to weigh their claims against competing pressures for highways, welfare, universities, and the like. Since 1957 a School Problems Commission had been established by the legislature to consider school needs. This consisted of the Superintendent of Public Instruction, the Director of Finance, five representatives from the state senate, five from the house of representatives, and five appointed by the governor (who traditionally appointed a member of the Chicago school board and representatives from the Illinois Educational Association, Illinois Agricultural Association, and the Illinois Association of School Boards). The commission held hearings throughout the state, considered educational needs, and weighed them against state fiscal resources. It consulted the governor concerning his proposed budget for the forthcoming fiscal year. Generally, its politically reasonable recommendations were approved by the state legislature. This arrangement, too, was designed to separate educational issues from obvious political pressures. As Masters, Salisburg, and Eliot have noted, the School Problems Commission "serves as a buffer, eliminating or reducing the conflict and pressure on public school matters, particularly those concerned with finance, to a minimal level."[19] However, in the late sixties, this arrangement began to break down under the pressures of enormous increases in educational costs. The governor began to play a more open and direct role in determining education finance, Mayor Daley himself sought funds for Chicago, and the School Problems Commission became a marginal institution.[20]

If the Chicago school system was generally isolated from state political pressures, its formal structure also gave it at least partial protection from local politics as well. In the first place, the Chicago school board was a legal entity separate from municipal government, with its own power to purchase or condemn property for school purposes, to erect buildings, issue bonds, and conduct referenda. Moreover, the school system was fiscally independent of municipal government. Although its budget had to be presented to the city council, the council had no authority to change it.[21] In fact the state school code specifically excluded any linkage between the board and city council: "No power vested in the board or in any of its officers, agents or employees shall be exercised by the city council."[22] The single but important exception to this formal isolation of the schools from other municipal authorities was the mayoral power to appoint the eleven school board members, each to a five-year term, with at least one position becoming vacant each year. But as we have seen, even this formal connection between the schools and city hall was hedged. The mayor selected appointees from a list submitted to him by the Advisory Commission on School Board Nominations.

Board Procedures

Board procedures reflected and accentuated its isolation from external political forces.[23] The public could attend board meetings, but virtually no provision for audience participation existed. Only at certain designated periods were groups and organizations permitted to make presentations before the board. During the preparation of the budget, employee groups at one meeting and citizen groups at another could present their views of what should be included in the financial plans for the forthcoming year. But these hearings were held after the "tentative" budget had already been prepared by staff members, and few changes were made as a result of the public sessions. One other session at which citizens' groups could present their views on school issues and problems was held each year; the only other time public hearings were held was when some great controversy seemed to require it.

Board members themselves hardly welcomed public intrusion into their deliberations, as was revealed at an October 1967 board discussion of their next public meeting. President Whiston introduced the topic, saying:

> I should like . . . to receive instructions from the board with reference to whether on school issues and problems we wish to have a meeting on October 26. . . . I must say that we had two meetings on school issues and school problems in April this year. . . . This would be a third meeting this year. . . .

One of his allies on the board, Marge Wild, opened the discussion:

> Quite frankly, I don't see why we are having this additional meeting. We certainly know the problems of the schools from the last meetings. . . . I cannot imagine anything that could be added.

President Whiston:

> We now have ninety applications for time to present their issues and be heard. . . . You might just as well know; frankly, one evening is not going to do all this work.

Bernard Friedman proved only slightly more interested in the meeting: "I agree with Mrs. Wild," he began. "I move that we cancel the meeting and write nice letters to the ninety people." But he added, "Before we vote I would like to hear from Dr. Redmond as to how he feels this would be a measure of human relations or poor human relations." To which the cautious superintendent responded: "I think the very fact you raised the question means there is some doubt in your mind." John Carey also demurred: "I don't think it would be wise for the impression to be created that the board is not willing to meet with the people who express their opinions."

The matter was settled by postponing the meeting until next April rather than canceling it altogether. Friedman suggested the "first part of April when I will be out of town." Wild seconded the motion with the comment, "I might be out of town too." Though reluctant to abandon meetings altogether, the board hardly enjoyed the democratic ritual.

Limiting formal opportunities for the public to express its views before the board was not the only mechanism by which the school system isolated itself. The board chose to hold its meetings on the afternoons of every second and fourth Wednesday of the month, a time not obviously convenient for the general public. Although general committee meetings, at which major policy questions were discussed, were held once a month (sometimes at 10:00 A.M., sometimes at 1:00 P.M.), no regular procedures for informing the public about these meetings existed. Information about other committee meetings was usually simply unavailable, even though by law these were open to the public.

Once a spectator found the board meeting, he was confronted with a variety of problems in understanding the course of events. If he came at all late, he was likely to hear the school clerk droning a series of numbers, after each of which a board member responded, "omnibus," "received and placed on file," or "roll call vote with eight votes need to pass." The numbers called referred to the items that comprised the bulk of the board agenda, which had been prepared by the superintendent and his staff and handed to board members the previous weekend. Large expenditures or special items that required a two-thirds vote (eight numbers) were acted upon as soon as their number was called. Reports that required no immediate action were "received and placed on file." Everything else was placed in one "omnibus" category that was voted on together, unless a board member objected to a specific item as its number was called. Often the board in the middle of its meeting went into executive session (which could last anywhere from a few minutes to over an hour) in order to discuss personnel or real estate questions that were deliberated upon in private. The audience was expected to wait until the public meeting was called back in session.

The very layout of the board room accentuated the separation of the board from the outside world. Board members sat in a semicircle with their backs to the audience. The amplification system, not inaugurated until Superintendent Willis had retired, broadcast all voices through one speaker in the ceiling, making it difficult to tell which member was speaking. At one time the board members' backs could be seen fairly easily by most of the spectators, but in the late sixties a row of administrators was placed in front of the railing between board and public.

The move was appropriate, for if the board tended to isolate itself from the external political world, it hardly acted in a vacuum. On the contrary, its operations were highly structured by the work of its large professional staff. To begin with, the staff prepared the board agenda. Given the quantity of material submitted, it was surprising that the staff did not try to indicate which items were potentially significant or controversial. Perhaps this was one reason board meetings often were devoted to the exercise of approving scores, even hundreds, of routine purchases and other minor administrative decisions, rather than to discussions of major policy questions.

Certain formal regulations inhibited careful board supervision of school system operations. Except for personnel and real estate matters, board members were prohibited by state law from meeting privately to discuss school policy, a rule which reformers had passed to eliminate behind-the-scenes deals by machine politicians. Although the definition of personnel and real estate was stretched at times, it was impossible to turn executive sessions of the board into full-dress deliberations of school policy. As one board member said about these sessions, "We are not able to stop all conversations about policy questions, but we do our best." Board meetings, held only twice a month, were consumed by the need to decide many routine agenda items. If the meetings, which began at 2:00 P.M., lasted for more than three hours, board members became restless and efforts were made to curtail discussions. Even though a general committee meeting was held by the board once a month for discussion of policy issues, these two hours each month were hardly adequate for careful consideration of the range of problems facing the system.

Nor did board committees give members an opportunity to scrutinize the activities of its staff. With the exception of the collective bargaining committee, the extant committees did not focus on matters central to the operations of the system. In contrast to the Los Angeles school board, which, among other things, has standing committees on budget and finance, educational development, personnel and schools, buildings, etc.,[24] the Chicago board used committees only to handle noneducational matters or highly controversial problems. Its only two standing committees were Real Estate, which leased and sold revenue property, and Fiscal Policies, which invested school funds, secured revenue capital, and dealt in tax anticipation warrants. The most important special committee (other than the one on collective bargaining discussed in chapter 8) was the Area Attendance Committee, which mediated the controversial question of school boundaries.

The school board did surprisingly little to develop informal mechanisms to circumvent the inhibitions formal structures placed on communications among board members and senior staff. A board luncheon was held each Wednesday noon, but no board member identified this as a period when useful discussions were held. In fact representatives of the news media frequently attended these luncheons. Although telephone conversations cannot replace meetings, board members indicated that they seldom talked to one another by phone except during crisis periods. Neither the superintendent nor members of his senior staff filled this communication gap. In fact Redmond studiously avoided having private luncheons or meetings with individual or small groups of board members. This, he felt, was inappropriate behavior for a professional superintendent. And since the board president, the one man with whom a professional superintendent could properly communicate, was antagonistic to many of the superintendent's policies, board and staff had only the most limited means for exchanging ideas.

Board involvement in the preparation of the annual budget provides a marked illustration of the limits of its influence over policy. Typically, the administrative staff submitted an enormous document, running to nearly a thousand pages, to board members the weekend before a November meeting, at which time the board was expected to vote preliminary approval. After community hearings on the budget in December, the final budget was voted in January. But except for changes negotiated with the Chicago Teachers Union, the final budget was scarcely altered by intervening discussions. In 1971 the school superintendent volunteered that the preliminary budget would, for the first time, be submitted to the board and certain community groups ten days before it required approval. Accordingly, the Citizens Schools Committee spent many hours of staff time carefully examining the documents, which gave detailed plans for every school in the district. After struggling helplessly for a couple of days, they finally sought out a staff member who had helped prepare the budget. When they asked if they could compare the proposed 1972 budget with that of the previous year, they were informed that this was a meaningless exercise, because the 1971 budget did not include supplemental appropriations. The proper comparison was between the 1972 budget and actual appropriations during the 1971 fiscal year; this comparison, however, was impossible to make because the 1971 fiscal year had not yet expired.[25]

Board members, if they made an effort, very likely had similar problems with the budget. The superintendent had informed them that $100,000,000 had to be cut from the tentative budget in order to balance it. The board could find no way to undertake this task, begged the administration for more intelligible data (which when supplied proved as obscure as the budget), and finally simply asked the superintendent to recommend which items in his judgment could most easily be cut. The power of the administrative staff to shape allocations within the school system was never more vividly portrayed.

Board members were lay citizens with other responsibilities. Although some devoted forty hours a week to school affairs, most limited their efforts to ten or twenty hours a week. Even then, much of their time was spent resolving disputes among themselves or in public relations efforts. They could in no way compete with the time that a complex bureaucratic organization could devote to policy questions.

Professional Valuation of Autonomy

School administrators were quite willing to assume the burden of policy formation. The field of educational administration had become highly professionalized, with most leading big-city administrators acquiring doctorates in the field at leading universities. Most administrators felt that through such specialized training in the direction of the educational enterprise they had acquired "a monopoly of . . . [an] esoteric and difficult body of knowledge" that enabled them to divine objective, efficient mechanisms for educating the next generation.[26] Ever since Taylor's ideas about scientific management had invigorated the study of school administration, educators had an elaborate ideological justification for asserting their superior capability for exercising autonomously their professional prerogatives.[27] As the American Association of Superintendents proclaimed in 1963:

> The superintendent of schools is the chief administrator and the executive officer of the school system. He is a teacher. . . . His position requires that he exert educational leadership . . . without fear of criticism and with confidence in his position. . . . It is imperative that the superintendent give leadership in all matters relative to personnel and in presenting proposals to the school board.
> We strongly urge that boards . . . continue to recognize . . . the superintendent as administrative head of the schools . . . .[28]

Like their counterparts elsewhere, Chicago administrators believed in sustaining a professional leadership within the policy-making system. As one assistant superintendent commented to the study's participant observer: "Very frankly, when we become involved with agencies that are more politically motivated than the Board of Education, we are in trouble."[29] And principals regularly expressed opposition to greater involvement of community groups in policy formation. Said one principal, "The board would become a group of political people bidding for power and it would be just power politics."[30] Similarly, another principal asserted, "The community people can't see the whole picture. . . . Hiring and staffing is a professional matter.

. . . Curriculum is a professional matter except that the community should be heard.[31]

In rejecting lay influence administrators did not perceive themselves as denying the desirability of democratic processes. Expertise was not antagonistic to democracy as long as the experts committed themselves to fulfilling the aspirations of the citizenry. And administrators had little doubt that they served parents and community, given their dedication to doing what was best for the children. In rejecting community pressures, administrators felt, as one said, that they were only avoiding becoming "obligated to the vocal portion of the structure. You then have a political structure like many years ago."[32]

As a concomitant of this commitment to professional autonomy, Chicago administrators preferred universalist and achievement criteria in making allocative and personnel decisions. Teachers and supplies were allotted to districts and individual schools according to a set of formulas used to determine the needs of the system's component parts. For example, the allocation of teachers to specific schools was determined by formulas such as the following:

> The total number of pupils in grades 1 to 8 divided by the total number of teachers in grades 1 to 9 should give an average class size of 34.5.
>
> A division [class] may be opened when the average class size will not be below 34.5, except that if the division were not to be opened the average class size would be greater than 36. A division is to be closed when the average class size is less than 34.5 and closing the division will not raise it beyond 36. . . .
>
> In the elementary school the class size from room to room should not deviate any more than is absolutely essential. As a "rule of thumb," the class size from room to room should not deviate by more than 10 percent—15 percent as a maximum. In a large school this deviation should be far less than the 10 to 15 percent.[33]

These rigid formulas did not guarantee equality of educational opportunity for Chicago school children, of course. For example, the disparities between the salaries of beginning and advanced teachers, together with the permissive transfer policy that allowed teachers to migrate according to their seniority, meant that far greater sums were spent per pupil in outlying than in inner-city schools.[34] But the formulas did preclude charges that political favoritism of an ad hoc variety influenced within-system allocations.

Similarly, recruitment and promotion was carefully controlled through the Board of Examiners, who determined through written and oral examinations who were the most qualified individuals to serve at various administrative positions. Scores on what was said to be an objective test, not contacts with ward politicians, determined the rate of advancement within the Chicago school bureaucracy. Once again, the mechanism did not guarantee an utterly open, unbiased system for recruiting the best talent available. For one thing, the system rigorously precluded lateral recruitment from external sources by requiring that appointment to higher levels depend on successful service at the lowest ranks in the system. Only teachers could become assistant principals, only assistant principals could become principals, and only principals could become district superintendents, and so on. As a result, Redmond recruited only one outsider to a major administrative position during the period July 1967 to July 1970. Moreover, this system of recruitment sharply limited the number of administrators from minority backgrounds; for example, in 1968 only 7 percent of Chicago's principals were black. Nonetheless, these procedures vitally protected the administrative staff from external pressures. When Superintendent Redmond was confronted with demands for more black administrators, he was able to respond, "While we can appreciate the idea of providing a positive image for blacks and other children, . . . the assignment of teachers and administrators must be made on the basis of competency."[35]

Organization of Administrative Staff

Quite aside from the professional staff's claim to expertise, the very size and complexity of the system for which the board was responsible precluded its close supervision. In 1970, 26,884 teachers were responsible for the education of 596,375 students in nearly five hundred elementary schools, forty-seven high schools, ten vocational schools and four elementary schools and one high school for the physically handicapped.[36] Nonteaching employees numbered at least 14,257.[37] In addition, there were child-parent, evening vocational guidance, and adult education centers. Total operating expenditures that year were $579,257,000, with an additional $45,739,000 expended on capital outlay and payment on debts incurred. The current expenditures per pupil in average daily attendance was $1,043.09.

As in all American cities, the system was organized around the concept of the neighborhood school, which all children living within a certain geographic area were expected to attend. Principals of these neighborhood schools reported to one of the twenty-seven district superintendents, who had certain limited authority over budgetary allocations, curricular development, and personnel selection within their district. After a plan for decentralization, recommended by a management consultant firm, was inaugurated in the fall of 1967 by

Superintendent Redmond, the twenty-seven districts were grouped into three areas, directed by three Area Associate Superintendents. They, in turn, reported to a deputy superintendent, who also had a large staff of assistant and associate superintendents with responsibilities in specific functional areas. At the apex sat the general superintendent, who had the responsibility of managing the entire school system; only the school clerk and the school attorney reported directly to the board of education independent of the general superintendent.

Chicago's administrative structure was thought to be highly centralized.[38] Most budgetary policy was formulated centrally according to a set of formulas illustrated earlier. Teachers were examined, certified, hired, and deployed through the central office's department of personnel, and pupil-teacher ratios were used to determine numbers of teachers assigned to specific schools. If a principal wanted to recruit a teacher seeking a transfer, the principal had to examine the transfer list in the central office, copying by hand the names of teachers he might want to interview. Curricula were set in guides developed in the central office, and textbooks had to be selected by principals from an approved list in the office of the director of instructional materials. Any departure from standard practices required the prior approval of a principal's district superintendent. As a result, principals and district superintendents often felt helpless, unable to control situations within their sphere of responsibility. To quote one district superintendent:

> The things that make a big difference are not in my prerogative, namely, the allocation of funds, the provision of adequate facilities, [and] the power to place people in positions that in my judgment suit them best. I have little control or influence over the engineering situation, very little influence in the operation of the lunch rooms and yet I am held responsible.[39]

Echoed a principal in a separate interview: "There is no authority. The principal is a whipping boy and only is supposed to serve a glamorous public relations purpose. He should display a superficial serenity."[40]

On the other hand, Chicago's school system, as compared with other administrative structures, had "structural looseness" in the sense that central office personnel were poorly informed about events taking place within specific neighborhood schools.[41] The critical interactions among administrators, teachers, and pupils, which apparently shape the educational process most directly, were not easily inspected by top-level administrators. Information necessary to hold subordinates accountable for their most important activities was virtually impossible to obtain, and for this reason alone the board of education necessarily had limited impact on the educational processes in the city of Chicago.

SUMMARY

Chicago's school system was thus in many ways isolated from external political forces and highly dependent on its educational staff for information, recommendations, and policy execution. The formal autonomy of the schools from state and local politics, the isolating tendencies of board procedures, and the difficulties a lay board confronts when attempting to oversee the operations of an enormous organization, all tended to make the system another "island of functional power," cut off from the battles on the political mainland.[42]

Given these characteristics, an organizational model of policy making, which understands the system as an undifferentiated, isolated, unitary whole, committed to a specific set of interests, values, and operating routines, might appropriately be applied. Indeed, in the three case studies presented in part 3 we shall use this model to analyze the Chicago school system's desegregation, collective bargaining, and (especially) its decentralization policies. But an organizational model, which stresses the way in which bureaucratic characteristics limits the capacity of the school board to achieve its objectives, is itself dependent upon another model of policy making. To show that autonomous organizations, responding primarily to their own internal needs and values, are the major determinants of public policy, the organizational theorist must implicitly or explicitly demonstrate (1) that the organizational head has a set of objectives to which it is more than merely rhetorically committed, and (2) that the policy option chosen by the organization is less than the most efficient means of achieving this objective. In this respect, the organizational model requires the construction of a model which assumes that policy makers are rational actors who seek efficient ways of maximizing their objectives.

Six

SCHOOL BOARD AS A RATIONAL
DECISION MAKER

In Graham Allison's study of the Cuban missile crisis, which has greatly influenced the shape of the analytical constructs advanced here, he begins with a model of rational decision making; I have saved this model until the end. Allison's analysis departs from studies of the foreign-policy-making process which depend heavily on a rational decision-maker model; my analysis departs from literature that has thoroughly discarded the model. Allison sought to debunk the rational decision-maker model; I seek to rehabilitate it. In criticizing rationality models, Allison can present an extreme, indeed stereotypical version of the model; I shall try to define it carefully to prevent misuse and misunderstanding.[1]

UNITARY MODEL B: THE RATIONAL DECISION MAKER
Scholars like Allison, skeptical of rationality models, define rationality very stringently, demanding that the actor rationalize both his goals and the means he chooses to pursue them. At a minimum the actor must have a value system which is consistent and coherent, and which gives precise guidelines for action in practical situations. Critics can then point to the difficulty—in fact, the virtual impossibility—of maximizing all values that are important to actors and to the imprecision of their attempts to establish a hierarchy among them. For example, a school board may want to pursue universalist policies, respond to local needs and problems, minimize costs, hire well-qualified teachers, win and maintain public support for the schools, instruct the children according to sound educational principles, and assure a rapid flow of information among system units. All of these and other goals are part of what board members may mean by good education. Yet these values may in many instances compete with one another, and no clear hierarchical relationship

128

among them exists for board members. The very plurality of values seems to make rational decision making nearly impossible.

The apparent impossibility of objectively rational action has induced defenders of rationality models to offer an alternative, more subjective, definition of rationality, which avoids the Scyllian rock that destroys any actor's claim to rationality only to be sucked into the Charybdian whirlpool that reassures every actor that he is acting rationally, thereby reducing rationality models to meaningless tautologies. Utility theories in economics and, more recently, in political science provide instructive examples of the advantages and problems involved in completely subjective definitions of rationality. An individual acts rationally, utility theory assumes, whenever he adopts a strategy which *he believes* has the greatest probability of maximizing the values which *he believes* to be relevant to his situation. According to this definition, a man may be acting rationally even when to an outside observer the actor appears to be destroying his own cherished goals; so long as the actor himself does not perceive the error of his ways, the actor may be presumed to be acting in a subjectively rational fashion.

The subjective notion of rationality has been offered as a solution to a difficult problem for microeconomists. Economic theories of the firm have assumed that the firm acts in an objectively rational manner so as to maximize profits.[2] Empirical studies of the market behavior of individual firms, however, indicate that in some instances firms have clearly not been maximizing profits, thereby calling into question some of the basic assumptions of microeconomic theory. Utility theory has been offered as a response to this difficulty. It argues that firms only maximize their utilities—those things that the members of the firm value. While profit maximization may be among the utilities that firms seek to maximize, it cannot be said that it is in all cases the only utility of the firm. The point is clearly valid. Yet the theory which says that firms seek to maximize utilities cannot be verified, for as Kelley has pointed out, by definition "an actor will always choose . . . outcomes with highest utility."[3]

An analogous debate has occurred recently among political scientists. In the discussion of the pluralist bargaining model in chapter 2, it was noted that Anthony Downs assumed that political leaders rationally seek to maximize votes. Mistakes and errors are due to the lack of information available to the political leader. The theory faces the same difficulties that profit-maximizing theory in microeconomics confronted; observable behavior at times is obviously inconsistent with the theory. In that chapter the pluralist model of bargaining was consequently supplemented with an ideological model. With a subjective definition of rationality, however, it is possible to collapse such models into an overarching framework, by assuming that political leaders are only interested in maximizing utilities, not winning elections.[4] Only in certain cases are the two identical. Some political actors receive greater utility by remaining in permanent opposition than they would receive if they gained office. Yet once again the assumption cannot be disproved, for utilities cannot be measured independently of the political choices a leader makes.

The circularity of the argument for a subjective understanding of rationality reveals it to be a Charybdian whirlpool. To avoid its strong but ultimately disastrous currents, I shall steer a middle course by offering an objective, though purely instrumental, definition of rationality as the most useful for our analytical task. Instrumental rationality does not assume that actors have a consistent hierarchy of values; it only assumes that a rational actor selects from the alternatives available to him the one that is most suited for achieving whatever goals (rational or not) the actor has in mind. In any given policy situation, certain goals can be identified which board members are seeking to maximize. In developing a policy affecting the racial distribution of pupils in a school, for example, the board may be seeking to stabilize the white community. In decentralizing the management of a school system, it may seek to coopt groups threatening system cohesion. In determining teacher salaries, it may wish to pay no more than is essential for attracting adequately qualified teachers to the system. Even though one or more of these goals may not be rationally selected (in the sense of fitting consistently within the board members' overall value systems), the board in making specific policy choices may be acting in an instrumentally rational fashion so as to maximize one or another of these particular goals in a defined policy context.

Two principal criticisms to this objective but instrumental definition of rationality can be made. First, as Parsons points out, there is nothing in this conception of rationality that deals "with the relations of the ends to each other."[5] By treating only "the character of the means-end relationship" this definition assumes "that there are no significant relations [among ends], that is, that ends are random in the statistical sense."[6] But as Parsons himself further suggests, this criticism carries weight only if the theory "is held to be literally descriptive of concrete reality rather than being consciously 'abstract.' "[7] For analytical purposes, assumptions of instrumental rationality can be of great heuristic value. Microeconomists have found one such assumption (that firms are rational maximizers of profit) useful for analyzing the market economy, even though the same assumption may not be helpful in understanding the detailed behavior of a single firm. Similarly, Downs's theory is not an accurate description of the activities of individual politicians, but the simplifying assumption that politicians are rational maximizers of votes may be useful for analyzing the operations of a democratic polity. In our case, we shall examine the utility of assuming (for example) that the Chicago school board is rationally maximizing racial stability in white neighborhoods, is rationally maximizing the recruitment of the best teachers at the lowest possible salaries, and so on.

Second, choosing the best alternative in a complex situation is extremely difficult, even when one's goal is clearly in mind, as the analogy of a chess game clearly illustrates.[8] Selecting the best of all possible alternative moves in a chess game is a task which exceeds the capacities of the most sophisticated of contemporary computers, to say nothing of the limited capacity of the human brain. Moreover, even if the information could theoretically be obtained, the costs of collecting additional information might exceed the benefits to be gained through adopting the most efficient strategy. But if the one best alternative is not obvious, certain alternatives are clearly unattractive. A computer can be programmed to play tolerably decent, if not outstanding, chess. If no one course of action can be seen to be the most viable strategy for maximizing profits, votes, or racial stabilization, certainly some strategies are foreclosed. The concept of rational decision making identifies the limits to the range of alternatives that will be considered, even though it may not determine which alternative is selected within that range.

The utility of such a rational decision-making model is probably limited to cases where goals can be reasonably well defined by a single political head. Widespread use of rationality models in interpreting American foreign policy is possible only because there exists some minimum level of coordination in the determination of policy. Although foreign policy decisions are made through a network of complex relationships, at the peak of a fairly well-defined hierarchy stands the president who, according to the Constitution and modern practice, plays a preeminent role. Although Allison correctly shows that organizational processes and political bargaining within the executive branch undermine the explicit authority relationships established in organizational charts, if no such hierarchical relationships had existed, other students of foreign policy making would not have found the rational decision-making model useful in the first place.

Rational decision-making models are notably absent from interpretations of American domestic policy making. At the national level, power and authority are diffused so widely among congressional committees, party leaders, interest groups, executive agencies, the White House, and even the judiciary that policy-making processes seem to lack the necessary coordinated relationships for successful application of this model. No single actor has presidential-like authority and power to impose a settlement. Domestic politics resemble the international political system more closely than the foreign-policy-making processes of a single government. There is no central policy-making authority and there are few, if any, goals upon which most powerful participants can agree.

SCHOOL BOARDS AS RATIONAL DECISION MAKERS

Urban policy-making processes also seem to defy any useful application of a unitary, rational decision-making model. Policy outcomes are influenced by mayors, governors, city councils, agency heads, interest groups, the news media, business and labor leaders, party organizations, and other groups and institutions. Power is so decentralized, so divided among a wide variety of competing participants, that even in Chicago, which has more centralizing institutions than many cities, use of a unitary model seems precluded. And most policy makers seem too distracted by immediate passions and concerns to pursue rationally a clearly defined objective.

So decentralized are policy-making processes, in fact, that only elitist interpretations of urban politics have even implicitly relied upon any form of the rational decision-making model. Whenever lists of influential individuals are constructed or the socioeconomic backgrounds of those in official governmental positions are determined, any conclusions about public policy that can be reached from such data necessarily build on the assumption that these influentials and officials are in substantial agreement on "important" strategic objectives which they rationally attempt to effectuate. Of course, all serious analysts have recognized that opinion among such influentials is far from uniform. Yet some elitist theorists of local politics, just as some theorists of international politics, have concluded that the areas of common agreement are more decisive than any "minor" conflicts which other theorists, often called pluralists, typically emphasize. However, few analysts writing from an elitist perspective have shown such connections between the strategic objectives supposedly commonly held and specific policy outcomes.

A number of considerations suggest, however, that just such a connection can be drawn in the case of urban school politics. In the first place, a board of education does constitute a single head that has the ultimate responsibility for determining policy. Within its functional purview, a school board has the formal authority to execute a policy consistent with any strategic objective it has in mind. It is true that in Chicago the school board consists of eleven individuals, but even this does not necessarily obviate a useful application of the rational decision-making model. Whenever a preponderant majority of the board members agree on a specific goal, both they and the other participants seeking to influence them are constrained to keep their recommendations within certain limits. An advantage is given to some arguments over others in the decision-making process. Board members will be interested as much in the quality of the argument being developed as in the amount of political pressure behind it. To be sure, the more this goal is vague and obscure, the less useful the rational decision-making model will be. Allison shows that any number of alternatives to the blockade of Cuba in 1962 could be and were defended as serving the national interest quite as well as the action Kennedy chose. Similarly, if boards agree only that they are interested in high-quality education at low cost, few limits are placed on the suggestions that can be made. But school boards often agree on more precise goals than these, and the more precise the goals the more applicable the rational decision-making model becomes.

Secondly, the competitive relationships among local units of government define a policy-making context which rational decision makers cannot ignore. Widespread use of the rational model by foreign-policy analysts has been a function of the competitive character of the international political system. Each nation-state finds its options significantly limited by an external world sufficiently *foreign* to its desires that policies must be carefully calculated within limited parameters. In trying to achieve a strategic objective, nation-states find external constraints so powerful that internal debates are often confined within rather narrow limits, precisely the context in which rational models are most useful. This critically important aspect of the foreign-policy context of nation-states is equally, if not more, characteristic of urban contexts as well. Each city is constrained by external social, economic, and political forces that it can influence only in marginal respects. And if this has always been true, the point has become increasingly obvious in the case of large, aging central cities that find their competitive position vis-à-vis other local, territorial units of government constantly weakening.

Chicago, like most big central cities, cannot easily control the socioeconomic forces shaping its destiny. As powerful as the Democratic machine appears to be, especially in comparison with other political groups, it has not been able to prevent great social changes from affecting the city's long-range health. If at one time its monopolistic control over the most valuable land in the region enabled it both to dominate other locales and to make most decisions without considering the consequences for transactions across its territorial boundaries, today migratory movements of industry, homeowners, retailers, and consumers must be anticipated by any rational central-city government. If federal policies once affected local functions only slightly, power sharing among federal, state, and local governments is now so intricate that both potential law suits and external agency actions must continually be considered before new initiatives are undertaken. If at the turn of the century wealth was so concentrated in big cities that only unrealistic attempts to lure railroads to their environs could destabilize their financial condition, central cities today must carefully estimate the effect of their fiscal policies on the complex interactions among taxes, property values, delivery of services, and the cities' standing in credit markets.

As managers of one of the city's critically important service-delivery systems, Chicago's school board had to anticipate the impact of its policies on the socioeconomic welfare of the city. Whether members of the machine or the reform faction, all board members were responsible for maintaining social order in the schools, conducting operations so as to minimize the system's jeopardy before the law, forming the school budget with a tolerable degree of fiscal integrity, and as we shall see, balancing the flow of prosperous and productive citizens and industries in and out of the city. Intelligent men and women could disagree about the precise ways of solving these problems. But since the problems could hardly be ignored, disagreement within the board was in some ways less important than the common challenges board members faced. And it is in contexts where problems are to be resolved that rational models of decision making are most likely to be useful.

Thirdly, a rational decision-making model is not dependent upon the presence of school board members with sophisticated understandings of economic, educational, and social processes. Neither this nor the other three models can be taken as an exact description of the processes of policy formation. Indeed, those processes are so complex they escape complete definition and characterization, the very reason construction of abstract models becomes necessary. Haphazard though the actual events by which policy is formed may seem to be, the rational decision-making model may still prove useful if it demonstrates that outcomes are constrained within limits defined by the board's objectives. The model cannot be validated by trying to show that individual board members reasoned in an instrumentally rational manner. Instead, its usefulness depends on showing that board members agreed on certain objectives, that reference to these objectives was made during the course of policy making, and that policy outcomes were consistent with these objectives.

RELATIONSHIPS BETWEEN UNITARY AND BARGAINING MODELS

The theoretical relationships among the unitary and bargaining models that have been presented are stated most succinctly in figure 2. It displays vertically the contrast between the unitary and bargaining models along the elitist-pluralist dimension. Bargaining models see numerous component parts of the system as independently significant explanatory elements. Unitary models consider the system of action under investigation as a single unit, finding no distinction among the parts of the unit of theoretical relevance. Bargaining models always imply that alternatives remaining open are important; unitary models suggest that the most important factors are parameters external to the system which necessarily limit outcomes to within a narrow range. Analyses of urban politics that focus on negotiations and bargains among groups and institutions internal to the system imply that a broad spectrum of possibilities are viable; the one that is selected is said to be a function of power relationships among these internal forces. Unitary models point away from internal disputes toward external or organizational realities that cannot be easily altered.

Horizontally are displayed the differences among the models in terms of the directness of the connection they identify between manifest policy objectives and actual policy choice. The organizational and pluralist bargaining models see policy choice not as a function of stated organizational or individual policy objectives, but as by-products of unstated desires for political survival. Both tend to be cynical, tough-minded analytical constructs for interpreting political action. Both emphasize the way in which unstated, self-serving, self-protective, defensive considerations shape public policy. Inasmuch as both perceive policy initiatives suspiciously, both tend to be conservative lenses through which to view social behavior. Not surprisingly, both were developed and applied most adeptly after World War II, when social scientists most acutely recognized the dangers and limitations inherent in schemes for social reconstruction. Yet all these similarities should not obscure an important distinction. The bargaining model sees policy as formulated through open, adaptive processes with numerous exchanges among system components. The organizational model, as constructed here, treats policy as a function of an organization which is an undifferentiated whole and which therefore has a single set of interests, values, and routines. As used in many studies, this model emphasizes the isolation, even entropy, of policy-making systems.

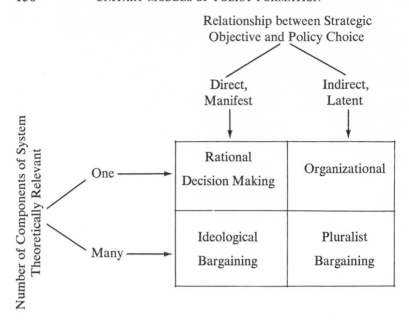

FIG. 2. Relationships among four models of policy formation.

Rational decision-making and ideological bargaining models also are similar in that both take stated, manifest objectives as decisive determinants of political action. Both models rather optimistically assume that explicitly stated goals and overt commitments to broad social goals can be rationally pursued, that such commitments to social goals can in fact shape individual behavior and policy choice, and that planned social change can in fact be executed in accord with intentions. Indeed, the two models are so similar that, under some circumstances, the ideological bargaining and rational decision-making constructs are simply duplicates of each other. Where an ideologically committed majority controls all the relevant levers of power, it can rationally and efficiently pursue the ideological objectives to which this dominant majority, as a whole, is committed.

In other circumstances, however, the very applicability of the ideological bargaining model would seem to vitiate the utility of any unitary construct. Where policy makers are divided along ideological lines, it is difficult to see how any model which takes the policy-making system to be a single cohesive unit could usefully account for policy outcomes. Ideologues in conflict would seem to be so opposed to one another they could hardly be said to hold any significant, relevant policy objectives in common. Indeed, the very label "ideologue" connotes such a fundamental cleavage. We shall discover, however, that even school board members with competing ideologies can agree on certain objectives.

Ideological conflict does not require such a wide gulf of opinion between two parties that no common, shared values can be identified. The understanding of ideology presented earlier sees ideologies as manifest expressions of the interests of certain social roles encompassing large segments of the population. From this perspective, an ideologue can articulate the interests of a particular role in opposition to another ideologue without necessarily disagreeing with him on all policy objectives. Even as a socialist ideologue expresses worker interests in opposition to a conservative's defense of business, the two may agree on the need to conserve energy, to promote economic growth, or, in the case of Great Britain during World War II, to defend the homeland against a Nazi invasion. Agreement on such objectives does not necessarily mean either that the conflict is too insignificant to be labeled ideological or that the agreed-upon objective is hopelessly vague and amorphous.

CONCLUSIONS

Both bargaining and unitary models have been widely utilized to understand and interpret public policy formation in either domestic or foreign-policy contexts. What distinguished Graham Allison's study was the simultaneous use of these alternative conceptual frameworks. By applying varying approaches to much the same body of factual material in order to understand a single set of important events, Allison illuminated with special clarity the way in which the lenses we use affect our understanding of the phenomena we study. In Allison's study, he was able to show the limitations of excessive dependence on a rational decision-making model. Through careful study of a single case, he showed that even in a crisis situation where the president and his innermost advisers thoroughly discussed nearly all aspects of the policy alternatives under consideration, this model was not a satisfactory predictor of policy choice. Bargaining and organizational models proved far more convincing.

Although in my opinion the rational model is more useful than Allison implies, no single model accounts for more than one facet of the totality of the situation. Each is only a snapshot of a multidimensional event. By interrelating the four, one achieves a more exact interpretation. In doing so, however, the tension among the four models must be taken into account. In the first place, each pair of models provides explicitly competing explanations. To the extent that patterns can be characterized by an ideological bargaining model, one can dispense with the pluralist perspective. Likewise, to the extent that bargaining processes are pluralist, a model of ideological conflict provides little explanatory help. To be sure, in every policy-making process both pluralist and ideological elements can be found, but in most cases one or the other model will best organize and give coherence to events under investigation.

Much the same can be said for the two unitary models. To the extent that outcomes are consistent with the objectives pursued by a rational, unified policy maker, the characteristics of the organization through which the policy is being implemented will have little explanatory value. Conversely, to the extent that organizations modify or undermine these objectives, to that extent the rational model becomes only a reference criterion from which to compare actual with hypothetical outcomes. In most cases, both models are likely to be of some, though not necessarily of equal, importance. The objectives of the central decision maker will shape but not perfectly determine outcomes that are nonetheless modified by characteristics of the organization through which he must operate.

The relative value of the unitary as compared to the bargaining models also varies with the context. In some cases, either a single policy objective upon which all important participants agree will decisively determine specific decisional outcomes, or policy alternatives will be considered only within the interstices of a highly structured, autonomous policy-making institution. Little in the way of bargaining, negotiation and compromise will be evident. In other cases, power may be shared by competing groups and institutions so that only through complex interactions of a more or less conflictual character will policy emerge.

But even though the relative utility of each of the four models varies with the issue and context, choice among these explanatory models also depends on the substantive concerns of the analyst. Because of differing opinions about what seems important, two interpreters of a single set of events may rely on two quite different models. The choice between the rational and organizational models, for example, depends in part on whether the analyst regards the deviation in actual outcomes from apparent policy objectives as significant or not. Selection of the rational model emphasizes the correspondence between goals and outcomes; selection of the organizational model focuses on the disjunction between the two. Since in every case there will be some discrepancy, the analyst's subjective assessment of its significance will influence his choice of models. Also, in the case of the two bargaining models, there will always be some aspects of a conflict more amenable to compromise than others and questions which divide some contestants differently. Whether one understands the conflict as pluralist or ideological, therefore, will depend on the significance one attaches to various parts of the bargaining process. One analyst might treat the highly conflictive aspect of a controversy as central, all other aspects as minor and peripheral; another analyst might weigh all divisions equally. Characterization of the conflict will differ accordingly.

The investigator's sense of what is important even more decisively shapes his choice between unitary and bargaining models of explanation. Indeed, the simultaneous use of both types of models in part 3 will, it is hoped, demonstrate the durability—and futility—of the controversy between elitists and pluralists over the structure of power in urban politics. Both can enter scholarly debate so confidently only if both had found much to convince them that their frameworks yielded correct findings. But neither has appreciated the extent to which their findings are a function of their analytical, not necessarily just their methodological, lenses.

One cannot choose between unitary and bargaining models simply on the basis of whether or not there are single or multiple factors shaping policy. Since one can almost never find in any policy-making context only one factor affecting outcomes, approaching the problem from such a perspective nearly always yields a bargaining solution. The question instead depends upon the precision with which the analyst wants to predict policy outcomes. The unitary model may predict outcomes within a sufficiently narrow range so that the analyst may feel that what is lost in exactness is more than offset by the explanation's theoretical simplicity and elegance. On the other hand, complex bargaining models require the introduction of numerous variables, complicating and elaborating the analysis, but the interpreter may feel they are necessary to provide a sufficiently complete understanding. Clearly, the trade-off between simplicity and precision will vary from case to case. But disagreements about what questions are significant will also affect judgments concerning the utility of the two types of models.

Although in the conclusions to each of the case studies that follow, the merits of each approach will be considered, in the end the reader's own values will inevitably govern any conclusion he may wish to draw. In no case is this clearer than in the bitter, value-laden conflict over school desegregation which in the sixties plagued most of this country's big-city school systems.

Part Three

BARGAINING
AND UNITARY MODELS
APPLIED

Seven

THE POLITICS OF DESEGREGATION

Chicago schools were segregated. Only 28 percent of its white students were in schools more than 5 percent black, and only 4.7 percent of its black students were in predominantly (more than 50 percent) white schools.[1] Whether by accident or design, Chicago schools failed to provide the integrated educational experiences which many felt were constitutionally required. After Benjamin Willis had retired as superintendent, black and white Chicagoans thus waited quietly but expectantly to see what moves James Redmond would make in this conflict-ridden policy area. In August of 1967 Redmond revealed a plan that called for the adoption of a number of highly regarded, if rather expensive, desegregation proposals, including "magnet schools," educational parks, financial incentives to teachers working with black children in the inner city, altered attendance boundaries, and pupil busing. In keeping with a new spirit of racial comity that had arisen since Willis's departure, the school board unanimously approved "in principle" this document, which rapidly became known as the Redmond plan. Encouraged by this response, the superintendent recommended the following December that the plan be initially implemented by busing pupils from a few schools in two Chicago neighborhoods—South Shore and Austin—to schools in South Chicago and Belmont-Cragin. It was proposed that more than a thousand black children be bused some distance from their homes.

This proposal encountered bitter opposition from white parents and neighborhood groups, and after some delay the board revised the superintendent's recommendations. It rejected the South Shore–South Chicago proposals altogether, asking Redmond to develop an alternative one instead, and it decided that busing in Austin-Belmont-Cragin should be limited to those children whose parents consented to the arrangement. Compulsory busing, it determined, was not feasible.

The significance of substituting voluntary for compulsory busing can scarcely be exaggerated. If school desegregation on a large scale were to be achieved, the board could not leave pupil placement decisions to parents. This would only perpetuate the neighborhood school pattern to which parents, teachers, and administrators were deeply attached. Moreover, the controversy itself dulled further efforts to implement the large and comprehensive Redmond plan. As late as 1976—nine years after it had been announced—scarcely any detectable progress had been made toward its implementation. The significance of the controversy thus was far greater than its impact on the 1,035 black children who were originally to be sent to predominantly white schools or on the same 10,000 white children who attended those schools.

Interpreting Desegregation Decisions

Why was the initial effort to implement the Redmond plan rejected by a board that had approved it only a few months previously? Following the theoretical frameworks developed in earlier chapters, both bargaining and unitary lines of argument can be developed. First of all, the decision can be seen as a result of political bargaining in which various groups and institutions in the city struggled to achieve their varying political objectives. From this perspective, power relations in the city permitted board adoption of a desegregation plan "in principle" but not its implementation. Although integrationist forces could secure symbolic concessions, they were not able to defeat the defenders of the neighborhood school when plans were about to be implemented. Two variants on this bargaining interpretation—the pluralist and the ideological—are possible. The first sees the outcome as a function of the decision makers' desire to take into account the political power and the intensity of the preferences of the participating groups. The second sees it as a function of the ideological preferences of the dominant coalition on the school board. In the case of the desegregation controversy, we shall discover that the ideological bargaining perspective was most relevant.

Secondly, the failure to implement Redmond's plan can be seen as a function of characteristics of the school policy-making system, taken as a unitary whole. Once again, two variants of this unitary perspective are possible. The organizational one emphasizes miscalculations made by the administrative staff of a large, complex school system. Significant facts include the following: the staff was badly informed about community opinion, it did not confer adequately with community groups, it did not keep school board members properly informed, and it overlooked possible strategies for implementing the plan that had a better prospect of succeeding. This interpretation stresses the extent to which these "mistakes" were not accidental but characteristic of a large organization responsible for hundreds of schools in a big city. However, a second unitary perspective can show that the school board acted consistently and rationally in pursuit of a commonly shared objective that gave direction and purpose to its decisions. The Chicago school board had on many occasions declared that one of its major goals was to stabilize the racial composition of the city of Chicago. The Redmond plan was developed with that very purpose in mind, and the board adopted it in principle because of its own commitment to racial stabilization. But as the details of implementation became available to the school board, new information caused it to reassess the plan and reject the busing scheme designed to implement it.

Chicago's decision to leave its schools as segregated as before was typical of northern school systems in general. Whereas schools in the South slowly and painfully integrated under court order and federal pressure, in the North the percentage of blacks in schools 90 percent black or more actually increased between 1950 and 1965 and again between 1968 and 1970.[2] Interestingly enough, this pattern of increasing segregation occurred even while great efforts were being made by civil rights leaders and school reformers to increase school integration. A number of interesting and informative studies of these efforts offer several explanations for the failure of northern schools to desegregate. Indeed, the interpretations offered in the most analytical of this literature parallel in many respects the several interpretations of Chicago's school decisions just summarized. Although no single study fits neatly into any one of the models we have developed, a review of the literature reveals a distinct tendency on the part of the most significant previous scholarship to follow, however implicitly, either a political bargaining, an organizational, or a rational decision-making model.

The most familiar framework for analysis, of course, is the pluralist bargaining model. It was this model which Frederick Wirt implicitly drew upon in his early review and interpretation of the politics of northern school desegregation. Consistent with a pluralist perspective, Wirt emphasized the array of interest groups active in the development and resolution of the issue, the multiplicity of access points available to such groups, and "the impulse to compromise" in the American system.[3] Although Wirt recognized that "if interest groups are of equal force and their claims of equal validity, then under these conditions there is a correspondingly greater freedom for the play of the personal values of officials,"[4] his analysis does not emphasize the significance of the commitments of public officials themselves but rather concludes that "group action is one of the critical keys of social change."[5]

In contrast to this rather traditional pluralist study, Robert Crain, in perhaps the most insightful of the desegregation studies, cast doubt on many of the assumptions of the pluralist bargaining model. Although Crain did not explicitly develop any countermodel of ideological bargaining—indeed he at points even asserted that board members were pragmatic and did not have an educational philosophy —he nonetheless found in eight northern cities that boards acted primarily on the basis of their own convictions about racial matters without paying much attention either to civil rights or neighborhood-school pressures.[6] For example, Crain stated that the "acquiescence of the school system" to civil rights demands was "not greatly affected by the amount of civil rights activity that takes place."[7] Also, "the board operated independently of the attitudes of the white population."[8] And, elsewhere, Crain observed that "the size of the Negro population does have an effect [on school board behavior], but it is not a very large one."[9] Instead of these factors, Crain found that the acquiescence of the board was largely a function of the board's "civil rights liberalism."[10] Upon reaching this conclusion, Crain made some partially normative comments that show he is aware that his findings point towards a pattern of political bargaining quite different from the pluralist variety which Wirt had found:

> This finding does raise some disturbing questions. We would like to believe that the . . . interaction of board members in the solution of school problems should cause a group consensus to develop which would play down the importance of the subjective attitudes of the board members. We would also like to believe that the negotiation process itself affects what the board does—that there are some ways of influencing the board which are more effective than others. Instead we are continuing to find the school integration outcomes virtually predetermined before the negotiation process begins.[11]

Crain nonetheless saw bargaining among board members as the dominant factor affecting school integration policy. The administrative staff of the school system, though it blocked initial consideration of desegregation demands, played a minor role in formulating overall policy.[12] In this regard, David Rogers's massive study of New York City's school desegregation policies developed a significantly different perspective on the issue. Although Rogers described the pressures emanating from a myriad of groups seeking to influence the policies of the New York City school board,[13] the most original section of his study demonstrated the way in which the characteristics of large, complex organizations affect policy formation.

> The New York City school system is typical of what social scientists call "a sick" bureaucracy—a term for organizations whose traditions, structure, and operations subvert their stated missions and prevent any flexible accommodation to changing client demands. It has all those characteristics that every large bureaucratic organization has, but they have been instituted and followed to such a degree that they no longer serve their original purpose.[14]

Rogers then illustrated in detail the impact these organizational characteristics had on school policy. I only doubt whether the New York bureaucracy was any "sicker" than most large, complex organizations whose interests, values, and standard operating procedures inevitably influence the kind of policies it will either recommend or implement.

Given the paucity of studies applying rational decision-making models to domestic policy information, no detailed interpretation of school desegregation politics from this perspective could be found. However, those black power writers who have discussed desegregation policies in passing have tended to see these policies as formulated by a unitary actor rationally pursuing a consistent set of objectives. For example, Stokely Carmichael and Charles Hamilton, boldly identifying a unified set of values and interests for all of middle-class white America, have asserted that the "middle class manifests a sense of superior group position in regard to race. This class wants 'good government' *for themselves*; it wants good schools *for its children.* . . . They will fight off the handful of more affluent black people who seek to move in; when they approve or even seek token integration, it applies only to black people like themselves—as 'white' as possible. *This class is the backbone of institutional racism in this country.*"[15] Although Carmichael and Hamilton did not support this contention with a detailed policy analysis, they did define a distinctive perspective for explaining integration policies: the white middle class is racist and will accept only token integration, and that only when it serves the interests of their children. Such a perspective, like the rational decision-making model, assumes a high degree of shared purpose, concentration of power, and capability of using governmental power to achieve preferred objectives.

Studies and interpretations of school desegregation have thus implicitly used one or more of the several models of decision making we have elaborated. But no previous study has sought to use each of these models—bargaining and unitary—simultaneously to account for the same set of outcomes in a single city.

BARGAINING OVER DESEGREGATION POLICY

As seen from a bargaining perspective, the Chicago school board's failure to implement its own plan for pupil desegregation was due to the distribution of political resources among varying political interests in the city. We found the ideological version of the bargaining model the most relevant to the study of school desegregation policies. From this perspective, the outcome was a function of the commitment by a majority of school board members to a system of neighborhood schools even at the cost of a high degree of racial segregation. The minority of board members committed to racial integration at the expense of maintaining a system of neighborhood schools did not have enough resources to achieve anything more than symbolic victories. Although not every detail of the decision-making process fits comfortably within the ideological bargaining model, many facets of the controversy are well characterized by some such perspective. Specifically, the processes were marked by (1) principled stands taken by many leading participants; (2) use of public channels of communication to address other participants; (3) a high level of "socialization" in which third parties and "outside" governmental units became involved in the dispute; (4) a board decision surprisingly uninfluenced by the intense public pressures that were mobilized; and (5) great difficulty in achieving compromises minimally acceptable to the competing sides.

Neighborhood School Defenders

Participants in the debate saw that the issue was a matter of principle, not a question of technique or detail that could be compromised easily. This was true even for those contestants, especially the defenders of the neighborhood school, who emphasized techniques, details, and small problems raised by the busing plan because they felt it important to avoid being labeled racists and bigots. Thus, some leaders only asserted that "Taxpayers' money could be used [instead] to build better schools."[16] In this vein, leaders regularly insisted they had no ill feelings toward Negroes as such and issued orders to demonstrators not to use racist language or talk to newsmen when participating in an antibusing campaign.[17] But at times the larger concerns, clearly animating the agitation, crept into public discussion, as for example when one community leader argued, "Our children are not checkers to be moved about on a board at the whim of social experimenters, or chemicals to be tossed into a test tube to see how the mixture will turn out."[18]

If neighborhood-school proponents did not always publicly give such an ideological tone to their utterances, they certainly took their case to the public in the manner that the ideological bargaining model expects. Indeed, they mobilized their political forces to a far greater extent than did any of the other participants in the controversy. Shortly after the busing plan had been announced, one group presented to board members an antibusing petition with fifty thousand signatures, and another group produced a petition with seventy-five hundred names attached. Six weeks later, just before the decision was to be reached, sixty thousand signatures to still another petition were produced by a third neighborhood-school organization. Although more time-consuming forms of participation than petition signing necessarily involved fewer people, some eight hundred to a thousand citizens either attended or picketed outside the school system's central offices at every school board meeting during the months of January and February. When the school board decided to hold hearings throughout the city, high school auditoriums in white receiving-school areas were filled to capacity by local citizens. Although the school board allowed only representatives of recognized community groups to speak, the chorus of opposition to the busing plans was at times overwhelming at these hearings. Altogether, there were nearly twice as many speakers opposed to the busing plans as were for them.

After the voluntary busing plan had been approved by the school board, neighborhood-school proponents further displayed their intense displeasure first by boycotting the receiving schools for two days (with 75–80 percent and 58 percent effectiveness for the first and second days, respectively) and then by picketing (relatively peacefully) the receiving schools each morning for the first several weeks of the program. When a bus carrying black children arrived late one snowy morning, members in the crowd jeered, "You're late, you're late for school," and one woman commented, "There goes our neighborhood." Quite clearly, neighborhood-school proponents were concerned about larger, deeper issues than the optimum means of spending a marginal $125,000 of the taxpayers' money.

Blacks, Busing, and Racism

Initially, black leaders were not enthusiastic about the desegregation plan that Redmond proposed in August 1967. Indeed, the Coordinating Council of Community Organizations (CCCO) which had spearheaded the civil rights attack on Superintendent Willis, strongly objecting to the use of racial quotas, filed a report with HEW's civil rights compliance office stating that this plan did not show "good faith" in moving toward an integrated system.[19] Even those black organizations that generally supported the plan did so in a qualified manner. At first Edwin Berry, executive director of the Urban League, declared that Redmond's plan "makes some significant moves towards quality and equality of education in Chicago,"[20] but after giving the matter more attention, his organization spoke more critically, saying, among other things, that "more emphasis should be put on improving education in ghetto schools."[21]

If black support of the Redmond plan was at first half-hearted, the white hostility to busing subsequently provoked sturdier black support. Berry observed that "anyone who can stand against such a little busing plan as this must be in favor of reinstating slavery."[22] Asserting that the "busing plan though a minor step is nevertheless a necessary first step to [sic] the rocky road to school integration," the *Daily Defender* claimed that "the agitation against the plan is the work of small-minded, misguided people who are bereft of social conscience and a sense of justice."[23] After the board finally rejected compulsory busing, Warren Bacon, the black community's leading representative on the school board alleged that it had "retreated in the face of bigoted opposition."[24]

These black leaders addressed the issue in highly moralistic terms. Their language was sprinkled with words such as "racism," "bigotry," and "social conscience," words that connoted a belief that the question involved a choice between right and wrong, rather than a technical or practical matter where principles gave little guidance. They were the more ready to do so, it would seem, because commonly accepted ideals, including equality before the law and tolerance of racial differences, seemed to favor their side in the dispute.

Given the moral significance with which the busing issue was invested, it is surprising that black civil rights groups did not do more to mobilize community support for Redmond's plans. Aside from issuing statements, testifying at public hearings, and filing petitions with HEW's civil rights compliance office, black political activity was marginal. Local black leaders in Austin were the one group of blacks who were active in supporting the busing plan. But these leaders, primarily concerned about a local problem of overcrowding, received little backing from the wider black community. While white neighborhood groups active in the receiving schools were joined by many other white homeowner and taxpayer organizations from throughout the city, civil rights groups, which at one time had mobilized thousands of citizens to demonstrate against Benjamin Willis, were now strangely quiescent.

In part this was due to the modest nature of Redmond's busing plans, which, after all, hardly ushered in an integrationist's utopia. Black leaders in South Shore in fact objected to the plans developed there on the grounds that they provided only for one-way busing of blacks to white schools rather than mutual or two-way busing for blacks and whites alike. But the modesty of the Redmond proposal is only part of the explanation. In addition, it was not only easier to mobilize citizens against a policy than for it, but black leaders, by 1968, had lost some of their earlier enthusiasm for integrationist goals.[25] Redmond's desegregation campaign came somewhat too late to capitalize on the strength of the civil rights movement; as a sign that times were changing, Redmond, even while promoting integration in Austin and South Shore, was defending a white principal in another neighborhood against black community demands that he be replaced by a black administrator better able to reflect community concerns. Perhaps the Woodlawn Organization best reflected the sentiments of black civil rights leaders when it said that the Redmond plan was a first step, but "a complete end to segregation in the schools will come only when Negroes achieve political power."[26]

White Reformers and Integration

While black leaders qualified their enthusiasm for the Redmond plan and only eventually came to support the busing proposals as "a first step," white liberal and reform groups hailed the Redmond plan from the very beginning. The Citizens Schools Committee (CSC), for example, "strongly endorsed the major provisions of the Redmond plan" and urged "immediate implementation of the recommendations for stabilizing racially changing neighborhoods by busing students" as early as October 1967.[27] And when Redmond proposed implementing his plan by busing, the CSC once again gave it full backing: "The neighborhood school is not the exclusive property of the neighbors. . . . School problems must be solved with reference to the whole system and the good of the entire city."[28] Although the Parent-Teachers Association for the entire Chicago region, aware of the diversity among its constituent elements, equivocated, its reform-minded activists did ask the board to "give vigorous leadership" for carefully prepared plans, saying it "deeply regrets the climate of intimidation which has been created . . . by self-seeking public officials."[29]

Even though strongly supportive, white liberals were unable to match neighborhood-school proponents in the size and militancy of their political undertakings. Reformers in Chicago, though politically alert, were too few in number to match the crowds mobilized by aroused portions of Chicago's Northwest and Southwest sides. In this ideological struggle, they therefore mobilized the one asset they had —contact with other citywide organizations. As a result, a host of community groups not usually involved in school matters issued pronouncements on the school busing matter. The busing plan was praised by the Chicago Conference of Laymen, Northwest Chicago Human Relations Council, the Anti-Defamation League of B'nai B'rith, the Young Men Jewish Council, the American Friends Service Committee, the Church Federation of Greater Chicago, the Catholic Inter-racial Council, the American Jewish Congress (which actually held a joint press conference on the matter with the Independent Voters of Illinois), the Chicago Conference on Religion and Race, the Chicago Youth Centers, and other religious and civic groups. In short, school reformers "socialized" the issue by encouraging entry of potential allies into the dispute.[30]

These groups did not hesitate to characterize the issue in clear-cut moral categories. For example, the American Friends Service Committee declared, "It would do immense harm to the cause of education and equal opportunity . . . if the present proposal should fail because of a highly vocal opposition of a frightened and bigoted minority."[31] And a representative of the Anti-Defamation League endured boos and heckling at a public hearing to insist that "if the Board of Education decides here on the basis of the fears of people who are more concerned with fanciful damage to their real estate values than the welfare of all children, Chicago is in even deeper trouble than events of the past several weeks would suggest."[32] Although white reformers were not able to mobilize mass demonstrations to support their integrationist objectives, they clearly viewed the matter as having the highest moral significance.

Socialization of Conflict

The conflict over busing had rapidly become a two-party, zero-sum confrontation. Although at the beginning blacks had made their own, quite distinct criticisms of the Redmond plan, once a busing plan was proposed, blacks and white liberal integrationists joined in opposition to neighborhood-school groups.[33] Because this ideological conflict was so intense, pressure was placed on third parties with little immediate stake in the outcome to identify with one or another side in the two-party conflict. And as we have seen, other liberal and reform groups came to the support of the school reformers. But backing for the busing plan also came from groups not usually part of the liberal-reform coalition—labor, business, and the Roman Catholic archdiocese. Except for the last, the support was token and pro forma, but it is nonetheless interesting that the Chicago Federation of Labor was moved to pass a resolution endorsing the busing plan, that the Leadership Council for Metropolitan Open Communities (a progressive business organization established to encourage desegregated land use) issued a statement in favor of Redmond's proposals, and that the Chicago Teachers Union at the last minute gave the proposals its endorsement even though its president had earlier criticized spending "money in this fashion when our schools are crying for lower class sizes."[34] Cardinal Cody, head of the archdiocese, acted more vigorously by not only saying that "busing represents an important step in the development of quality education" but also by announcing that Catholic schools would in the near future institute their own busing plan.[35]

With this one exception, these third-party expressions of support were not backed by any substantial expenditure of group resources on behalf of the scheme, and their significance should be appropriately discounted. Perhaps the most significant backing integrationists received was the favorable, if not outright biased, news reporting in the two Field newspapers.[36] Consistent with their reports of events, the *Sun-Times* editorialized that "the proposal to bus Austin and South Shore grade school pupils is more moderate and sensible,"[37] and the *Daily News* commented that "there is . . . mounting evidence that busing helps to sharpen the minds of all the children involved."[38]

If integrationists secured the half-hearted backing of powerful and prestigious citywide groups, neighborhood-school groups mobilized much more active support from lesser known but still potent centers of power—locally elected public officials.[39] Both Republican and Democratic aldermen and state legislators from South Chicago, Belmont-Cragin and similar white neighborhoods found the issue so politically significant that they ignored the usual "keep schools out of politics" rule and moved quickly to "lead" the protest against the school board. On the early January day when the school board was first presented with specific busing proposals, twelve elected officials first attended the school board meeting, securing from President Whiston permission to sit within the wooden railing that divides the board and its staff from the general public, and then were allowed to participate in an extraordinary semiprivate session with board members after the regular meeting. As a direct consequence of these pressures, the school board modified its original decision to hold only citywide public hearings in favor of holding a series of hearings in high schools within the communities affected by the busing proposals.

This was only the most dramatic move made by the local political leadership of the white communities. They attended antibusing rallies, spoke against the proposals at public hearings of the board, and introduced resolutions in the City Council as well as the state legislature (which threatened to investigate the schools and hold back needed funds). Most significantly, the neighborhood-school forces recruited to their cause the active support of a United States congressman, Roman Pucinski, who occupied a position of some prestige within the Democratic organization. Pucinski sat on the House Committee on Labor and Education, was regarded as somewhat of a liberal in Congress, had played an important role in securing federal funds for Chicago schools, and was well-enough regarded by the party leadership to be slated as the Democratic candidate for the U.S. Senate two years later. When Pucinski testified that his constituents felt that "busing may ultimately lead to the kind of block-busting which has destroyed many of Chicago"s finest communities,"[40] it was abundantly clear that the machine was not interested in protecting the school board from white opposition to its plans.

The entry of third parties into an ideological dispute is frequently accompanied by the activation of other governmental units who may have direct or indirect authoritative powers relevant to the dispute. Thus the city council was urged to delay approval of the school board's budget and the state legislature considered bills and resolutions calling for an investigation of the busing plan, a state law forbidding busing to achieve racial balance, and an elected school board.

While neighborhood-school forces relied on these local and state institutions, integrationists appealed to the federal government. Originally, the Department of Health, Education, and Welfare approved Redmond's plan as an "encouraging first step," although it indicated that its investigation of Chicago's integration policies would continue until it could "see specific steps taken towards implementation."[41] With the emergence of the busing controversy, the director of the civil rights compliance office of HEW threatened to activate his investigation unless busing was instituted. Finally in the week after the board had rejected the compulsory busing plan and before a voluntary one had been approved, the director reiterated his threat to open up the investigation. Indeed, some might even see this implied threat to withdraw federal funds as the critical instrument that produced a compromise in favor of voluntary busing.

Resistance to Pressure

All of these actions by neighborhood-school groups, black civil rights leaders, white liberal reformers, third parties, and state and federal governments finally eventuated in a decision by the school board to reject both of Redmond's proposals in favor of a voluntary busing program in Austin. It is tempting to attribute to such activities a good deal of causal impact. Groups make demands, mobilize supporters, activate political representatives, threaten electoral retaliation, scrutinize decisions taken by office holders, and thereby achieve at least some of their objectives. One reporter chose to interpret at least part of the events under discussion in this manner: "The ability of indignant citizens to make elected officials listen—and even retreat—was apparent once again this week as white parents gathered in the board of education building to protest student busing."[42]

If not examined carefully, some facts lend credence to this interpretation of the board's decision. As pressure from neighborhood-school forces mounted, support for integration steadily declined. In late August of 1967 the board of education voted ten to nothing, with one abstention, in favor of adopting "in principle" the Redmond plan. In late December the board approved by an eight-to-two margin a recommendation that $150,000 be set aside for busing students in two neighborhoods to "achieve a viable racial balance."[43] By a seven-to-three margin the board rejected at that same meeting a request to defer action on the budgetary allocation until a later date.[44] At the next, early January meeting of the board, Superintendent Redmond proposed a specific plan to bus children from schools in South Shore and Austin to schools in South Chicago and Belmont-Cragin. At this meeting, attended by hundreds of neighborhood-school defenders plus a number of their local aldermen and state representatives, President Whiston recommended postponing the decision until public hearings had been held. The board agreed to hold public hearings but by a six-to-four vote insisted that a final decision be made by February 28. On that day, they voted nine-to-one to *reject* the superintendent's proposals with respect to South Shore and failed by a five-to-five vote to approve a compulsory busing plan for Austin. A voluntary busing plan for Austin was also rejected by a five-to-five vote. One week later, at a special meeting the board finally did approve nine-to-one a voluntary busing plan for Austin. In short, a mere summary of the voting behavior of the board indicates continual slippage in the support for compulsory busing.

But before assuming a causal connection between outside pressure and board behavior, one needs to look carefully at the actions of each of the ten active members of the board. It is only individual board members that can bow to group pressure, not a board as a whole. That done, it is difficult to assert that political pressure had much effect on what board members did. In the first place, four board members—Bacon, Friedman, Malis, and Oliver—voted consistently in favor of integrationist plans throughout this period, even though clearly aware of opposition to them.

Secondly, two neighborhood-school proponents—President Whiston and Vice-president Murray—voted to delay or defeat the busing plans at nearly every opportunity. It is true that they voted for the Redmond plan "in principle" in August 1967, but their support was highly conditional. Although Whiston said that it was "a fine package and I concur with it," he also observed, "I have some misgivings, and I want it completely understood as we implement this report . . . that I have a right to vote 'no' and to express myself."[45] Similarly, Murray stated that his support of neighborhood-school policies did not mean "[I am] a member of the Board who cannot change my mind," but he only admitted to being "on the borderline [of changing] now."[46] In the circumstances, it is probably fair to suggest that at least these two board members approved the Redmond plan "in principle" because they knew that the only practical consequence of the vote was to place Chicago in compliance with a directive of the federal government.

Thirdly, Marge Wild and Mrs. Green were hardly less consistent in their opposition to the superintendent's compulsory, quota-based desegregation plans. It is true they voted in favor of allowing $150,000 to be included in the budget for busing, but even when they cast their ballots in favor of this budgetary allocation, they indicated that they were "opposed to Redmond's concept of busing and . . . [might] reject the final plan."[47] At that December meeting, before community protest had erupted, Wild indicated that she did not favor "moving children out of their own community involuntarily 'because I wouldn't want my own child moved in this fashion.' "[48] Green's objections had to do with the provision in Redmond's plan that black students bused into white schools would never total more than 15 percent of the student population. At the time Green approved the Redmond plan "in principle" she expressed reservations about the legality of using racial quotas, promising that "as we come to matters of implementation . . . where we think we are in conflict with the law, I shall vote 'no.' "[49] In sum, both Green and Wild voted on the substantive questions in February exactly as they had said they would vote months earlier, before neighborhood-school groups began their campaign.

Fourth, John Carey voted in favor of all the desegregation proposals—he even voted for the South Shore scheme rejected by the rest of the board—but cast his votes with the neighborhood-school faction on an important procedural question. He supported President Whiston's desire to postpone indefinitely a decision on busing until after public hearings had been held. As a labor leader, he had ties with the machine faction on the board and in the city, and he helped maintain these relationships by giving Whiston and Murray his vote on this procedural question. But Carey was also a leader of an industrial union with many black workers, and he was very much committed to Redmond's integrationist proposals. On the same day he cast his vote with Whiston on this procedural question, he aggressively and angrily attacked the antibusing politicians who had obtained a special, private session with the board. Among other things, he told these elected officials he "was bothered by the 'negative' attitudes of the antibusing contingent and that he resented efforts to make 'a political football out of a serious situation.' "[50]

In sum, five board members—Bacon, Oliver, Friedman, Malis, and Carey—voted in favor of Redmond's proposals on virtually every substantive occasion. They did not cave in under intense pressures from neighborhood-school supporters. On the other side, four board members—Whiston, Murray, Wild, and Green—all indicated opposition to a compulsory, quota-based busing scheme even before Redmond's specific proposals were announced and community opposition was aroused.

This leaves one key board member, Cyrus Adams III, who in the end cast a decisive vote that prevented the board's approving Redmond's plan for Austin. He had voted for the Redmond plan "in principle," voted in favor of allocating funds for a busing plan, and voted against delaying a decision by holding public hearings. Moreover, he stated in late December, before community opposition had surfaced, that busing "may or may not work, but we must give it a try to attempt to retain and attract people who are moving to the suburbs." Only after opposition mounted in early January did Adams change his mind and state that "the plans will not accomplish their purpose."[51]

Even though the sequence of events implies that this board member responded to public pressure, the evidence is not conclusive. In the first place, as vice-president of a major downtown department store planning to retire from both his business and civic responsibilities a few months hence, Adams was hardly vulnerable to political pressure. Secondly, the head of the department store with which Adams was associated was also president of the Leadership Council for Metropolitan Open Communities, which endorsed Redmond's plans the same week Adams announced his opposition to them. Thirdly, when Adams announced his change in position, he quite candidly but scornfully spoke of the neighborhood-school activists as follows:

> I don't think the spirit of Jesus Christ could change the minds of people or allay their anti-Negro fears and prejudices. To me they have just confirmed their philosophy about their schools: "suffer little children to come unto them, as long as they aren't black."[52]

In the circumstances, it is probably appropriate to pay attention to Adams's own explanation of his change of opinion. Earlier, he had said that the plans "may or may not work, but we must give it a try" so that Chicago could "retain and attract people who are moving to the suburbs." In January he showed the way in which the demonstrations had affected his thinking: "If plans intended to retain middle-class people in the city are going to drive a larger number of middle-class people out of the city, they don't make sense."[53] Between these two statements, Adams had evidently recalculated the consequences busing would have for racial stability within Chicago, a value to which he attached a great deal of weight. Only in this sense can he be said to have been pressured into withdrawing support for the superintendent's integration plans.

Reluctance to Compromise

In many ways, the school desegregation controversy followed a course anticipated by the ideological bargaining model. The antagonists took what they believed were principled positions on the issues, they engaged in open confrontations using public testimony, boycotts, demonstrations, pickets, and law suits to convey their positions on the issues, socialized the conflict by bringing in third parties, and induced other governmental agencies to enter the conflict. In these circumstances, one does not expect political compromise—unless power is so shared among authoritative decision makers as to force a compromise.

On two occasions during the course of the controversy, efforts to compromise in fact proved impossible. When integrationists in South Shore wanted a two-way busing plan bitterly opposed by whites in nonintegrated parts of the area, the administrative staff proposed a compromise one-way busing plan. When it was then criticized vigorously by both sides, the board rejected the plan altogether. On the school board itself, the voluntary busing plan was agreed upon only with great difficulty. Long before the February 28 meeting it was clear that Adams and Wild were willing to support a voluntary busing plan; newspaper reporters wrote background accounts forecasting a consensus developing behind the voluntary plan. At the meeting itself, however, an effort to amend Redmond's recommendation by making the plan voluntary was rejected on a five-to-five vote, with the integrationist faction voting against the compromise. When compulsory busing in Austin was then put to a vote, it also failed to obtain the necessary six votes. Outraged and disgusted, Warren Bacon moved to adjourn, and no compromise was worked out. Instead, the board had to be called into special session the following week to vote the Austin voluntary compromise—even though the votes for this compromise probably existed all along.

The refusal of the five integrationists to reach a consensus before the February 28 meeting indicated their reluctance to compromise on a matter of principle until the power relations within the board had been firmly delineated. Once Adams had announced against compulsory busing in early January, it was clear that Redmond's proposals were doomed. Newspaper reporters said so in their background analyses of events before any public hearings had been held. Yet integrationist board members apparently hoped that in the end they could pick up a sixth vote from one quarter or another; only after the decisive vote was taken were they willing to settle for less than compulsory busing. The compromise occurred because voluntary busing was, from their viewpoint, better than no busing at all, and because Adams and Wild had all along been willing to approve voluntary busing to relieve overcrowding in the two Austin community schools. A compromise was reached, but that compromise came about only because power was equally divided between the two sides, and neither side could impose its will on the other. Except possibly for Cyrus Adams, board members were not interested in compromise for its own sake.

Mayor Daley and School Desegregation

Chicago's school board had the *authority* to formulate school policy, but most liberal reformers in Chicago doubt they have *independent power* to make the decisions. No analysis of the bargaining processes would be complete without consideration of the mayor's involvement in the episode, although actually the story can be related satisfactorily without mentioning Daley's involvement.

Mayor Daley publicly commented on Redmond's desegregation plans on three occasions. Each time he indicated that school policy was something in which he did not want to become involved, and that he thought the board should be open and responsive to public opinion. When the Redmond plan was first announced in August 1967, Daley commented:

"It is bold, imaginative, and challenging. It presents something that is unique and new. I know the board of education will give every possible consideration. There will be public hearings. They'll accept suggestions. I'm confident the decision they will make will be the right one."[54]

What did he think of busing pupils? "It is before them. I'm not an educator."[55] Does this mean an end to the neighborhood school system? "I'm not a member of the board."[56] Is there too much federal interference? "I said when I was first elected mayor I would not interfere in school administration. But we hope there always will be local control of schools, no matter who contributes."[57]

In early January, after the busing proposals had aroused great opposition, Daley spoke to this matter a second time:

"While I think this is a matter for the board—and I said constantly that matters of the board should be resolved by the board and the superintendent of schools—I feel very strongly that any program today should have maximum participation by the people of the neighborhoods."[58]

He was asked, "Are you saying that if the people don't want any proposal, the government should listen to them?"

"I think it is basic. Who has the right to determine? Everyone serves the people, and if the majority of the people don't want a certain thing, who in government has the right to set themselves up above the majority?"

"I am a democrat with a small 'd,' and I can put my record alongside anyone else's. It's up to the people to decide finally because they are the ones who make up our city."[59]

What about Roman Pucinski's opposition to the plan?

"Pucinski's opposition is an individual matter. He does not represent the Democratic party. The school children of Chicago should never be the object of politics."[60]

"It's a matter for an individual in public office. No one wants conformity."[61]

A couple of weeks later, Daley added,

"Some organizations on both sides of this are paper organizations speaking for no one. And some try to make this a Negro-white situation, which it is not."

"One of the things wrong with our society today is that too many mothers are working. I can't really criticize them for earning a living, but I guess I'm old-fashioned. It used to be that people wanted to see their children home for lunch, and discuss what happened in school with them."[62]

And with that the mayor was silent.

He is here quoted at length, almost in toto, so that the reader can see for himself the cues Daley was providing other participants in the controversy. In my opinion, Daley's words suggest a lack of enthusiasm for the busing proposals but at the same time a reluctance to become involved directly in the issue on one side or the other. Although he distributed his clichés on both sides of the question, the balance of his comments seemed to favor the neighborhood-school groups. He defended the board's autonomy and independence, but he still felt "very strongly" that "it's up to the people to decide." He criticized any mixing of politicians into the affair, but with respect to Pucinski, Daley said that "no one wants conformity." Perhaps most revealing was his little noticed comment that children should be "home for lunch," a practice not easily arranged if children are bused to school.

If Daley did not influence the school board, why did he comment at all? Why did he say that it was "up to the people to decide?" In this case, the pluralist bargaining model seems to provide the most satisfactory explanation. As a consummate politician, Daley realized that he could not remain silent on such a politically explosive issue as school busing. Yet if he took a clear position on the question, he would only disturb one or another component of his Democratic coalition. If he were to declare his support for busing, he would outrage many of the party faithful in white sections of the city and county. If he were to oppose it, blacks would be insulted and white liberals would accuse him of mixing schools with politics. His issuance of somewhat delphic comments, filled with proverbs that could scarcely be disputed but which nonetheless were weighted in the direction of preserving the neighborhood school, was the politically most profitable course to follow. As a key board member commented to an interviewer, the mayor's comments were "a typical political statement which was in the middle and wishy-washy and didn't say a thing. . . . That's the way we have to be too. *But* he has to get elected and *we don't*."[63]

Limits on a Bargaining Perspective

Quite clearly, desegregation politics in Chicago provoked extensive political bargaining. Yet there are some aspects of the policy-making process for which this bargaining model does not provide a satisfactory answer. Why did Redmond choose to initiate implementation of his plan by means of a busing scheme, in Austin and South Shore? Why did the board overwhelmingly endorse desegregation "in principle," only to reject a plan for South Shore by almost an equally overwhelming vote? Why was Redmond unable to frame his proposals in ways that could have maintained the eight-to-two majority he received on his initial busing recommendations to the board? Why was this closely fought contest never repeated in subsequent years? To answer these questions we shall turn to two unitary models of policy formation.

UNITARY MODEL A: AN ORGANIZATION DESEGREGATES

From the perspective of the organizational model, the behavior of the school board is not the outcome of bargaining among board members and their reference groups, but a function of the constraints which a large, complex, formal organization places on board behavior. Board members are dependent on an administrative staff with interests, values, and standard operating procedures that are valuable for achieving routine organizational goals but often hinder solution to unusual and difficult problems such as school desegregation. As a result, the decisions of the school board are best conceptualized as the outputs of a unitary organization incapable of maximizing its policy objectives.

Three major sets of tactical miscalculations reduced the likelihood that the Redmond plan would ever be carried into effect: (1) the staff selected as its initial proposal a scheme unlikely to promote eventual acceptance of the overall plan; (2) the staff did not communicate effectively with community groups in the areas affected by the busing proposal; and (3) the staff failed to prepare the school board for the controversy that eventuated. Significantly, these miscalculations were due not so much to the personal deficiencies of individual staff members as to values widely shared by educational professionals and to structural features characteristic of most large school systems.

Choosing the First Step

Shortly after the announcement of the Redmond plan in August 1967, the superintendent and his staff chose school busing as the initial means to implement it. A more controversial beginning could hardly have been selected, as prior school busing conflicts in other cities had made painfully clear. Indeed, by 1967–68 George Wallace had not only organized one surprisingly successful presidential campaign around the busing issue but he was on the verge of launching a second. Although alternatives were not easily identifiable, at least one proposal contained within the Redmond plan was far less controversial than busing. Formation of "magnet schools" with special facilities, favorable faculty-student ratios, and controlled racial composition would doubtless have been hailed by many as a significant educational improvement. Because admission to these schools would be voluntary, at the very least their creation in certain transition areas of Chicago would not have generated great controversy.

Given these political virtues, it seems in retrospect to have been a serious miscalculation to proceed with a busing plan. Although we can only guess at the thinking of the administrative staff during this period, it seems unlikely that any conscious choice between these two alternatives was ever made. Instead, the administrative staff selected the alternative for solving its problems that created the least disturbance to the existing structure. And in this regard, busing had a great advantage, because it involved only a minimal departure from a neighborhood-school pattern of organization. By comparison, the magnet school idea presented many hazards. Such schools would disturb attendance patterns at existing neighborhood schools in unpredictable ways. Resources would have to be allocated to magnet schools in ways inconsistent with the standard formulas familiar to administrators. Relations between magnet schools and neighborhood schools would be complicated by the overlap of territorial jurisdiction: if children elected to attend the "magnet school," would that not reflect poorly on the local neighborhood school? In the Redmond plan prepared by long-time administrative officials, it was suggested that magnet schools could be created in from five to seven years, because by that time construction of new buildings with special facilities would make magnet schools feasible. It is doubtful that the system needed new buildings so much as it needed time to adjust. After the disastrous attempt to bus children in South Shore had been rejected by the board, the staff quickly designed a magnet school to open the following September. Under extreme pressure, the magnet school concept was discovered to be compatible with facilities in existing buildings. As organizational theorists have asserted, organizations do learn to modify their behavior, but they learn most quickly after severe "output failure" has occurred.[64]

In contrast to the magnet school concept, busing, though disturbing to parents and children, involved relatively minor modifications in the system's standard operating procedures. A determinate number of identifiable children in certain blocks of a school attendance area would be transferred to a new school. The size and location of change was predictable enough so that the school system could digest it. Even so, organizational imperatives dictated that busing could not be comprehensive but had to be implemented on an experimental basis in only two communities.

According to the logic of the Redmond plan, comprehensive busing was needed. If Austin and South Shore really could be stabilized by the busing plans, the pressures on racially changing neighborhoods elsewhere would inevitably increase. A comprehensive plan for controlled racial integration in previously all-white schools throughout the city would be far more effective than these modest plans for just two neighborhoods.

Nor would a comprehensive busing plan have been much more controversial. For one thing, a plan aimed at only two neighborhoods appears to be discriminatory. By selecting two neighborhoods for such "invidious" treatment, the administrative staff invited strong opposition from community groups in these neighborhoods. Had every school in the white areas been similarly integrated, every neighborhood would have been treated equally.

Even if such a comprehensive busing plan would have encountered serious opposition, it would also have gained greater support. The political arena would have been the city as a whole, not just the specific communities affected. A more general policy would have invited more extensive and effective support from blacks, white liberals, religious leaders, and the business community, than did this token program.

Once again, it is doubtful that the administrative staff consciously chose to limit its plan to two neighborhoods because it calculated the political and educational situation and determined that a two-neighborhood plan was best. The most likely reason for the modest busing proposal was the difficulty with which organizations develop and implement programs that call for major organizational change. Any busing plan required extensive fact-gathering and preparation. Classroom availability, selection of students to be bused, identification of curricular needs of bused pupils, transfer of teachers: all these and a host of other organizational details had to be arranged. Equally important, local community leaders had to be consulted.

In theory, personnel were available within the organization for this purpose. Aside from the large number of administrators in the central office, the system had twenty-seven district superintendents who with their principals could have worked out specific plans for their communities within the guidelines laid down in the Redmond plan. In practice this was hardly feasible. Not only would this have given district superintendents a responsibility far beyond anything they had previously undertaken, but it was known to central office administrators that many principals and district superintendents throughout the system were extremely dubious about the viability of integration plans.[65] In order to prevent any deliberate sabotaging of the busing scheme, Redmond gave the entire assignment to Francis McKeag, assistant superintendent for facilities and planning, who took upon himself and his four-man professional staff the responsibility for developing detailed plans and discussing them with community groups in South Shore–South Chicago and in Austin-Belmont-Cragin. Even a modest busing scheme for just these two areas taxed the resources of this office to their very limits. Organizational incapacity precluded any more comprehensive busing plan.

Organizational theorists point out that the best predictor of organizational behavior at time $t + 1$ is organizational behavior at time t. This observation does not say very much. But it suggests that even when major changes are as politically feasible as smaller changes, they may still not be viable simply because they depart too dramatically from the system's operating norms. Organizations are clumsy animals; they do not deftly leap through the forest but measure each step before taking it.

Developing a Plan for South Shore–South Chicago

If busing students in only two selected neighborhoods was not the most auspicious manner of inaugurating a comprehensive desegregation plan, the proposal still might have had a greater chance of success if the staff had communicated more adeptly with community leaders. In this regard, the clumsy, inappropriate behavior of school administrators was particularly evident in South Shore.

The South Shore community has since 1960 steadily become increasingly black. As the number of blacks in Chicago increased by over 325,000 in the decade of the fifties, they migrated southward almost to the city limits. The South Shore community, which bulges eastward into Lake Michigan (see fig. 3), was bypassed in the early stages of this migration, but by 1960 blacks were beginning to cross Stony Island Avenue and move east toward the lake. A liberal, relatively highly educated community, with a high percentage of Jews living within it, South Shore did not build powerful neighborhood organizations that vigorously fought further black encroachments.[66] On the contrary, an increasingly powerful group of community leaders were proclaiming by the mid-sixties their strong commitment to a stable, integrated community. By 1963 these integrationists achieved a dominant position within the neighborhood's most significant community organization, the South Shore Commission.[67] In order to achieve their goal of maintaining a "quality, integrated" community, the commission developed a number of conservation programs designed to keep the area an attractive locale for in-migrating whites. Among other things, they established a tenant referral service for screening prospective tenants, pressed city agencies to enforce building codes, and manned a radio patrol system to minimize local crime.

The commission also sought to maintain sufficient numbers of whites in local schools so that these important community institutions would not become all black. In the November following the announcement of Redmond's plan, the president of the commission proposed that South Shore be the setting for a pilot two-way busing program.[68] Significantly, this plan, which involved sending white children to previously predominantly black schools (and vice versa), was agreed upon only after some liberal members of the commission had criticized a proposed one-way busing as unfair to black children. Instead, two-way busing was agreed upon as the fair way to provide "a stabilized integration of our school population."[69]

The South Shore Commission, though the strongest and most enduring community organization in the area, was not the only one which could claim to represent the community. Smaller neighborhood organizations and PTAs in the white portions of South Shore and in South Chicago, a more predominantly working-class white area to the south and east of South Shore, were far less enthusiastic about a desegregation program. Residents in these all-white areas, especially those living in South Chicago, felt that school busing, particularly two-way busing, threatened the stability of their neighborhoods. While the commission might argue that South Shore as a whole faced these changes, those living in parts of south Shore further from the points of black in-migration (to say nothing of South Chicagoans) felt that the best way to maintain their neighborhood was to keep their schools as white as they already were.

As South Shore became increasingly black, a third perspective found organized expression in the community. An emerging group of black leaders questioned whether the commission's goal of a stable, integrated community was in the interest of blacks. They noted that most policies designed to achieve this goal, such as gifted-child programs, integration schemes, and careful screening of prospective house buyers, worked to the advantage of whites rather than blacks. In order to maintain racial stability, whites, not blacks, had to be attracted to South Shore, and public policies had to be designed accordingly. As the Concerned Parents of Bryn Mawr would argue at one of the public hearings on busing, "Nowhere in this plan is the black community assured that their children will receive a better education in the receiving school."[70] "Using Negro children to maintain a racial balance at Bryn Mawr," their spokeswoman continued, "is total racism and shows a lack of respect for black people as human beings."[71]

Since such a broad range of opinion within any one community was highly unusual, the values governing school-community relations and the routines typically followed by administrators were not appropriate to the South Shore–South Chicago situation. School-community relations, as understood and practiced by school administrators, generally assume that a community has a "consensual elite" structure of power that the professional properly consults when making major decisions. Administrative officials acted in South Shore and South Chicago as if this pattern held for that area as well.

To begin with, the school system recognized the South Shore Commission as fully representative of community opinion in the area. When the commission proposed to administrative officials a two-way busing plan, they accepted the proposal as a basis for secret discussions. After considerable discussion and revision, school and commission officials agreed upon a two-way busing plan that involved nearly 3,500 students; each school was to have a population that would be 60 to 70 percent white.

The secret, pluralist bargaining out of which this plan emerged assumed a consensual elite within the community. Since school officials and the commission shared a common commitment to a stable, integrated community, a compromise reasonably satisfactory to all could be arranged. But before long, the unreality of these assumptions became too obvious to ignore. When a newsman was barred from attending a secret meeting in South Chicago where plans were being explained to leaders from all-white areas, he strenuously objected that his removal was in violation of a state law requiring open meetings. Eventually, the group had to adjourn to a private home. Not surprisingly, the contents of the meeting leaked out in any case, and over the New Year's Day weekend parents and community groups continuously called school administrators to protest two-way busing.

Although such opposition was to be expected, Francis McKeag, the assistant superintendent in charge, rapidly developed a new plan in the hope of building a consensus. Without consulting the South Shore Commission, he dropped two schools entirely from the plan and decided simply to bus 463 blacks from three schools in South Shore to nine schools further south, as shown in figure 4. In replacing two-way with one-way busing, the staff tried to find a compromise between the position of the Commission and the whites in South Chicago.

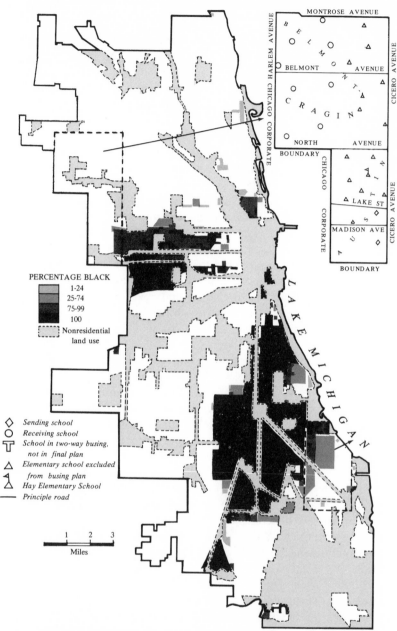

FIG. 3. Racial distribution, by city block, of children attending Chicago
public schools, November 1967. After a map in *Race and Housing: The Chicago Housing Market, 1967–1972*, by Brian J. L.
Berry (Cambridge, Mass.: Ballinger Publishing Co., 1976), by
permission of the author. *Inset*: Sending and receiving schools
in desegregation plan for Austin and Belmont-Cragin, 1968.

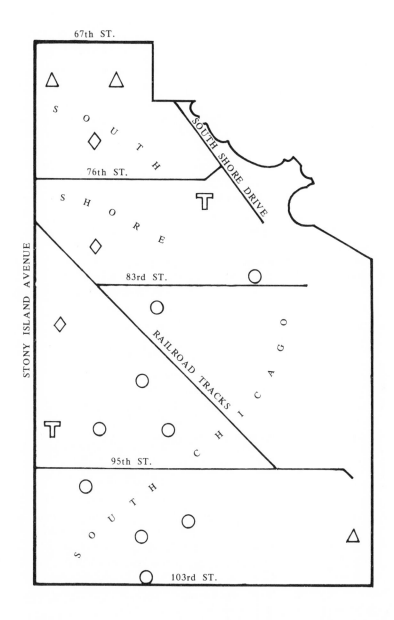

FIG. 4. Sending and receiving schools in desegregation plan for South
Shore and South Chicago, 1968.

The move was disastrous. Given the character of ideological bargaining, the white neighborhood-school groups, rather than seeking to arrive at some consensus, increased their opposition. Their initial victory only whetted their appetite for a more complete one. The South Shore Commission, finding the school system no longer adhering to the two-way busing plan, said the new scheme was "so meager the commission would prefer that the board drop it."[72] A number of black leaders, suspicious of the plans from the beginning, proclaimed their distaste for plans which used black children to solve the needs of a white community. At the hearings which the school board held in South Shore hardly a group testified in its favor. The school system, by trying to seek a consensus which everyone could support, announced a plan which no one would support.

In ideological conflict, as in war, the crucial problem is not to placate the enemy but to keep the alliance intact. But since the consensual elite myth was internalized in the operating code of the administrative staff, officials rejected such a battle plan. In so doing, they prepared the ground for the board's decisive rejection of busing in South Shore. As the president of the South Shore Commission observed, "If the superintendent's staff had deliberately set out to kill the busing program, . . . it could not have done a better job."[73]

Developing a Plan for Austin-Belmont-Cragin

Although the administrative staff made fewer miscalculations in Austin-Belmont-Cragin than in South Shore, even in this area it failed to maximize its objectives because it failed to communicate effectively with groups in Belmont-Cragin. By this we do not mean that the staff should be held responsible for the vigor of the opposition to the busing plans; there is probably little that the system could have done about that. Rather, their miscalculation involved a serious underestimation of the strength of this opposition.

Prior to the public announcement, PTA presidents at the eight receiving schools shown in figure 3 were approached. When these presidents were assured that busing would be carefully controlled so that less than 10 percent of students at each elementary school would be black, one or two presidents nonetheless suggested that opposition would develop. However, most said they thought the plan would work and they would help see the plan successfully implemented. As one newspaper reporter commented later, "Staff members met with PTA leaders in all the affected schools and discussed the possibilities. First reactions were favorable."[74] Acting on the basis of a consensual elite model of the community, administrators approved the plans for submission to the school board. Although some administrators did anticipate opposition, detailed planning as to the way in which such opposition would be countered was not undertaken. On the contrary, when demonstrations occurred they "came as a rude shock" to Redmond himself.[75] The miscalculations in Austin did not involve acts of commission, as in South Shore, but acts of omission. Acting on dubious evidence that the receiving schools would support the plan, the officials developed no contingency plans in case they did not.

Adverse reaction to the busing plan developed rapidly. Within a week of the meeting between administration and receiving-school leaders, PTA presidents which had predicted community support for busing either resigned or were voted out of office by their members. A telephone grapevine among mothers in the area had transmitted the unhappy message to nearly everyone on the Northwest Side of Chicago. Large numbers of residents attended protest rallies and demonstrated before the school board. The board eventually retreated to its voluntary busing plan.

The Staff and Its Board

If the administrative staff had not been acting on the basis of a consensual elite model, they might have taken special pains to prepare board members for the extent of the opposition. The staff, however, discussed the busing plans with community groups without ever discussing its plans with board members. Strange as it may seem, Redmond and his staff did not provide board members with detailed information concerning the plan they were developing, nor did they inform board members privately of the reasons for the kind of plan that was being proposed. And they gave board members no hint of the kind of opposition likely to develop in South Chicago and Belmont-Cragin. Instead, board members by reading newspaper accounts discovered that secret meetings were being held with community groups.[76] Thus a storm of protest broke about the heads of board members even before they heard the details of busing plans. The staff failed either to inform the board adequately of the potential opposition or to prepare an appropriate strategy for dealing with it.

In part this was due to the model of school-community relations which the system valued. But it was also in part due to the standard manner in which the staff typically communicated with its board.[77] The reforms of the Hunt and Willis eras, designed to protect school administration from political influences, had isolated the board from the administrative staff—and, what was equally important, the staff from the board. Where the superintendent was strong, dominating policy making, as during the Willis era, this did not handicap the staff's capacity to implement its decisions. But where the superintendent was new, not as influential, and certainly less aggressive, he was left without an efficient mechanism for developing a coalition on the board in support of his policies.

Given the ideological convictions of board members, it would not have been easy to sustain a board majority throughout the controversy, even if the superintendent and his staff had acted with maximum efficiency. Yet there is some evidence that school boards that act decisively and quickly can forestall white opposition and carry into effect at least modest desegregation proposals.[78] Had the superintendent discussed with his board the plans in Austin and South Shore, emphasized the support integrationist groups were providing, insisted on the need for decisive action so that plans could be inaugurated to coincide with the beginning of the second school semester, secured a commitment privately from a majority of board members, and vigorously discouraged holding any public meetings, then he might have, by obtaining an early commitment from Cyrus Adams and the solidly prointegration board members, held at least a six-vote majority on key issues.

Clearly, these maneuvers would not have been easily negotiated. The superintendent, who at the time was in the midst of complex bargaining negotiations with his union, would have had to have controlled all relevant facts and utilized them to persuade the board in private sessions. To say that this is too much to expect of any superintendent responsible for a far-flung school system is only to reveal the way in which school systems must have standard operating procedures and accredited ways of relating to problems which permit orderly division of organizational labor. In crucially difficult decision-making situations, these procedures and arrangements often preclude gaining important objectives.

In summary, policy formation occurs in an organizational context that powerfully shapes what the system can do. The organization has interests, values, and standard operating procedures that subtly influence the assumptions administrators make when framing recommendations. While these organizational characteristics are essential for orderly functioning of the system in routine matters, they lead in unusual circumstances to serious miscalculations. In this instance, the Chicago school system failed to implement Redmond's plan for school desegregation because its organizational characteristics prevented it from: (1) selecting among alternatives the best means of initiating this school desegregation plan; (2) building the strongest political alliance with its community allies in South Shore; and (3) not preparing adequately either the board or the superintendent for the level of community opposition that eventually occurred. No two or three individuals within the organization can be blamed for stupidity or sabotage. Indeed, it is unrealistic to expect any school system or other large, complex organization to perform any more efficiently in such difficult circumstances. Although some scholars think errors of this magnitude must be due to organizational "pathology,"[79] it seems likely instead that the very routines that enable a school system to function well in ordinary circumstances preclude maximum achievement of newly defined objectives.

UNITARY MODEL B: THE SCHOOL BOARD AS RATIONAL DECISION MAKER

To assert that organizational characteristics preclude maximum achievement of school system objectives in Chicago presupposes that the board of education "really" intended to execute Redmond's plan in the first place—that the board, as a unit, had an objective which its administrative staff failed to maximize. This assumption may seem to be confounded by the foregoing interpretation of school desegregation policy, which saw outcomes as the result of ideologically based conflict between two factions on the board and in the community. If the board was deeply divided, can we then say that it held objectives sufficiently explicit, and to which it was sufficiently attached, that these could control specific decisions? After all, does not first the approval, then the de facto rejection, of Redmond's plan beautifully illustrate the futility of any assumption that public institutions are capable of rationally shaping their decisions so as to achieve definable objectives?

A persuasive case to the contrary can be made from a rational decision-making perspective. From this vantagepoint, the school board was committed to a specific goal which shaped the way in which it examined issues, gathered information, and selected alternatives. Used successfully, the model identifies an objective to which the board seems committed and then shows how board behavior can be satisfactorily explained as a series of efforts to maximize that objective. As the utility of the model in foreign-policy studies shows, its power lies in the simplicity of its explanation. In brief, the rational decision-making model simply assumes that the board carried out its intentions.

Rationale for Redmond Plan

The Chicago Board of Education was both implicitly and explicitly committed to stabilizing the racial composition of the city of Chicago. Put more harshly, the board wanted to discourage blacks from entering, whites from leaving, Chicago as a place of residence. Redmond's plan was conceived with this goal in mind, and the board's subsequent decisions seem to have been a consistent application of the same objective. As early as 1964 the school board asserted that its "policy [was] to seek and take any possible steps which may help to preserve and stabilize the integration of schools in neighborhoods which already have an inter-racial composition." Since the major threat to the preservation of interracial schools was the flight of whites from a spreading ghetto, the policy statement clearly implied a commitment on the part of the board to keeping whites in the interracial community. What was implicit in the 1964 policy statement became explicit in the Redmond plan. Indeed, the plan's elaborations on this point were so sharply spelled out that its line of reasoning is worth quoting in detail:

> Unless the current exodus of whites from the city is quickly arrested, the question of school integration may become academic. Chicago will become a predominantly Negro city unless dramatic action is taken soon. Anyone who carefully analyzes the block-by-block neighborhood patterns of Negro in-migration and white flight cannot help but see the handwriting on the wall for Chicago as well as other large cities. The immediate short range goal must be to anchor the whites that still reside in the city. To do this requires that school authorities quickly achieve and maintain stable racial attendance proportions in changing fringe areas. If this is not done, transitional neighborhood schools will quickly become predominantly Negro as whites will continue to flee. One does not have to be a sage to predict this result. This has happened to dozens and dozens of schools in Chicago and other urban areas.
>
> In Chicago the pressure to integrate often has been placed on those elements of the white population that are least prepared. Working class whites who are often just one step ahead . . . of the rolling ghetto are less secure economically and socially than their middle class counterparts. The Negro is perceived as a threat and appears to jeopardize their tenuous economic security and social status. We . . . propose . . . that Negro enrollments in the schools in these changing sections of the city be limited and fixed immediately. If this is not done by the Board of Education, . . . long range planning for racial integration of schools within the city of Chicago's boundaries will be a futile exercise.

Although the Redmond plan affirmed other values and goals as well, these were stated in such generalized terms they gave little policy guidance. Specifically, the plan declared that "integration is desirable for white and Negro children alike." But it nowhere defended this claim in any way whatsoever; moreover, it expressly indicated that the goal could not be entirely realized and therefore the system must concentrate as well on improving education "particularly in ghetto schools" that were a concomitant of "the present housing segregation pattern in this city [which] will probably continue for some time." Given the acceptance of these all-black, ghetto schools, the plan's vague commitment to integration for its own sake provided no criteria for determining which children and how many children would experience an integrated education.

The racial stabilization objective, on the other hand, provided guides for action throughout the entire document. In making pupil assignments, the plan insisted "that every effort should be made to retain the white population and promote stabilization in integrated school situations." In order to attain this goal, "responsibility for integration should be shared by all of the white community by maintaining fixed racial proportions in all schools," a strategy which must include, among other things, "transporting of students by the school system."

Many details followed from these general guidelines. According to the Redmond plan, it was necessary to "limit the Negro or other minority percentage in the fringe area schools" so whites would not flee. The board should select black children in the threatened neighborhood and bus them some distance away. Moreover, the board should insure that schools to which students are bused never become more than 15 percent black. Finally, in anticipation of what was proposed in South Shore, the plan provided that in one area of the city the system might even transport white students so as "to equalize the minority percentages in the selected schools." This was proposed only on experimental basis, however, because of the danger that parents of transported white children would leave the city.[80]

Racial stabilization was not simply the foundation for Redmond's overall plan as submitted to the board in August 1967. It was also the explicit justification given by board members for adopting the plan "in principle." For example, Cyrus Adams, the board member whose swing vote proved in the end to be decisive, asserted:

> The principles that are involved in this report, which are non-contiguous attendance areas, the transportation that is involved, the problem of quotas . . . in my mind is the only way that we can prevent the exodus from the city.[81]

Louise Malis in explaining her enthusiasm for the report said that she would like to "inject a note of urgency. Three years from now or two years from now will be too late to do anything, maybe, for Austin or Lincoln Park or South Shore." John Carey also observed,

"I don't know whether the busing is going to help stabilize Chicago or not, but we have to try something."

Members of the neighborhood-school faction, though more skeptical of Redmond's proposals, also indicated that stabilization was a major concern. Although Thomas Murray seemed to regret that the board was "going to have to depart from the neighborhood school policy," he admitted that the plans, "if they are ever put into effect immediately, [will] solve the problems. If you wait, I'm afraid it is going to be too late." And, some months later, Marge Wild, a South Shore resident, while reserving her final judgment on Redmond's proposals, observed, "I'm for anything that will stabilize our community."[82]

Interests Served by Racial Stabilization

This overwhelming commitment to racial stabilization by members of both integrationist and neighborhood-school factions on the board is to be expected, given the array of interests dependent upon preserving "racial balance" in Chicago. To begin with, many of the already integrated neighborhoods along Chicago's lakeshore and on other edges of the expanding black community hoped to halt further movement into their areas. For any Chicago neighborhood, the costs to the indigenous white population of racial transition are high. People are uprooted from their homes, property values are at least temporarily jeopardized, racial conflict increases, community institutions decay, businesses falter and go bankrupt, churches and synagogues lose their members, and local political leaders lose office.

What is true for a neighborhood can prove true for cities as a whole, when the extent of racial change citywide reaches a high enough level. Property values throughout the city can decline to the point that city property taxes become a severe burden on citizens. At the same time the cost of city services may increase both because poorer citizens are more dependent on governmental services than more affluent ones and because civil service employes expect higher levels of compensation in return for servicing a minority clientele.[83] As significant as racial transition is for city government, its impact on central business institutions is probably greater. As the central city becomes black, fewer people shop downtown, firms and office headquarters migrate to suburban locations, and cities develop a hollow core. As a result, advertising revenues of metropolitan dailies decline, support for art museums, symphony orchestras, fine restaurants, and other cultural institutions falters, and United Fund drives that sustain a host of private welfare activities of the city are jeopardized. Finally, substantial racial change threatens the dominance of

Irish and other ethnic group leaders within the urban Democratic party. As diverse as these interests are, they and many others have a common stake in Chicago's racial stability. For Chicagoans, Newark, Gary, Washington, and Detroit were potent, negative images.

Given these interests, a goal of racial stability dominated policy formation in many contexts. City leaders vigorously supported state-wide open-occupancy laws in order to facilitate black migration into the suburbs; opposed desegregated public housing within the central city, lest such housing endanger additional white neighborhoods; promoted urban renewal in transition neighborhoods in order to attract white families to these parts of the community; apparently permitted (encouraged?) a higher quality of public services (including park maintenance, street cleaning, and fire protection) in white than in black portions of the city; and pushed the development of regional shopping centers within the black community in order to reduce rapidly increasing black use of the central business district (which threatened to drive white customers away).

Widespread as were the ramifications of the concern for racial stabilization, school policy remained the area in which the commitment was most dramatically clear. The reasons for this are fairly obvious. Schools are compulsory institutions that force individuals to interact with one another in close proximity. The individuals affected are children and adolescents who cannot be expected to exercise the same self-discipline and self-control which adults usually can take for granted. Parents are quite naturally more concerned about the character of the schools their children attend than about the operation of most urban institutions. If parks, playgrounds, or beaches are thought to be dirty, disreputable, or dangerous, they can be avoided, even if this means a deprivation in public amenities that are enjoyed. Only by incurring the substantial cost of sending one's child to a parochial or other private school can parents similarly avoid the public school.

Since many white parents have in fact been willing to incur even these high costs in order to control their children's educational experiences more directly, the problem of racial transition in schools is further complicated. With much larger percentages of white than of black children attending nonpublic schools, and with the lower age structure of Chicago's black community, racial change in public schools has been much more rapid than the rate of change in the city's overall population. By 1970 Chicago was still only 32 percent black, but when the public schools took their first racial headcount in 1963 school officials discovered that black pupils already accounted for 46.5 percent of the school-age population. By the time of the school busing conflict in 1967 this had increased to 52.3 percent, and by 1970 blacks amounted to 55 percent of all pupils.

If this pattern was evident citywide, it was even more apparent in communities experiencing racial transition. Schools were virtually the first community institutions to become black-dominated, forecasting and apparently causing racial transition in the area as a whole. Austin High School increased from 15 percent black in 1965 to 75 percent black in 1968, and by 1970 it had become more than 90 percent black—even while Austin, as a community, remained nearly 50 percent white. South Shore High School increased from 25 percent black in 1965 to 90 percent black in 1968 and virtually all black in 1970 —even while South Shore, as a community, continued to be only marginally more black than white. Quite clearly, public schools change before community populations as a whole do. Although these changes are obviously influenced by differing age structures of the black and white communities and their differing propensities to use nonpublic schools, it is clear that residents can at least perceive the cause of racial transition in their area as school-related. Consequently, they ask school officials to act to stabilize their schools in order to "save" their community.

Racial Stabilization and Busing

Redmond's desegregation plan was clearly a product of white concern for the racial future of the city. It remains to be shown whether such concern can explain the subsequent twists and turns in board decision making throughout the busing controversy. Here the problem for the rational decision-making analyst would seem to be greater, for the school board amid contentious, ideological debate shifted its policies from one month to the next. Given that strife-ridden, erratic behavior, how can board policy be interpreted as a function of a commitment to any one, single objective?

Theoretically, the answer to this question is threefold: (1) even when policy makers disagree, a shared objective places limits on options considered; (2) the objective shapes the kind of information collected and the weight members attach to various arguments used by participants; and (3) changes in policy will follow from changes in available information and changes in available interpretations of previously existing information. Empirically, the answer to the question requires that we show how each step taken in the course of working out the busing plan seems to have been made with racial stability clearly in mind.

The school administration's initial plans were clearly consistent with Redmond's previously announced plan for racial stabilization. In choosing Austin and South Shore as the initial sites for implementing the plan, Redmond was aware that he had selected the areas in which the "biggest racial shifts during the [preceding] year" had occurred.[84] In South Shore the early, two-way busing plan was designed to preserve a substantial white majority in all the affected schools; it was hoped that this would keep any school from "tipping" toward becoming an all-black school. In Austin, schools close to the area of racial transition were deliberately eliminated as receiving schools so as not to jeopardize community stability. Instead, black students at May and Spencer were bused to schools in Belmont-Cragin, which was thought to be far enough away from the black community so that white stability could be safely assumed (see fig. 3). Moreover, the plan for Austin insured that no receiving school would have a black population greater than 15 percent. When the board approved an allocation of funds for busing, they were approving "in principle" early, tentative plans that the staff said were designed with racial stabilization as a foremost objective.

In January and February, however, the board received information from residents of the affected communities which indicated that white stabilization might not be enhanced by these plans. Residents in South Chicago and Belmont-Cragin insisted that even though they were not on the immediate edge of the black belt, they nonetheless felt their property values and neighborhood stability threatened. They argued that even if only 10 to 15 percent of the student body were black, it would mean "an exodus of whites to the suburbs."[85] The school system, far from slowing down the rate of racial transition, would only be speeding it, because the real estate market, even in areas not on the edge of the black community, would weaken. As long as parents have all-white suburbs into which they can move, it was argued, the school system could not maintain white stability simply by limiting the proportion of blacks to less than 15 or 20 percent. As the *Chicago Tribune* editorialized, "The current busing program, which was put forward partly to arrest the flight of white families to the suburbs, has had only the opposite effect."[86]

These criticisms of the plan by neighborhood groups had an impact on board members. This was most obvious in South Shore, when the board decisively rejected the one-way busing plan eventually submitted to it by a nine-to-one vote. Indeed, without seeing racial stabilization as the board's objective, there is no convincing explanation for this overwhelming vote. The compromise, one-way busing plan provided for as much integration in the previously all-white receiving schools as did the earlier two-way plan. Yet the plan was still condemned by the South Shore Commission and a number of board members as "token." One anonymous letter writer explained the basis for this charge: "If the purpose [of the plan for South Shore] is to stabilize a currently integrated area, the proposal is a mockery. It would not improve the stability of our school or our community."[87] These criticisms were well taken; as finally proposed to the school board, one-way busing would have only marginally reduced black percentages in schools undergoing racial transition. As Bernard Friedman commented in an interview,

> Those who were for busing in South Shore, but not for that particular plan was what impressed me, and that is if you are going to use busing as a way to help an integrated community stay integrated . . . then you had better have at least the acceptance of the pupils to be sent and their parents. The people involved and the other important leaders in the community [felt] that it did not accomplish [enough] to warrant the busing plan.

Information on the consequences of the busing plan for Austin was not as clear-cut and board members divided more evenly. Yet even here the intensity of white opposition to busing gave at least one key board member—Cyrus Adams—grave doubts about the scheme's capacity. Board actions with respect to Austin, taken as a whole, indicate that it, as a group, shared Adam's judgment. Redmond's plan was carefully enough designed so that if busing from the overcrowded May and Spencer schools was made voluntary, the board decided by a nine-to-one vote that it would alleviate the pressure on Austin without adversely affecting Belmont-Cragin. But the board also found it necessary to reject (if only by a close vote) compulsory busing—even of black children—in order to demonstrate to all parents, and especially white ones, that transfer from one's neighborhood school would only be done on a voluntary basis. Significantly, this decision endured throughout subsequent years—even though minority, reform-minded representation on the school board continued to increase.[88] The next year, when elementary schools in Austin became overcrowded once again, no more children were bused to Belmont-Cragin; overcrowded schools were instead placed on a double-shift schedule. All the conflict over busing demonstrated to the school board and school system as a whole that busing was not a viable means of achieving racial stability.

In sum, the school board shared a common objective that shaped its general approach to school desegregation and gave coherence to what at times seemed to be a wandering, inconsistent set of decisions. The board could approve the "principles" of the Redmond plan because it agreed that racial stabilization was necessary. When the plan was first proposed, the board could accept as conducive to that end a limited busing program in two transitional communities. But when the plan for South Shore was rejected by that community's leading force for racial stabilization, the board also turned it down. When white neighborhood groups in Belmont-Cragin, in South Chicago, and throughout the city attacked the proposals, the board decided to make the plan for Austin voluntary to demonstrate that busing would not be used in a generalized manner. It was willing to accept a modest, voluntary busing plan in one area because busing there might possibly help stabilize Austin without adversely affecting all-white neighborhoods receiving the black children.

CONCLUSIONS

These models of decision making have given three distinct interpretations of school desegregation politics in Chicago. According to the ideological bargaining model, the decision not to undertaken any more than a modest, voluntary busing program in Austin was a function of the predominant position in the city and on the school board of individuals and groups committed to preserving neighborhood schools. According to the organizational model, the failure to implement Redmond's plan for school desegregation was a function of the miscalculations of a bureaucracy committed to traditional values, interests, and routines in a novel, complex, controversial context. From the perspective of the rational decision-making model, the school board was above all committed to racial stabilization; when it became convinced that Redmond's plan, which promised such stability, could not in fact achieve it, the board quashed its most significant features. Three theorists writing from each of these theoretical perspectives could write equally plausible accounts of school desegregation decision making in Chicago. Given our dependence on case-study material, is there any way that we can choose among these perspectives or resolve the differences in emphasis among them?

The bargaining and rational decision-making models stand in sharpest contrast with each other. The former sees great conflict within the school board, the latter perceives a common objective to which most, if not all, are committed. The bargaining model sees policy as the outcome of a wide range of constantly changing political forces, the rational decision-making sees policy as the decision of a board choosing what it regards as the best means to a particular end. The one identifies great complexity in policy formation, the other has virtually a single-factor explanation. The bargaining model requires detailed exposition of the perspectives, resources, and activities of a host of political actors; the unitary model requires that one pay attention only to the goals of the school board and a few relevant environmental factors it takes into account. The former sees a dispersion of power among board members with distinctive commitments and reference groups; the latter treats the board as an elite maximizing its objectives.

By now it should be clear that these differing approaches to school desegregation in Chicago parallel closely (if not exactly) the differences between what have become known as the pluralist and elitest interpretations of urban politics more generally. Even though our ideological bargaining model sees more conflict and less "slack" than most of the pluralist literature, the model shares with pluralist studies an emphasis on political complexity. It sees a wide range of actors with varying perspectives each contributing something to the final political outcome. Our rational decision-making model, on the other hand, sees a unified elite carrying out its commitment to preserving a white city at the expense of socially, educationally, and politically deprived blacks.

In my opinion, both perspectives are partially correct; choosing between them ultimately involves value as well as strictly factual questions—which is why the elitist-pluralist debate has raged continually in one form or another within the literature of political science over the past several decades. The bargaining model correctly identifies the plurality of forces affecting the decisions with respect to busing in South Shore and Austin. The conflicting opinions of board members, the array of forces affecting recruitment to the school board, and the pattern of support and opposition in each community had their impact on decisional outcomes in complex ways not easily diagramed or explained. Moreover, it seems that genuinely significant alternatives were being debated and challenged. Quite clearly, residents of the affected communities felt that the choices open for discussion were important for values to which they were strongly attached.

The rational decision-making model, on the other hand, demonstrates that certain alternatives were never seriously considered, and all alternatives that were proposed had to be defended according to certain value criteria. No integration plan for Chicago would have been taken seriously by the decision-making elite—whether of machine or reform orientation—had that plan not been formulated with racial stability in mind. For this reason, the Redmond plan flatly asserted that there would remain in Chicago many all-black ghetto schools where improved educational services would have to compensate for their segregated character. Moreover, Redmond's desegregation plans contained within themselves what seems in retrospect to have been a fatal flaw. As much as they were based on the proposition that maintaining low levels of black children in transition-area schools would stabilize these areas, there was little empirical evidence to support this basic assumption. Neighborhood-school groups could persuasively argue that no matter what happened in the schools, Austin and South Shore could not be "saved." Continuing racial prejudices, an enlarging black community, lack of housing opportunities for blacks in suburban areas, and white preferences for suburban living might well combine to insure that Chicago, as well as other large American cities, would continue to have neighborhoods in various stages of racial transition. Far more comprehensive social planning than what could be proposed by any school superintendent seemed to be needed in order to control these forces. Because the theory upon which the Redmond plan based itself was at least dubious from the beginning, Chicago's school board, committed to racial stabilization, would find many persuasive arguments against implementing it.

This unitary model, like elitist theories, thus demonstrates that debates and controversies take place within certain limits. When an objective as precise as racial stabilization guides policy-makers, the model shows that differences over achieving that objective involve bargaining only within a narrow policy range. For some scholars (and some citizens), it is sufficient to know that a set of powerful interests agree that school policies or race will always be biased in favor of whites threatening to migrate elsewhere. On the other hand, some scholars (and many citizens) may find this model's predictions too general to serve as an adequate explanatory framework. They may feel the model is unable to specify which of several significant alternatives within parameters specified by the elitist model will be selected by decision makers. In these circumstances, one or another bargaining model must supplement a rational decision-making framework. For example, the unitary model does not predict whether or not buses will transport students from Austin to Belmont-Cragin. It only predicts that any such busing will be carefully structured to maximize racial stability. In order to know the more specific outcomes—which to many parents were very important—the bargaining model must be utilized.

The particular outcomes in the busing controversy were indeed so important that the issue provoked an ideological conflict between machine and reform factions on the school board. As much as the rational decision-making analyst may regard the debate between the neighborhood-school-oriented members of the machine faction and the integrationist-minded reformers as a farce, the board members themselves took the question so seriously they employed what they believed to be relevant ideologies to interpret the material they confronted. For one thing, both sides analyzed ambiguous empirical information on the relative merits of alternative approaches to racial stabilization in ways consistent with their ideologies. Machine-oriented board members were the first to question Redmond's plan, because its integration schemes threatened the kinds of neighborhood institutions to which machine members were attached and in which the machine's base of power was rooted. Reformers readily accepted the arguments of the Redmond plan because it seemed to show how their commitments to integration and racial stabilization could be honored simultaneously. In the course of the dispute, these ideological orientations affected the way in which board members examined the evidence, listened to the arguments, resisted compromise, and determined their votes. Even though both sides were committed to racial stabilization, differences between them were still great enough to produce an ideologically tinged conflict.

If asked to choose between the two unitary models, once again one must consider value as well as factual questions. In this case, the value question involves judging whether school system miscalculations and clumsiness affected *significant* outcomes or not. In this instance, organizational error did *not* change the board's goal of stabilizing white Chicago. But it did affect the way in which the board sought to achieve that goal.

More generally, a rational decision-making analysis exaggerates the accuracy of information available to decision makers and the precision with which they can find the best way of achieving their objectives. The organizational model stresses the fact that when decision makers work through large, complex organizations, their ability to maximize goals may be limited. In the desegregation case, it was unclear whether busing would stabilize or destabilize areas on the fringes of the expanding black community. Since good arguments and supporting empirical data could be presented on both sides of the question, the way in which the staff developed its proposals, processed information to the board, and communicated with neighborhood groups affected the board's ultimate decision to move extremely cautiously before using integration schemes to stabilize white communities. Whether the decision to bus or not to bus is regarded by the analyst as important will affect his judgment about the power of the organizational model to explain significant events.

Stated in this way, it appears that the organizational model competes with the bargaining model as a rival explanation for the way in which the board chose among a variety of proposals all designed to achieve racial stability in the city. The bargaining model attributes the choice to the power balance on the school board; the organizational model attributes the choice to the way in which the staff developed its proposals. But if these seem to be competing explanations, they can also be complementary ones. The question can only be resolved empirically by looking at the facts of the particular case. Indeed, the answers to the problem are different when one considers the South Shore–South Chicago and Austin-Belmont-Cragin cases separately.

In South Shore, the organizational model seems to provide the most powerful explanation for the board's almost unanimous vote against the superintendent's recommended one-way busing plan. In the course of developing the plan for that community, the administrative staff worked out such an unsatisfactory scheme that hardly any participants in the controversy were willing to support it. Had the balance of power been substantially different, organizational miscalculations would still have precluded the board's approval of this badly formulated recommendation.

In Austin, the bargaining model provides the more powerful explanation. Even though the staff worked out a more acceptable, less controversial plan for that community, it was still altered from a compulsory to a voluntary scheme by a school board that did not want to upset white residents concerned about their children being bused into the black ghetto. The vote on the board was very close, but the neighborhood-school faction prevailed. Had the power relations between the two sides varied even marginally, the outcome could well have been quite different. Even if the staff had made fewer miscalculations, it is not certain the original compulsory plan for Austin would have passed.

The relative predominance of organizational factors in South Shore and bargaining factors in Austin still does not reduce the alternative model to complete irrelevance in either case. Very likely, South Shore was not the first time the staff of the school system had submitted to its board a poorly developed set of proposals. Rejection in this case was not solely on the merits of the proposal; indeed, it is very likely that the board grew aware of its defects only because the proposal became entangled in a bitter, ideological struggle. In Austin, an opposite point can be made. Simply because the balance of power was so even, the way in which the staff communicated with its board affected the outcome. In the final analysis, however, it is difficult to see how the board's commitment to racial stabilization could ever have produced a significant change from the neighborhood-school pattern. Significantly, no sign of such change has appeared in the eight years that have passed since these events took place.

Eight

THE POLITICS OF COLLECTIVE
BARGAINING

Chicago teacher salaries increased dramatically in the late sixties and early seventies. From 1966 to 1972 beginning teachers' salary increased from $5,500 to $9,572, a 72 percent increase, or an average of 12 percent per year. Even controlling for inflation during this period, beginning teachers earned 7.4 per cent more per year, an increase considerably greater than the 3.1 percent annual increment in the per capita disposable income for the country as a whole. Significantly, these increments in teacher salaries did not occur evenly over the 1966–72 period. Beginning teachers received a 53 percent increase in salary the first three years but only a 14 percent increase, which just kept pace with increases in the cost of living, over the last three years.

The unprecedented character of these salary gains earned by Chicago's beginning teachers in the late sixties is shown graphically in figure 5.[1] Displayed in the figure are the increases in Chicago's minimum salaries in constant (1965) dollars on a year-by-year basis from 1955 to 1973. The figure also shows in detail the relationship between trends in teacher income and growth in overall disposable income in the United States. If one compares the solid line which presents the rise in teacher salaries in constant dollars with the broken line which illustrates the rise in U.S. per capita disposable income in constant dollars over this same time period, one can see that Chicago teachers' fortunes, as compared with other segments of society, varied considerably over the twenty-year period.

Teachers did marginally better than other groups in the late fifties, but from 1962 to 1966 their salary increases were so small and so widely spaced that they did not even keep pace with the cost of living, to say nothing of maintaining parity with other sectors of the economy, one possible explanation for the heightened militancy of

186

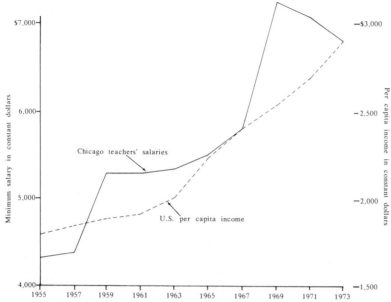

FIG. 5. Annual minimum salary for Chicago teachers with B.A. degrees *versus* per-capita disposable income, in constant dollars. (Sources: see n. 1.)

teachers during this period. After collective bargaining rights were won in 1966, teachers secured a three-year sequence of spectacular salary increases well in excess of the general increase in per capita disposable income. Figure 5 also shows that this breakthrough for Chicago teachers was short-lived, as the real-money income of beginning teachers began to decline in the 1970s.

These rather dramatic alterations in the economic fortunes of Chicago teachers constitutes the puzzle which this chapter seeks to explain in terms of the bargaining and unitary models previously developed. First I interpret the increased rewards teachers received from the political system in the late sixties as a function of the increased political effectiveness of teachers. From this perspective, it seems that after initial successes, teachers lost some of their early influence gained through collective bargaining, and teachers' salaries no longer continued to rise. Unitary Model A, drawn from organization theory, provides a different perspective on the events that affected teachers' salaries. It can be shown that immediately after collective bargaining began, the school system miscalculated in a number of ways, placing itself in a highly disadvantageous bargaining position in its negotiations with the Chicago Teachers Union (CTU). Only in later years did the board learn collective-bargaining techniques that effectively limited the salary increments given teachers. Thirdly, in applying Unitary Model B, the rational decision-making model, we shall explore the adequacy of an economist's perspective that interprets changes in salary schedules as a function of the laws of supply and demand.

POLITICAL BARGAINING BETWEEN BOARD AND UNION

To many political scientists, the prima facie cause of post-1966 increases in Chicago teacher salaries was a comparable increase in teacher power within the arena of school politics. Once teachers had been given the right to bargain collectively, they were able to pressure the board into making concessions that teachers previously had been unable to obtain. Since this viewpoint has much merit, it is appropriate to begin with a bargaining interpretation of board-union relationships.

Machines, Reformers, and the Chicago Teachers Union

To understand the relationships between the CTU and other centers of power in Chicago, the historical relationship of this union to Chicago's machine and its reform movement needs to be reviewed.[2] Chicago teachers became increasingly reform-minded in the 1930s, when the school system tried to balance its budget by paying teachers drastically reduced salaries and then often in "scrip," which merchants would not accept at its face value.[3] At the same time, teachers were disturbed by the extent to which administrative positions were distributed to persons who had connections with the dominant Democratic party. To protest their situation more effectively, teacher leaders established a Citizens Schools Committee (CSC) in 1933, consisting of teachers, parents, and other citizens concerned about education, which worked for restoration of salary cuts and elimination of patronage practices. Teacher organizations contributed substantially toward its budget in the early days, and even in the sixties the union continued to support CSC.

CSC's great triumph occurred in 1946 and 1947, as the machine-dominated school board and superintendent resigned, to be replaced by a school board dominated by reformers and by Herold Hunt, the Kansas City superintendent committed to professional values. The fortunes of the teachers union changed at the same time. In contrast to the thirties and early forties, when the CTU could not even secure an interview with the school superintendent,[4] Herold Hunt, upon his arrival in Chicago praised its strength, "its marked degree of professionalism, [and] desire for high standards and eagerness for the best possible education for Chicago's girls and boys. I hope to merit your confidence and support," he concluded.[5] Over the next two decades, John Fewkes, president of the CTU, relied on close ties with Chicago's two reform superintendents—Hunt and Willis—to win higher salaries for teachers.[6] Figure 5 indicates that he was reasonably successful, obtaining increments that, on the whole, kept pace with general increases in the standard of living.

Toward the close of the Willis administration, and even more obviously during the Redmond regime, CTU shifted away from the reformers, seeking political support from the machine faction on the board and its allies in the city. The reasons for this development are numerous, but are probably rooted in the reform commitment to rule according to the principles of professionalism, expertise, and disinterested assessment of the public interest. If this ideology was common to most reformers, it appeared in a particularly exaggerated form in the personality of Benjamin Willis, who vigorously opposed any challenges to his power to determine Chicago school policy.[7] Willis saw the union's accentuated efforts to win collective bargaining rights after 1963 as a direct challenge to his superintendency, and he steadfastly refused to consider these CTU demands—claiming that the state law forbade collective bargaining with public employees. Significantly, his concern for keeping educational decision making free of group pressures was shared by the reformers on the board, three of whom voted against recognition of the union even in 1966. Moreover, in subsequent bargaining negotiations, the reformers on the board were the most steadfast opponents of large salary increments for teachers.[8]

Opposition of reformers to union demands can be illustrated by examining the voting behavior of board members on those crucial votes when the board each year decided whether or not to accept a proposed union contract. In 1967, 1968, 1969, 1970, and 1972 the board was deeply divided on this question, and in each instance the opposition came from the reform faction. Of those board members who voted on at least one of these four contracts, eight voted in favor of the contract each year they had the opportunity, seven regularly voted against it,[9] and one member Bernard Friedman, wavered, voting in favor of the contract in the last three instances after having opposed it in the first two. All those who steadfastly voted against the contract were members of the reform faction of the board, and all members of the machine faction voted in favor of the contract.

Or, to put the division of the board into relevant sociopolitical categories, those opposed to the contract were two anti-Daley, civil rights–oriented black members, one Puerto Rican, two Jews, and two Protestant businessmen. The union supporters were three labor leaders, two Irish Catholics, an Italian Catholic, and two blacks who had closer ties with the Democratic organization.[10]

The explanation for their opposition given by reform board members themselves turned on their commitment to maintaining a balanced budget and upholding sound management principles. When interviewed, one of these members observed, "We just could not afford [the contract]. We didn't have the money to pay what they asked for. . . . Moreover, the union has now put us at the mercy of the . . . state legislature."[11] Another said, "I believe in good salaries to get good teachers . . . but I don't like going bankrupt." And a third gave as his public explanation for opposing these contracts a similar rationale: "We've allocated not only all the money we would have had but we've mortgaged any possible anticipated revenues in order to meet the union's demands."[12] Reformers also became increasingly concerned that salary increments were interfering with various plans for instituting "educational improvements." Said one member, "We couldn't hire any more teachers. We couldn't cut our class size . . . [or even form an] information office." Finally, reformers were just not in favor of determining educational policy by means of a bargaining process rather than the application of sound principles of educational administration. When one reformer was asked if he would still have voted against recognizing the union as a bargaining agent, he replied, "Yes, I would, because that is just not the way to make educational decisions." Another board member, when asked what were the advantages of collective bargaining, responded, "There are none for us."

While reform-oriented board members resisted CTU demands, the union gained the backing of the board's machine faction. After the teachers' union in New York City had won collective bargaining rights in 1961, Chicago's labor movement began to take more seriously the largest white-collar union in its midst. In fact the head of the Chicago Federation of Labor, William Lee, personally interceded with the mayor on behalf of the teachers, insisting they should have the right to bargain collectively.[13] The mayor, in turn, is said to have informed his closest allies on the school board that the CTU should be recognized, and, in 1966, the board, overruling Superintendent Willis, held an election among teachers to determine which organization should become their bargaining agent. The alliance between the union and the board's machine faction, however, was never overt and not perfectly stable, especially at the beginning. For example, only the labor members of the machine faction opposed using the injunction against the union when it threatened a strike in 1967. But as our voting data shows, in crucial votes to approve contracts, the machine faction provided the support for contracts which substantially increased teacher salaries. Moreover, the mayor himself intervened on four occasions to help reach a settlement between board and union, and in the first three times he made a personal commitment to raise money necessary to finance a settlement. Clearly, the union had solidified an alliance with a powerful political machine that a generation earlier teachers had bitterly opposed.

Mayor Daley and his allies on the school board backed the union for several reasons. First of all, the labor movement was an important participant within the Chicago Democratic party. Labor did not dictate party policy; in fact it seldom concerned itself with major public issues. But it was actively involved in matters directly affecting unions, such as licensing laws and salaries of unionized public employees. Prior to 1966 labor union leaders attended primarily to the interests of skilled, blue-collar workers. As long as CTU was closely aligned with Chicago reformers, union leaders in the city and on the school board did not act energetically on behalf of the CTU. Very likely, the atypical character of this white-collar union of professionals limited its influence within Chicago's labor movement, taken as a whole. But in the early sixties, after the Kennedy administration permitted collective bargaining in the public sector, labor leaders on the school board began taking a special interest in teacher's salaries and working conditions.[14] As Thomas Murray admitted in a personal interview, once collective bargaining had begun, he felt "awkward being on [management's] side of the bargaining table. This sometimes put you in a funny position when you have to say that the union doesn't have a right to make decisions in this area." He and other labor leaders on the board handled their role conflict by becoming CTU's strongest supporters.

Secondly, machine-oriented board members seemed more interested in "managing conflict" than in fiscal responsibility or educational efficiency.[15] Although they resisted union intrusion into nonfinancial policy areas, were reluctant to increase property taxes, and were not openly identified with the CTU, when the conflict over salaries intensified and strikes were imminent, machine-oriented board members quickly turned to the mayor's office for a solution. Like the mayor, they felt that a strike was unsettling and damaging to Chicago's image as an orderly city. President Whiston commented in an interview some time after the 1968 negotiations had been concluded without a strike:

> If they go on strike, who wins? You know that you're going to have to give them something anyhow. And . . . then you get a situation where it's very hard to make kids feel that school is worthwhile.

Thirdly, the union leadership fit nicely into the political style characteristic of Chicago's machine. John Desmond, union president throughout this period of collective bargaining, was almost a carbon copy of the mayor himself. Irish, Catholic, short, fat, good-humored, pragmatic, realistic, he understood the language of working people and machine politicians. Other analysts have stressed the importance that "style" plays in influencing Chicago decision makers. They argue that often the middle-class professionals active in Chicago politics are too formal, use grammar that is too proper, communicate too often in writing, have too many facts and figures, and are too sure that they are right and the other side is wrong.[16] Chicago teachers at times made these tactical mistakes, as, for example, when they lobbied the state legislature at Springfield en masse.[17] But former playground instructor John Desmond, whose working-class background and style closely resembled that of union leaders and machine politicians, seldom violated the accepted bargaining norms governing Chicago politics. One machine-oriented board member observed to colleagues: "If we don't deal with John, we'll find ourselves dealing with someone much worse." Such empathy between a faction on the board, the mayor, and the union president must have solidified CTU's relations with its new allies.

Finally, and perhaps most importantly, the mayor and his allies had a substantive political interest in arranging an alliance with the CTU. In the mid-1960s active forces in the educational sphere were almost uniformly opposed to the mayor and his Democratic machine. Besides the school reformers, the mayor endured the civil rights movement's attacks on school segregation. In the midst of the great struggles surrounding Benjamin Willis, Daley could ill afford to have the CTU, still another political force within the educational arena, activey opposed to his policies. If strikes were added to demonstrations, sit-ins, and boycotts, the turmoil in school politics could possibly once again disturb the stability of Chicago's political regime. Fortunately for the mayor, the reformers spurned CTU demands for collective bargaining. By bringing the CTU into the broad, eclectic alliance of the political machine, the mayor responded deftly to the dictates of the political situation.

Union Assets in the Bargaining Game

By changing its alliances in Chicago school politics, CTU found itself in the late sixties with several significant bargaining advantages. In the first place, CTU had mayoral support. As Daley mediated the 1967 negotiations, he commented, "There is no doubt that all of us recognize that for too many years teachers, not only in Chicago but all over the country, are underpaid."[18] Again, during the 1971 strike the mayor urged the two parties to resolve the dispute, adding, "My office will be open to the union and the board if they wish my aid in the settlement of the contract dispute and ending the strike."[19]

Secondly, the union had the support of the majority machine faction on the school board. From 1967 through 1969 they had the informal support of union leaders Carey and Murray and of President Frank Whiston, who had business associations with the Teamsters union. Whiston's support was particularly valuable, for he regularly appointed Murray and Wild, another CTU supporter, to the collective-bargaining committee. In the early years, he appointed himself as the committee's third member.[20] In short, not only did the union have two active labor members on the school board, but its allies were in the most potent official board positions.

Thirdly, Mayor Daley and his allies on the board had three new sources of revenue with which they could assist the CTU. During the 1966–68 period, it was possible for the school board to obtain voter support for an increase in property taxes. With Redmond's arrival as superintendent, racial controversy in school politics had temporarily receded. Taking advantage of the relative quiescence, the board in 1966 placed a school bond referendum before the voters and saw it pass by a 72.8 percent margin. During the next two years the board, with Mayor Daley's open support, twice proposed an increase in the school property tax, and once again the voters approved, though in the second case only by 52 percent of the vote.[21] Although the school busing controversy precluded further attempts at increasing the property tax, a second source of revenue appeared in 1969, when Illinois passed a state income tax. Finally, with the passage of the Elementary and Secondary Education Act of 1965, the federal government began to contribute to public education in a significant way. Although its finances were to be used for educational improvements rather than pay for standing obligations, astute administrators found ways of using these resources to ease their financial burdens.

As can be seen from these developments, CTU won its collective bargaining rights at an opportune moment, for from state, federal, and local sources, funds available for education increased more rapidly than they had for many years. In fact, whereas the Chicago school budget had increased by an average of only $17,600,000 per year during the Willis period (1953–66, a time of supposedly great educational expansion), in the first four Redmond years (1966–70) the budget expanded at the rate of $43,400,000 per year, from $388,000,000 to $560,000,000.

Internal Politics of the Chicago Teachers Union

CTU's bargaining position was also strengthened, ironically enough, by the strong opposition within the union to its president, John Desmond. Since he was popular in the mayor's office and among a number of the more powerful board members, he was able to use his internal problems as a reason for imposing especially strong demands on his external allies. In order to see the way in which this affected bargaining relationships, we shall explore the internal politics of the CTU.

Desmond was far from the omnipotent, undefeatable dictator of the CTU that one would expect from studies of union oligarchy.[22] In 1966 he won the presidency by only 50.7 percent of the vote, defeating the opposition candidate of the Teachers Action Committee (TAC) by just 116 votes. Two years later, in 1968, after he had negotiated solid salary increases, he won reelection by less than a two-thirds majority. Even after that victory, he suffered the next year a union rejection of a settlement he had negotiated and was forced into a strike he felt was a strategic mistake.[23] Not until 1970, after CTU had won spectacular gains, did Desmond approach an overwhelmingly powerful position within his union, winning the election that year by 75 percent of the vote.

In these internal battles, Desmond, as president, had many advantages over his opposition within the union. He controlled the union newspaper (distributed by the union to all members) and used this voice to extol the virtues of his leadership. The TAC opposition was given no access to the union newspaper and was totally ignored in its news accounts. Moreover, as the union won concessions from the board it obtained a certain amount of patronage, which was used to coopt TAC leaders. But even though these devices helped Desmond, they were offset by the competing interests among urban teachers, the absence of a union shop, and a history of bipartisanship within the union. Racial diversity within the union was especially significant. In contrast to New York City, where teachers were over

90 percent white,[24] Chicago teachers included in October 1967 a sizable black minority of 33 percent. Significantly, a high percentage of these black teachers were full-time basic substitutes (FTBs), who had not been certified as regularly qualified teachers by the school system.[25] The 6,147 teachers (or 28 percent of the teaching force) who in 1967 were FTBs remained at the first step of the salary schedule no matter how many years they had taught. Moreover, they could not select the school at which they would teach or earn tenure rights within the system.

In 1967 a group of "Concerned FTBs" organized to protest their condition. Inasmuch as somewhere between 80 to 90 percent of the FTBs were black, the group claimed that the certification requirements of the school system were racially discriminatory.[26] They therefore demanded virtual elimination of the FTB category by certifying as regular teachers all those FTBs who met state certification requirements and who had taught in the system for two years. They claimed that the "certification exams, written and oral, are based on white middle class values, so they automatically discriminate against blacks." And even though blacks failed the exams, they argued, "the board of education lets these black teachers continue to instruct children, paying them lower salaries. If these teachers are good enough to stay in the system, they're good enough to get tenure."[27]

Concerned FTBs were not only displeased with school policy; they were unhappy with the union as well. Prior to 1966, though they were invited to pay full union dues, they were not allowed to vote for union officers and were given proportionally only half as much representation in the union's house of representatives as certified teachers. Even after being given full union membership, FTBs were not convinced their union leaders were bargaining vigorously enough on behalf of their interests. As a result, after two bargaining sessions had yielded only token concessions from the board on the FTB question, Concerned FTBs in January, 1968 initiated their own wildcat strike against the school board.

Although this strike, opposed by CTU leaders, fizzled without winning any concessions from the board, Concerned FTBs remained a threat to the union leadership. The problem was not black opposition to Desmond and his allies in union elections—black participation in union affairs was too minimal for their votes to be decisive.[28] The primary problem for union leaders was keeping member support for the organization and its activities, a particularly salient consideration given the fact that CTU had no closed shop or union shop privileges.[29] And FTBs realized this was their trump card. In the words of one black activist: "We'll split this union on racial lines unless something is done about conditions in the ghetto schools." More significantly, in May 1969, when CTU first struck the schools, it was estimated that over 45 percent of the black teachers crossed picket lines to hold classes. At the height of this conflict, one reporter observed:

> There is a growing movement for the secession from the union. If enough resentment builds up, it could mean formation of an all-black union for teachers, administrators, tradesmen, and clerical workers.

Taking these threats seriously, CTU, in the course of the very strike boycotted by black teachers, negotiated a settlement of the FTB question that gave the Concerned FTBs virtually everything they wanted. It won for the FTBs an agreement from the board that FTBs could become regularly certified teachers after they had received satisfactory ratings from their principals for three consecutive years. Black teachers were evidently grateful to union leaders. In the next union strike, over 90 percent of all teachers honored the picket lines. Talk of a separate black union quickly died.

Apart from these racial problems, Desmond had to contend with a tradition of two-party, competitive politics within the union. Not surprisingly, the TAC opposition challenged him at his weakest points. In 1966, TAC claimed Desmond was not sufficiently militant and would not maximize the opportunities provided by the recently won collective bargaining agreement. In 1968, when the union had won two handsome contracts, TAC stressed Desmond's failure to secure educational improvements and an alteration in the status of FTBs. In 1969, TAC first said that it would not support a strike unless the issue was over educational improvements; later, it insisted on a strike because sufficient educational improvements were not included in the January offer that Desmond had accepted. Generally, therefore, TAC adopted the position of the militants, the educational reformers, and blacks. They ran more black candidates on their ticket, more candidates from inner-city schools, and, usually, encouraged strike action more readily. Not surprisingly, the machine faction on the school board felt that John Desmond was preferable to anyone likely to succeed him.

Union Liabilities

The CTU benefited in the late sixties from the solid backing it received from the mayor, from the support of machine-oriented board members, from the favorable financial situation, and from the claim Desmond could make upon his allies to help pacify restless elements within his union. Yet the union was not without liabilities, whose importance would become more significant over time. In the first place, tactics virtually essential to union success alienated reformers on the school board. Since union success required that it pressure the board into concessions that necessitated an unbalanced budget contrary to "sound business practices," CTU inevitably faced strong opposition from one segment of the board.

Secondly, the union's pressure tactics did not appeal to downstate legislators, who resented what they regarded as union dictation of state fiscal policy. Moreover, the union was a Chicago-based organization with strong links to other labor organizations and the Democratic party within the city. In Illinois as a whole, the American Federation of Teachers, with which the CTU was affiliated, competed rather unequally with the National Education Association, the preferred organization for most teachers in smaller towns and suburban communities. To downstate legislators, the CTU was a big-city union, not a group of professional educators. Also, the union in Chicago had been far more successful in securing higher teacher salaries than had Illinois teachers as a whole. The fiscal "crisis" in which the Chicago school board found itself in the late sixties was not shared by its counterparts elsewhere. Yet state aid policies were based on a formula that distributed money to all school districts throughout the state. Since other local boards of education did not seem to need the additional funds that Chicago's board demanded, Republican legislators and even downstate Democrats were likely to find more pressing needs on which to spend state funds.

Finally, the teachers' own rhetoric eventually undermined their position. As early as the second negotiations (1967–68), Desmond announced in the preliminary rounds that more money was necessary to pay for the kind of educational programs "needed in the inner city schools." Warning that "we are either going to find the money or we may not have an inner city to worry about," Desmond claimed that more than 75 percent of CTU demands "would benefit the children as well as the teachers."[30] And the following year, Desmond was even more explicit about the union's concern for the welfare of children: "The board must allocate the money it does have to make the educational improvements we're seeking," Desmond said. "Salary is secondary."[31] Desmond's private view of the matter was something else: "Salaries are the first thing. I want to get the highest salaries in the country. Then, we can work on class size."[32] And another union leader acknowledged, the emphasis on educational improvements is "something that we have to say."[33]

The emphasis on educational improvements was a useful, perhaps necessary, bargaining tactic. In the end, the money to pay the teachers had to be voted by the taxpayers or at least by an elected state legislature. Teachers' best claim to these funds was to cast the argument in terms of the children's welfare. But if this tactic was useful in the short run, certain long-range difficulties arose. Since the teachers too often settled for large salary increases with only minor alterations in educational practices, other interested parties increasingly discounted the emphasis on educational improvements.[34] After the negotiations in 1969 were completed, one board member commented to an interviewer: "They had three demands: they were money, money, money."

Changing Assets and Liabilities of CTU

From the perspective of the political bargaining model, the changing financial fortunes of the Chicago Teachers Union were a function of the changing power relationships among relevant actors in the bargaining game. Several factors can be identified that weakened the union's position after 1969. First, the financial constraints of the school board became much greater after that date. By the end of 1971 the school board no longer had sufficient funds to pay teacher salaries for the remainder of the year, and, as a result, the board borrowed money from its 1972 revenue. This financial crisis was a function of (1) the greater resistance of voters to new taxes (after 1968, when a tax referendum barely passed, the board was unwilling to risk submitting any further increases to the voters); (2) the sharp limits on further state aid for Chicago schools; and (3) the opposition of the Nixon administration to increased federal aid to urban schools. As a result, the school board, because of factors largely beyond its control, entered a period of comparative famine after three years of plenty.

Secondly, with greater financial limitations, the mayor's power to influence settlements declined significantly. The mayor played a critical role in the first three sessions because he could find additional funds. In 1971 he also entered the dispute after the schools had been struck, and teachers were given an 8 percent salary raise. But this time the mayor was not able to find the votes in the state legislature necessary to finance this increment, placing the school system in financial jeopardy. In 1970 and 1972, on the other hand, he simply let the board and the union settle the dispute on their own. In both cases, the union settled for minor gains.

Thirdly, the reform faction, predisposed to oppose union demands, gained in strength on the school board after 1969. As we have seen (chap. 4), Whiston and Murray died in office, being replaced by Carey and Preston as board president and vice-president, respectively. New members appointed to the board after 1968 were not as dependable machine allies as Daley and the CTU had once enjoyed. Signifying these changes in board personnel, the composition of the union negotiations committee was changed so as to include board members from both machine and reform factions. For example, the settlement in 1970 depended on the votes of Carey Preston and Bernard Friedman, reformers who had previously voted against the final settlements and were unwilling to support salary increases on the scale the union had previously been receiving. Simply because teachers did not have supporters on the board in the numbers they had in the late sixties, salary increases after 1969 were much smaller.

Finally, Desmond's own position within his union became stronger in 1970 than it had been in previous years. Not only had he won reelection that year by the largest margin yet, but the danger of defection by black teachers had also subsided, as was indicated by the 91 percent teacher support of the 1971 strike. With Desmond in a strong position within his union, Daley and machine-oriented board members did not need to give him special consideration. After all, they, not Desmond, were the ones in difficulty. For one thing, the mayor had to contend with salary demands from other city employees. For example, in 1969, Daley had allocated $9,000,000 that Chicago had received as its share of the recently passed income tax to help pay for a teacher contract settlement. In later years, however, he allocated these funds to pay for other city services. Evidently, the mayor decided it was time for Desmond to reciprocate the assistance that Daley had once provided the union leader.

Ideological or Pluralist Bargaining

To point out that power relations in a bargaining situation affected the outcome does not adequately elaborate the type of political bargaining that ensued. Throughout our analysis, we have found school board behavior best explained by an ideological bargaining model, while the mayor has seemed more of a pluralist decision maker. And the bargaining over teacher salaries once again reflects this pattern. Reformers consistently and regularly opposed major concessions to teachers. Except for one of their number, this faction opposed the final settlements on almost every occasion, even though circumstances and size of settlements changed considerably over the six-year period. The machine faction just as faithfully supported the demands of a union which had established itself as a significant, vested interest within Chicago's bargaining structure. Managing conflict was a more important political objective to them than initiating a variety of "reforms" that might or might not improve the quality of education in the city. And in this way the decisions of the board were not compromises that would win the support of all the diverse elements on the school board, to say nothing of the diversity of interests in the city, but triumphs of the majority coalition which the minority simply had to accept.

Mayor Daley's role in the conflict appears, in some ways, to be similar to that of his machine allies on the school board. Certainly, one cannot appreciate his support of the union unless one understands the mayor's recognition of the need to defer to its demands. But the mayor did not always respond positively to union pressure. As significant as his backing was for union triumphs in the first three negotiations, Daley did not provide city revenues (from, say, the income tax) to assist teachers in later years. Perhaps he knew power relations had changed on the school board; perhaps he realized the teachers did not want higher salaries with the same intensity as they had in earlier years; perhaps there were too many competing claims for him to consider. In any case, the mayor seemed to change his position with the political situation in the way that is expected of a pluralist bargaining politician.

As helpful as the political bargaining model has been in elucidating the sources of fluctuations in teacher salary increases, certain questions remain. Did the teacher's position within the bargaining structure change as rapidly over this period as did the outcomes of the collective bargaining process? Were there any changes in supply and demand factors that could have caused these price fluctuation? How about the collective bargaining process itself? Does it not have its own impact on financial outcomes? Or are they simply predetermined by the political context within which they are conducted? In order to elucidate these questions and to provide quite different perspectives on negotiations between board and union, we shall turn to the two unitary models of board policy-formation.

Unitary Model A: Organizational Processes and Collective Bargaining

From the perspective of a "natural system" model of organizational behavior, salary increments following the introduction of collective bargaining cannot be understood without considering the values, interests, and standard modes of operation that characterized teacher-board relations in prior years. Specifically, these relations were governed by a norm designed to maximize the autonomy of educators from outside pressures—a standard that called upon them to display, whenever possible, a unified front in public, whatever conflicts of interest might lie below the surface.[35] Unity was essential for any claim by educators that they were professional experts on school-related issues. Where professionals disagree, there are no experts. But where unity permits a successful claim to expertise, it justifies an autonomous system of educational decision making. To sustain this unity, it is important that a common objective be identified that legitimates the claim to professional expertise. For doctors, the common objective has been the health of their patients; for educators, it is the welfare of their children, a slogan which pervades discussions of educational policy by school boards, administrators, and teachers alike.[36] In sum, autonomy, unity, expertise, professionalism, and expressed concern for the welfare of the children were interdependent values, norms, and objectives.

But however well the standard of unity served the school system in earlier years, it undermined the interests of the school board once the board became involved in collective bargaining negotiations. After the CTU had forsaken the myths of unity, professionalism (in the sense sketched above), and common objectives, the school board could ill afford to remain operationally committed to them. Once a union had been formally recognized as the bargaining agent for teachers, the pretense of a united profession of educators undermined the board's bargaining position. With unionization it was inevitable that a conflict between labor and management would occur. While the myth of unity denied any conflict of interest between employers and employees, the reality of collective bargaining emphasized and dramatized the tension between them.

The organizational model predicts miscalculations at times when a system is changing from one set of procedures supported by one set of norms to another set of procedures for which old norms are inappropriate. According to this model, a school system is likely to adapt only after "output failure" has revealed clearly the inappropriateness of the old methods. The first three sets of negotiations between board and union, undertaken in the winters of 1966–67, 1967–68, and 1968–69, illustrate well the tendency of organizations to perpetuate inappropriate norms and routines in new, dramatically different contexts.

Pretense of Unity in Midst of Conflict

During these first three negotiations, the school superintendent continued to perceive himself as the leader of a united educational community, who had to protect the interests of his professional associates vis-à-vis lay outsiders. For example, in the midst of the second negotiations, he publicly stated that he saw it as his role to act as arbiter between board and union: "The general superintendent must be the pivotal point, consultant to both the teachers and the board." Consistent with this view of his role, Redmond declared in the first negotiations that the teachers deserved a $500 a year raise at a time when the board was claiming it could afford only a $100 annual salary increment. Even in the third negotiations, Redmond insisted, "It's not a collective bargaining crisis, it's a crisis of support for the common schools." Redmond throughout this period seemed to regard himself as a traditional professional superintendent, speaking on behalf of school interests to the whole community. It was difficult for him to assume the role of executive director of the management team in a bargaining situation between administration and the CTU. By contrast, in later negotiations, Redmond no longer supported the teacher's cause. In the fifth series of negotiations (1970–71), for example, Redmond straightforwardly denounced the 12 percent increase CTU demanded as "in excess of reasonable expectations since it results in a tremendous deficit."

Fear of Strike

As much as Redmond's explicit recognition of the justice of his opposition's cause damaged the board's cause, it was even more significant that the board itself greatly feared a strike against the "common school." In this regard, Mayor Daley set the dominant tone. As a strike loomed in January 1968, he publicly declared that "Chicago has never had a teachers' strike and I'm sure there won't be one now."[37] Privately, he told board members that his police department had informed him radicals might take advantage of a strike situation, and he did not want disruption of orderly governmental processes in Chicago. In order to avoid a strike, board members, committed to keeping the schools in session, responded to the mayor's appeals and made dramatic concessions to the union.

In retrospect, it seems that the school board exaggerated the negative consequences of a school strike. Although few adults positively enjoy such a forced school closing, children in fact do not attend school on a continuing basis throughout the year. Not only are long summer vacations normally enjoyed by teachers and students, but substantial holidays are taken at Christmas and in the spring. Moreover, it has yet to be established that the longer the school year, the more the children learn.[38] Indeed, in 1973 the school board actually agreed to a school "reform" demanded by the union, which *shortened* the school year. If the length of the school year is not sacrosanct, why be concerned whether it is shortened by vacations or a strike?

In assiduously striving to avoid a strike, the board overlooked a vital bargaining advantage it had in the negotiations. Whereas other wage earners (with a three-week vacation) work more than 245 days a year, Chicago teachers worked fewer than 185 days a year, and, as a result, each day on strike cut relatively deeply into teachers' annual pay. Teachers in fact lost more than one half of one percent of their yearly income each day they were on strike. Chicago's board of education, on the other hand, did not lose but gained money every day a strike continued—for a strike's first eleven days. Since Chicago schools had a longer year than was required by state law, they lost no money in state aid until the number of days in the school year ran less than what the law required. Consider the four-day school strike of January 1971, for example. During this time period, the board saved six million dollars, while teachers lost more than 2 percent of their pay. The 8 percent salary increase that they were awarded actually amounted to only a 6 percent increase in income received that year.[39]

Once the strike of 1969 had occurred, board members began to perceive it as a constituent component of the entire bargaining process. When the schools were closed for two days in May, the city did not suffer race riots, obviously higher crime rates, or any apparent decrease in educational achievement. One board member by this time was willing to observe privately, "I would not be afraid of a good, lengthy strike." And another noted that schools closed to forestall a flu epidemic when he was a boy—and no great harm was done.

Subsequently, the board adopted a more tough-minded stance in the negotiations. The following January (1970) the board simply refused to pay any increase in the starting salary of teachers (though it did agree to raise salaries for senior teachers, a far less expensive proposition for the school system). In January 1971 the board tolerated a school strike lasting four days before giving teachers an 8 percent salary increase and a promise of another 8 percent increase the following January (1972). And when January 1972 arrived, the board reneged on this agreement, claiming that Nixon's wage-price guidelines prevented them from paying any more than a 5.5 percent salary increase. Remarkably, the union did not strike in the face of this retraction of a previous agreement. Once the board no longer feared such a possibility, its bargaining position was greatly strengthened.

Change in Educational Practices: The FTB Problem

In every set of negotiations the board was faced with two types of demands—demands for salary increments and demands for changes in educational practices. Particularly in the early negotiations, the settlements granted generous teacher welfare concessions to the neglect of what were commonly called "educational improvements." Since school systems can change their standard operating procedures only slowly, financial concessions proved to be the easiest for the board to make. Prior to unionization, decisions with respect to class size, number of teaching assistants, use of special classes for disturbed children, and teacher qualifications had been left to the board and its administrative staff, and many of the nonmonetary demands of the CTU threatened these long-standing divisions of responsibility. Even Thomas Murray, CTU's most important ally on the board, said privately that he objected to union demands that "took away the board's right to make decisions. . . . This is not the kind of thing which the union should be able to dictate." Because of the board's firmness on these "educational" issues, it had to make all the greater concessions on salaries. In this regard, the case of the full-time basic substitutes was most revealing.

In 1947, as one of the reforms instituted by Herold Hunt, the board required that all certified teachers, in addition to meeting state regulations, pass both written and oral examinations administered by the Board of Education. Initially designed to eliminate any possibility of patronage in teacher hiring and to broaden the recruitment base for the system, these examinations, together with the modest salaries paid teachers, made it difficult to recruit an adequate supply of certified teachers, so that by 1967 FTBs constituted 28 percent of the teaching force. For reasons discussed above, CTU was eager to certify these FTBs as regular members of the teaching force.[40] At the very least, the union could not settle for less than "across-the-board" salary increases, which would give FTBs, at the first step of the salary ladder, the same salary increase that other teachers were receiving. In the first two negotiations, the school system nonetheless stoutly refused to revise in any significant manner its procedures for teacher certification.

One can appreciate the system's opposition to a proposal changing hiring procedures that had been established to insure school autonomy from corrupt political practices. Certifying teachers who could not pass the qualifying examination defied professional standards. It mattered little that the qualifications of teachers, as measured by such tests, cannot be shown to have much, if any effect, on the educational achievement of pupils. A change in these standard procedures was an attack on professional norms instituted with the reform of Chicago schools. But in fighting union demands on this issue, the board had to make concessions on other financially costly demands.

Standard Operating Procedures

Established routines, no less than established principles, also affected the bargaining process. In the first place, the very mechanisms by which the school system determined its annual budget weakened its position. The administrative staff submitted to the board a budget that was balanced—but *just* balanced. According to the earlier rules of the political game, such a strategy made good sense. The law required a balanced budget; too large a proposed surplus would call for a cut in the property tax at the expense of the educational empire. But after collective bargaining, this procedure made negotiations particularly difficult. The balanced budget was proposed in November, the union demanded much more, and the board was then forced either to refuse to bargain (in any meaningful sense) or face an unbalanced budget. As a result, every negotiation was followed by pleas to the legislature or to the voters to finance the increment that had been settled upon.[41] In later years, the board became somewhat more sophisticated. For example, although the board felt during the 1971 negotiations that it could finance more than a 4 percent increase in salaries, it offered no more than that until negotiations reached the mayor's office. As one close observer reported, "They decided to hold some money back for the mayor to give out." Yet such tactics were developed only slowly, after an initially painful experience.

Secondly, the school board relied on its staff of professional educators to conduct the bargaining with the union during the first two sets of negotiations. In the first negotiations, the system was particularly ill-prepared; the new superintendent had arrived in Chicago in October, and a contract was to be signed by January. Since the old superintendent had made few preparations for this major change in school practices, the new superintendent had to direct the negotiations personally. Lacking experience, he settled many minor issues having to do with grievance procedures in ways much more favorable to the union than at least one experienced negotiator felt was necessary.[42] And, conceivably, sheer inexperience with the collective negotiations process weakened the position of the board on financial questions as well. At any rate, the school board in later negotiations hired a professional negotiator, and eventually a member of the administrative staff trained himself in collective bargaining procedures, developing the skills the organization had needed from the beginning. Unfortunately, the system hesitated for two crucial years before hiring a noneducator: the practice was foreign to the traditions of the organization.

Organizational Model

Admittedly, no single miscalculation could by itself account for both the spectacular union gains in the late sixties and the sharp decline in further gains in the early seventies. Yet when a superintendent publicly admits the justice of union demands, when board members fail to perceive and act on the advantage a strike gives them in the negotiations, when financial demands are perceived by administrators as less threatening than modifications of previous educational reforms, when a superintendent fails to hold back funds for bargaining purposes and does not recruit professional negotiators to assist him, a board is likely to be in a relatively weak bargaining situation with its union. Such deviations from maximally efficient pursuit of board objectives are only to be expected, given the difficulty with which all organizations—not simply school systems—modify their behavior to meet new situations. Nonetheless, organizations, including school systems, do learn; they can perceive the error of their ways, and in fact the board and its administrative staff in later years changed their mode of operation. The board began to act more like management in a bargaining situation and less like a school board protecting educators from external political forces; it no longer conceded that union demands had merit; it became more willing to tolerate strikes; it hid money from the union to use in last-minute negotiations; it refused to let the mayor determine the nature of the settlement; it conceded to the union some influence over educational policies besides salaries; and, symbolic of these changes, it hired a professional negotiator. As a result, union success in later negotiations declined markedly.[43]

UNITARY MODEL B: SCHOOL BOARD AS A RATIONAL ECONOMIC FIRM

As compared with the lengthy, complicated explanations of Chicago teachers' salary schedules provided by political bargaining and organizational models, a rational decision-making model, by making a few not unreasonable assumptions can account rather simply for variations in Chicago teacher income. Consistent with the use of this model by economists, we may assume that the school board, like a private firm, seeks to obtain qualified personnel at minimum cost. This analogy with private business firms cannot be exact, of course, because boards of education do not earn profits in any ordinary sense of the word. Yet if boards of education, as governmental units, act rationally to balance their obligation to provide quality education against their obligation to taxpayers to minimize costs, payments to teachers, like payments to employes in the private sector, should fluctuate with changes in the supply of and demand for this type of skilled labor.

One expects such an economic law to be particularly applicable where financial policies are determined in a highly decentralized decision-making system. Were teacher salary schedules for the country as a whole determined uniformly by the national government, as in many European countries, prices paid for teacher services could possibly vary considerably from prices paid for comparable professional services in the private sector. Holding a virtually monopolistic position within the teaching market, the national government could allow political rather than economic considerations to govern its decisions. In the United States, however, salaries are determined competitively by local school boards, which, even though they vary in the salaries they offer prospective teachers, are nonetheless constrained by market forces beyond their direct control. If a school board offers subtantially less than other school districts, it either has to provide alternative inducements—such as pleasant working conditions or an attractive living environment—to attract its marginal (in the economic sense of the word) teacher or the board must lower the formal and informal qualifications that it expects of its teaching staff. On the other side, a board paying well above market price for its teachers will probably find itself so flooded with qualified applicants that it can be expected to increase further its teachers' salaries only with great reluctance.

From the rational decision-making perspective, then, it is apparent that a school board's salary schedule will (1) respond to overall changes in the demand for and supply of teachers and (2) fluctuate in tandem with salary schedules offered by competing employers. In the application of this model to Chicago's school board, we shall first examine changes in the demand for and supply of teachers in the United States as a whole and in the state of Illinois, which was the most immediate market for the Chicago school board.

Demand and Supply Trends

Changes in the national teacher market during the fifties, sixties, and early seventies were generally consistent with changes in prices paid by the Chicago school board for teacher services. As can be seen in figure 6,[44] the demand for teachers in the United States, as measured by school enrollment figures, climbed more rapidly than increases in the supply of teachers, as indicated by the number of B.A. degrees in education awarded by United States colleges and universities, during the decade from 1955 to 1965. Indeed, the chart underestimates the differential between trends in demand and supply, because even as

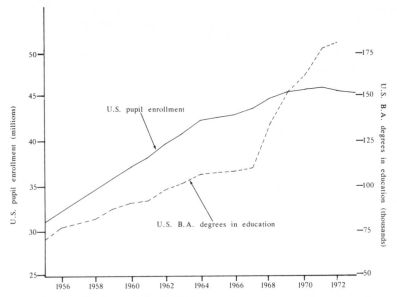

FIG. 6. Enrollment in U.S. public elementary and secondary day schools *versus* earned B. A. degrees conferred by U.S. colleges and universities in education. (Sources: see n. 44.)

enrollments were increasing, boards were striving to lower teacher-pupil ratios so that they could offer a wider range of specialized educational services and lower class sizes.[45] But if demand was outstripping supply from 1955 to 1965, the opposite trend is detectable beginning around 1967. As school enrollments began to level off, the number of degree holders in education rose steeply. The teacher shortage of the sixties gave way to teacher unemployment in the seventies.

The national pattern was also evident in Illinois, whose colleges and universities offer education diplomas that conform closely to state laws governing the certification of teachers. As can be seen in figure 7, the trend within this semiprotected state market was roughly similar to the national trend. We were not able to obtain data on the total number of Illinois graduates earning B.A. degrees in education, so we calculated the largest subcategory of that total—the number earning degrees in elementary education—in order to approximate the supply trend in the state. This measure probably underestimates the steepness of the rise in education degrees awarded in the late sixties and early seventies.[46] But whether or not one corrects for

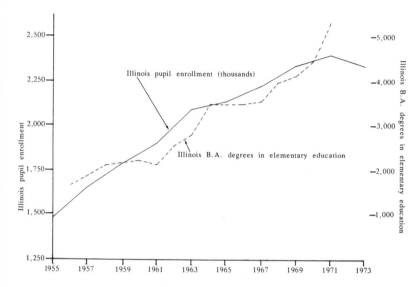

FIG. 7. Enrollment in Illinois public elementary and secondary day schools *versus* earned B.A. degrees in elementary education granted by Illinois colleges and universities. (Sources: see n. 44.)

this probable underestimate, it is clear that the balance between supply and demand within the state of Illinois shifted in favor of school boards after 1968.

If one examines once again the trend in Chicago teacher salaries given in figure 5, one can see that these price changes are generally, though not perfectly, consistent with the changes in teacher supply and demand. During the decade 1955–65 teacher salaries, consistent with increasing demand for teachers, rose steadily at a somewhat faster rate than did average per capita income in the country as a whole. The one major inconsistency is the downturn in teacher salaries (adjusted for change in cost of living) from 1962 to 1966, just as national and local demand was increasing much more rapidly than supply. Given this deviation from the expected price pattern during those years, one is not surprised to discover that the Chicago school board subsequently "caught up" by providing substantial salary increases during the next three years. What is unusual during these three years from 1967 to 1969 is not the increase in salaries, only their unprecedented size. Demand-supply relationships also seem to account for the leveling off and eventual decline in teacher salaries after 1969. As the number of teacher graduates continued to rise even when elementary and secondary school enrollments were flattening and beginning to decline, the school board no longer increased salaries at a rate in step with the increasing cost of living. Viewed broadly and over time, Chicago's school board seems to have responded to changes in market conditions in setting the price it was willing to pay for teacher services. In the early sixties it seemed to be risking a teacher shortage; in the late sixties it awarded rather generous salaries. But these deviations were within a general pattern that at first glance seems to fit comfortably within a rational decision-making framework.

Comparative Salary Figures

Although these figures on pupil enrollments and B.A. graduates in education help account for the trends in Chicago salaries, they do not show whether or not Chicago salaries were generally higher or lower than the teacher market as a whole. Moreover, as only rough indicators of teacher supply and demand, they do not yield very precise estimates of the salary schedules necessary to recruit a full complement of qualified teachers. To provide more exact estimates of the extent to which Chicago's school board was acting rationally in response to market conditions, we shall compare Chicago's school policies with those of other boards in comparable circumstances. Since no two school boards ever occupy exactly the same market position, one cannot use comparative data to establish conclusively whether Chicago paid its teachers more or less than their "market value." But by making a number of comparisons with different systems sharing some significant similarities with the Chicago school district, we should be able to determine whether its behavior differed dramatically from what might be expected of a rational purchaser of teacher services in a competitive market.

In some ways, Chicago salaries should be compared to other school districts within the state of Illinois. Although Chicago required that its teachers pass special written and oral examinations to qualify for certification, its base requirements were similar to those of all other Illinois school districts operating under the same state certification requirements. Since these differed from other states, thereby inhibiting teacher mobility across state lines, Chicago competed most directly for teachers within the state market. From this perspective Chicago's school board was by 1972–73 clearly overpaying its school teachers. In that year, the average school district in Illinois with an enrollment of more than 6,000 pupils paid its beginning teachers only $8,127, whereas Chicago teachers were earning $9,571—15 percent more than the typical district found necessary to recruit a qualified staff.[47] No other Illinois school system approached Chicago's starting salary.

As comparatively high as Chicago teacher salaries were, Chicago's salary schedule might still have been rationally determined. For one thing, Chicago restricted the supply of regularly certified teachers available to it by requiring that teachers pass written and oral examinations. It might be claimed that Chicago paid more because it set particularly high standards for the teachers working within the school district. Moreover, teachers had to be recruited for some Chicago schools where many factors adversely affected the ease with which a teacher could perform his or her duties. In these schools, textbooks and other curricular materials were in short supply; the physical plant was antiquated and unattractive; students were overtly hostile toward school authorities; pupil performance on tests and in daily work was well below the norm; and racial unrest led to psychologically painful and sometimes even physically dangerous personal experiences. Of course, not all schoolteachers endured such adverse conditions—indeed, some enjoyed situations as attractive as those of teachers in a middle-class suburban school. But the school board, committed to paying the same wage to all teachers,[48] had to pay a high enough salary to attract the marginal teacher, that is, an economically rational teacher who would accept employment in the most unpleasant working conditions in the system.

Comparisons with other Illinois school districts may thus be misleading. Instead, to control as much as possible for the particular working conditions faced by Chicago teachers, we collected a variety of data on the salary schedules of other big-city school systems. Since nearly all big cities are reputed to have within some of their schools highly undesirable working conditions comparable to Chicago's, we felt that with respect to this critically important factor enough similarity could be assumed so that meaningful comparisons were possible. Admittedly, given the cost of moving long distances and the varying certification laws among states, not many teachers are likely to be recruited from one big-city school system to another. Although this limits any claim that all big-city school systems are in exactly comparable market situations, this does not preclude comparative analysis. As figures 6 and 7 on supply and demand in the U.S. as a whole and in Illinois have shown, national and local trends were similar enough that conditions in Illinois very probably were typical of conditions elsewhere. If cost-of-living differences among cities are taken into account, comparative salary analysis can reveal whether Chicago's salaries were substantially above or below what was required by the teaching market as a whole.

Figure 8 compares Chicago teachers' salaries with those of teachers working in the four other largest U.S. cities, the six largest school districts represented by the American Federation of Teachers in collective negotiations, and the fourteen largest central-city school districts in the continental United States for which both teacher-salary and cost-of-living data were readily available.[49] The dollar figures presented in the chart are not the actual dollars paid by any school district but a salary figure corrected so as to eliminate differences in cost of living among cities. Also, the data are presented in constant 1965 dollars, so that increases in salaries that simply kept pace with increases in the consumer price index are not shown. In other words, all comparisons are controlled for consumer-price differentials both over time and among cities.

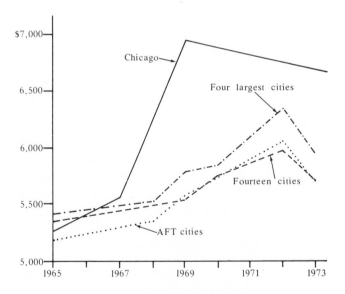

FIG. 8. Minimum salaries for teachers with B.A. degree in selected cities. (Sources: see n. 49.)

As a glance at the chart reveals, Chicago teacher salaries, though below the average for all fourteen cities prior to 1967, rose dramatically in comparison with other cities in the late sixties, then lost a portion of their relative advantage after that date. But even after losing some ground Chicago teachers remained in 1973 far better paid than teachers in other big-city school systems. Whereas the beginning teacher in the average big city received $5,693 (in 1965 dollars) in 1973, Chicago teachers received $6,673, or 15 percent more, the same advantage they enjoyed over teachers in the average Illinois school district. Further examination of the graph reveals that Chicago's relative advantage cannot be attributed in any simple sense to collective bargaining, for teachers in other cities with AFT unions did little better (in real money income) than teachers in the average city. Teachers in the four largest cities, whose working conditions probably most closely approximated Chicago's, did receive a generally higher salary than teachers in other big cities, but even in this context Chicago beginning teachers in 1973 received 11 percent more than beginning teachers in these cities.

The maximum salary earned by Chicago teachers with B.A. degrees also outstripped those of other cities, in this instance by an even larger margin. Figure 9 shows that before collective bargaining, Chicago teachers earned maximums only somewhat higher than in other cities. But with unionization Chicago's position as compared with other cities improved dramatically. Whereas in 1965 the Chicago B.A. teacher with 15 years' experience earned only 14 percent more than the maximum B.A. salary in the average city. In 1973 the Chicago teacher could reach a maximum 20 percent higher than the teacher in the average big city. As is also shown in figure 9, differences between Chicago and other AFT cities and other very large cities were also substantial, indicating that neither unionization nor city size provides an adequate explanation for the peculiarities of Chicago's salary schedule.

So in the end, the rational decision-making model cannot entirely account for the great increase in Chicago teachers' salaries in the late sixties. It is true that salaries increased as teacher demand outpaced teacher supply, and it also is apparent that as teacher supply increased rapidly in the seventies, further salary increments for the beginning teacher came slowly. But the salary increases that were given Chicago teachers in the late sixties were much steeper than elsewhere in Illinois as well as other big cities. Even if the comparison is restricted only to the four other largest cities whose school problems were most similar to Chicago's, Chicago teachers were in 1973 paid from 11 percent (for beginning teachers) to 16 percent (for most experienced B.A. degree holders) more. Although market forces were not irrelevant for Chicago teacher salaries, they by no

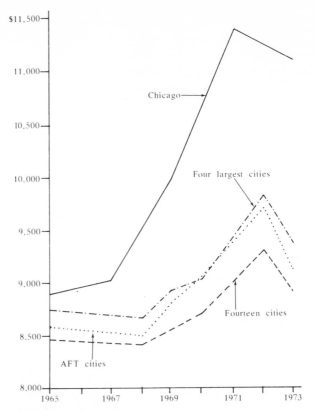

FIG. 9. Maximum salaries for teachers with B.A. degree in selected cities. (Sources: see n. 49.)

means shaped them precisely enough so that one can avoid considering the interrelationships among and the relative merits of both unitary and bargaining models of policy making.

CONCLUSIONS

Although unitary and bargaining models of school decision making have given quite different interpretations of the way in which collective bargaining processes affected the financial policies of Chicago's school system, one model, the rational decision-making model, seemed on its face to err substantially in predicting the size of the increments Chicago teachers would earn. Does it nonetheless have any utility in an analysis of collective bargaining?

Three considerations suggest a positive response. First of all, the rational decision-making model seems to be useful in predicting outcomes in other collective bargaining situations. However limited its applicability to the Chicago situation, this does not deny its general validity. For example, the fact that union and nonunion systems both paid their staffs approximately the same salaries (figs. 8 and 9) suggests that unionization by itself does not necessarily alter the workings of the marketplace. Secondly, even for Chicago, the great rise in teacher salaries was due at least in part to a nationwide teacher shortage in the late sixties. And it is important to note that Chicago salaries peaked and began to decline after 1969, as the supply of teachers increased substantially. Better paid as Chicago teachers were, it seems their organization could not isolate them altogether from external market forces. Indeed, some analysts might be willing to predict that Chicago teachers, who were only 10 to 15 percent better paid than teachers elsewhere, may not be able to sustain this advantage over the long run. Moreover, rational decision-making models seldom predict exact outcomes; an error of 10 to 15 percent hardly demonstrates that a model is of no value. Thirdly, the rational decision-making model provides a standard against which actual behavior can be compared. Even if the model does not predict exact outcomes, it provides a baseline which shows what aspects of a situation need to be explained by alternative perspectives. In this instance, only by demonstrating that Chicago teachers were unusually well paid can we claim that the school system miscalculated or that teachers had unusually powerful political allies. In short, it is by showing the limitations of the rational decision-making model that other interpretations become persuasive.

As valuable as the rational decision-making model is for these purposes, in the end one cannot escape value judgments in one's final evaluation of the model's utility. In this case, we feel that the increases paid to Chicago teachers above salaries paid elsewhere were substantial enough so that Chicago teachers should regard themselves as particularly well-represented by their union and taxpayers and parents should judge the board critically for emphasizing salaries at the expense of other educational options. We therefore believe the other two models add a fullness to the explanation that is well worth the detailed investigation which their application required.

As for the relationship between the bargaining and organizational models, the interdependency that we found in the previous chapter once again becomes apparent. The board's errors during negotiations especially undermined its bargaining position, because the CTU had such powerful allies in the mayor's office and on the school board itself. But even these allies of the CTU might not have been willing to make so many concessions if the myths of an educational past had not committed them to norms and practices inappropriate to a collective bargaining context. No matter how the school board's composition shifts in the future, the CTU can never again expect to achieve the spectacular gains of the late sixties. But no matter how sophisticated the superintendent and his professional negotiations team become, the CTU in Chicago will probably continue to possess the political muscle needed to win contract settlements providing its members with more money than other big-city teachers. Chicago teachers were so well paid in the late sixties because both political considerations and organizational factors simultaneously worked to the teachers' advantage in three critical bargaining sessions.

Nine

THE POLITICS OF POLITICAL
DECENTRALIZATION

Upon his recruitment, Superintendent James Redmond was expected by his school board to "open up the system." The board had come to feel that Benjamin Willis during his tenure had isolated the school system from the external political world and, internally, had concentrated great powers within the central office.[1] By the end of his administration, Willis had broken contacts with other municipal agencies, ordered his staff to communicate with board members only through his office, resisted board efforts to decentralize the system's administrative structure in any but the most formal terms,[2] and even opposed placing telephone numbers of individual schools in the directory. Whatever differences board members had had with respect to school integration and teacher unions, board members generally agreed that the new superintendent should pursue a less autocratic, more flexible decision-making style.

Even before Redmond was offered the position, as we have seen, the school board had asked a management consultant firm, Booz, Allen, and Hamilton, to conduct a study and recommend ways of decentralizing the system's administrative structure. Redmond had once worked for this firm, and he was able to influence the shape of the final report which was submitted to him nine months after becoming superintendent. In particular, he endorsed the study's recommendations that the board appoint an area associate superintendent for each of the city's three new administrative areas. Somewhat later, he advised the board to appoint a deputy superintendent with the responsibility, under Redmond himself, of coordinating the three area offices.

NOTE: This chapter was written in collaboration with James G. Cibulka.

However significant this decentralizing move would prove to be, it could not have guaranteed a school system open to concerned parents or community groups. Although the Booz, Allen and Hamilton report recognized that "there is a need to establish, through the organizational structure, an increased capacity to deal with educational and administrative problems at the local level," and Redmond himself said in a speech delivered in July 1968 that "decentralization, as I see it, must bring about that overworked cliché—sensitivity,"[3] the report in fact called for no changes at all in the governance of Chicago's schools.

The school board's move to provide political as distinct from simply this administrative decentralization was initiated quite separately.[4] As early as the spring of 1965 the board had ordered the formation of education councils in several school districts "to develop a cohesive community working actively and constructively together on projects which would result in the development of community pride and satisfaction."[5] In September 1969 the board ordered the extension of these District Superintendent's Education Councils to all of the twenty-seven districts in the city.

In the beginning, these councils were appointed by the district superintendent and their powers were carefully circumscribed. But by 1971 the board had insured that district councils be selected by somewhat more democratic means and given more independence under the district superintendents. More importantly, the board extended the principle of citizen participation to the individual school level by requiring that every school have a local council which, among other things, would be involved in the recruitment of any new principal appointed to serve that school. At the same time the school board cooperated in a variety of other programs designed to facilitate citizen participation in school affairs. Most significantly, under Title III of the Elementary and Secondary Education Act of 1965 (ESEA), it established the Woodlawn Experimental School Project, which provided for a tripartite governing arrangement, including representatives from the school system, the University of Chicago, and a neighborhood group called The Woodlawn Organization.

Although these formal structures for political decentralization were established by the Chicago Board of Education, hardly any substantively significant political decentralization occurred in Chicago during the first five years of the Redmond administration. Although the board, by its public pronouncements, committed itself to this goal, little of operational significance followed. To be sure, a set of district and local school councils were created, some of which gained marginal influence over the recruitment of administrative personnel. Yet compared with the political decentralization achieved in New York and Detroit, Chicago's structure for policy formation changed only slightly after the arrival of James Redmond.[6]

In this chapter, we shall for a third time construct both unitary and bargaining models, each of which offers an apparently persuasive explanation for this outcome. But instead of beginning with a model of political bargaining, as we did in earlier chapters, we shall first utilize the organizational model to explore the way in which an administrative staff responds to an issue which profoundly challenges its interests and values.

ORGANIZATIONAL MODEL: UNDERMINING DISTRICT AND LOCAL COUNCILS

The interests, values, and routines of the school system's administrative staff profoundly shaped decentralization policies. To show the extent to which these characteristics of Chicago's school system sharply curtailed the degree of political decentralization, a number of analytical distinctions need to be made from the beginning.

Formal and Substantive Representation

Whereas administrative decentralization can be achieved simply by increasing the duties and responsibilities of lower-ranking members of a bureaucratic structure, political decentralization, the concern of this chapter, can occur only insofar as the governing structures of the school system are altered. Since it was clearly impossible for all citizens to participate in the formulation of policy within even decentralized decision-making units, the only way in which political decentralization could be achieved was by some system of communicating citizen wants and desires through representatives. In assessing the extent of political decentralization, therefore, it is necessary to determine whether representation schemes provided more or less of a political link between citizens and a bureaucratic structure. In this regard, both the forms and the substance of the representational arrangement are important.[7]

Formal representation refers to the mechanisms for selecting community representatives. In this instance, one discerns greater political decentralization, that is, more effective representation of neighborhood interests, when representatives are selected by neighborhood residents themselves. The least formal representation occurs when council members are selected by school authorities; the most formal representation occurs when members are chosen in well-institutionalized electoral contests conducted according to democratic norms. An intermediate case is selection by indigenous community organizations.

Whatever the manner of formal representation, the *substantive* relationship between representative and constituents also is relevant to any determination of the degree of political decentralization. Although in this regard both the representative's orientation and his influence are relevant considerations, data limitations restrict our attention to the latter factor.[8] If a representative has very little influence over school policy, we shall conclude that his role is largely *symbolic*; on the other hand, if a good deal of power is shared by the school system with any particular representative body, we shall conclude that *actual* substantive representation occurs. Where high levels of both formal and substantive representation of neighborhood interests are found, substantial political decentralization has occurred. In these instances, the central board of education will have shared its governing authority with other, locally based, decision-making institutions.

Forming the District Superintendent's Education Councils

In Chicago a few halting steps toward political decentralization were taken in the face of considerable organizational resistance. Efforts in this direction began as early as the last year of the Willis administration, when the superintendent finally recommended establishing education councils in six pilot districts. Formal representation was carefully controlled by the school system; the first 25 percent of the membership was appointed by the district superintendent, with that 25 percent then selecting the additional members. Moreover, it was specified that membership be divided equally among the following four categories: teachers and principals, business and industrial personnel, representatives of youth-serving agencies or civic, improvement, service, or professional groups, and parents of children in the district. Under the circumstances, it was unlikely that the council would be in any way socially descriptive of the community it purported to represent. Substantively, the councils had no authoritative control over school policy, and it was not clear that they could exercise much influence. The original guidelines approved by the board in January 1966 specified that "the Council should be under the leadership of the District Superintendent and advisory to him." The topics upon which the councils were expected to give advice were limited to such matters as the adequacy of staffing ratio and facilities, extra programs that were needed, and recreation programs provided outside of regular school hours. Quite self-consciously, council concerns were directed away from such basic policy areas as determination of curriculum, allocation of budgetary resources, and recruitment of personnel. Given the councils' limited functions, one district superintendent warned: "If the prospective members sense that this is a shadow boxing game, it may take the District Superintendent years to mend the rupture in good faith which is sure to result."[9]

Modest as this pilot program was, the school system's administrative staff resisted board suggestions, made in late 1968, that the councils be extended throughout the system. In a lengthy report submitted to the board, the staff argued in March 1969 against extending the pilot program because there was some question about their "function and efficiency at the present time, particularly in view of increasing militancy against schools and in view of the present trend toward wanting not to serve in an advisory capacity, but in a policy-making role."[10] Supporting this conclusion were quotations from several district superintendents. "Such a council in my District would do more harm than good and create more bitterness and divisiveness than harmony and union," said one.[11] Another complained that "the more vocal persons who might become members of the Council have refused to follow the guidelines set up by the Board of Education. They have insisted that their Council be a District Board of Education with the power to make policy decisions."[12] Although some district superintendents were quoted as being more favorable to the idea—"the exposure of people with opposing views . . . is beneficial and broadening"—the report in the end simply commended district superintendents for having "adopted many multi-faceted substitute methods for vital communication between schools and their patrons."[13]

At its March 1969 meeting, the board, led by several of the reform-oriented members, rejected these recommendations, ordering instead that the staff establish superintendent's education councils in each district. A progress report within six months was demanded. In the face of these board expectations, the superintendent and his deputy, by continually raising the subject at weekly staff meetings in the spring and summer of 1969, brought considerable pressure to bear on area associate and district superintendents. As one top administrator summarized the situation at that time:

> We have been deliberately stalling in our answer to the Superintendent, but we can't any longer. In the last board executive session, the board was 100 percent against us. We'll have to do the best we can.[14]
>
> Basically, it [the report to the Board] will center on what we're doing for communication. . . . We have to do anything

we can to avoid the final decision, but it's on the wall. Our strategy is to give them so much information that they can't possibly read it. We will wait 'til June so the schools will be out and will start in September.[15]

The six-month progress report submitted in September 1969 reflected these tactics. In a report with twenty-three pages of appendixes, the fact that councils had been established in barely half the districts was carefully disguised.[16] Also, the report, in adding to and modifying the functions of the district councils, allowed for advisory participation in the determination of "qualities desirable in persons who might be candidates for administrative positions" but kept from councils any general capacity to comment on budget, curricular, or other personnel questions.

By this time, Superintendent Redmond had been in office for over three years. Yet his only progress toward "opening up the school system" was to extend district superintendent's education councils, which had only the most limited advisory powers, to little more than half of the city's school districts. A school board that seemed unanimously favorable to expanding the role of these institutions had made only the most halting progress toward achieving its goal.

Obviously, the slow rate of change was due to organizational opposition to encroachments upon its autonomy. As administrators well knew, strong district councils could limit the discretion of the educational professional. Many of them also seriously questioned how such structures could serve educational processes. In a series of interviews conducted in 1969–70 with fifty-nine principals and district superintendents in seven of the city's districts selected to maximize variance in their social and racial structure, administrators were asked whether they favored greater efforts to involve community residents in the formation of school policy. Only 15 percent favored even the most moderate suggestions of greater citizen involvement; the vast majority were satisfied with the existing patterns of communication and consultation.[17] In other words, the board was confronted with the arduous task of inducing its professional advisers to develop political mechanisims that most of them were opposed to in principle. Since board members lacked the ability to formulate a plan for citizen participation themselves, they were forced to accept as gracefully as they could a half-implemented plan for district councils involving minimal participation by citizens. In the circumstances, further changes could occur only when the school board took policy formation out of the hands of its administrative staff.

The Administrative Staff Loses Some Autonomy

During the next year the board intervened in the administrative processes through the establishment of two committees to inquire into the nature of citizen participation at the district and local levels. Although the committees were formed for other purposes, the board used their reports to make specific, detailed recommendations on matters previously left within the autonomous sphere of the system's professional staff. As a result of these procedural changes, a considerably greater measure of both formal and substantive representation was introduced between 1969 and 1971.

All this began in November 1969, when board members discussed heatedly racial unrest in two all-black communities, where neighborhood leaders demanded the removal of two white principals. To investigate the matter, the board formed a committee consisting of three board members, two moderate black community leaders (one of them the executive director of the Urban League) and the superintendent and his deputy. Perhaps because five of the seven members of the committee were black, the committee, though of moderate political complexion, adopted an ameliorative stance toward the boycott and disruptions experienced in these schools. Although it rejected the assignment of administrators solely on a racial basis, it recommended that current and prospective administrators be selected in a manner that took into account community opinion.[18]

A second board committee, also appointed in late 1969, began studying ways of improving the board's own communication with the public. In the beginning, this committee proposed only that explanatory brochures be distributed to those attending board meetings and that information concerning the board agenda be written in a more readily understandable style. However, the committee, by incorporating representatives from many civic and community organizations (including the PTA of the Chicago region, the League of Women Voters, and the Citizens Schools Committee), laid the grounds for a wider-ranging inquiry. When these representatives were asked to form a subcommittee to explore additional ways of improving school-community relations, they quickly turned their attention to the district superintendent's education councils, which had been the focus of a comprehensive, critical study by the League of Women Voters. Drawing on this document, the subcommittee developed several policies for broadening both formal and substantive representation of parents and neighborhoods residents. Most importantly, it recommended that in addition to strengthening district councils, local school councils, formed at community meetings, be given authority to discuss and advise on a wide range of local school policies. Most of these subcommittee proposals were in fact legislated by the school board.

In short, during the 1969–70 school year, the school board exercised considerable initiative on its own, using community organizations and its own committees to develop a set of policies calling for greater citizen participation than Redmond had devised over the preceding three years of his superintendency. The board required that communities be involved in the selection of principals, that the district councils be given more structure and independence of the district superintendent's office, and that local councils be established. If these actions did not by themselves constitute high levels of actual representation of community opinion, the board at least showed more concern for establishing linkages between school and community than its administrative staff had ever displayed.

Organizational Response to Board Initiatives

These board initiatives to increase substantive representation, made possible by more direct board intervention into administrative processes, still required interpretation and implementation by the professional staff. Because of the unusual involvement of board members in the details of this issue, the staff could not subvert the policies altogether, no matter how distasteful they may have found them. But in subsequent months, the staff modified these policies in ways designed to minimize their participatory impact.

The initial staff response dealt with the selection of principals. Instead of giving this power to district councils or any other permanently organized body, the superintendent recommended that district superintendents be given the responsibility of getting in touch with representatives of community organizations so that they might interview eligible candidates. Significantly, it was left to the district superintendent's discretion which organizational representatives were to be approached. Moreover, the group was called into being on a temporary basis for that purpose only and would not be able to perpetuate itself once the principal had been selected. In other words, no representative group with authoritative powers would subsequently be able to determine whether a principal fulfilled his or her promise. Finally, neighborhood representatives were forced to confine their consideration to those candidates ranking highest on the certified eligibility list, thereby perpetuating a pattern of internal recruitment of administrative staff; indeed, in the original recommendation Redmond promised nothing more than "to the extent possible, community preferences will be honored."[19]

Although at the time most board members praised the staff for its good efforts to implement citizen participation in principal selection, it soon proved very difficult to find positions for all formally "qualified" candidates and at the same time respond satisfactorily to community representatives. In 1971 the board no longer considered variations in performances on the qualifying examination but allowed community representatives to consider candidates from the entire list of applicants who had passed the examination at any level. The Principals' Club vigorously opposed the policy, asserting that

> the actions of local selection committees operating under the guidelines of the Board of Education have failed to inspire the confidence of Chicago Principals in the validity of the selection process.[20]

Noting that such a selection process encourages provincialism and demeans principals seeking new positions, the article concluded by asking: "As this function [the selection of principals] is formally relinquished to lay leadership, is not the general superintendent abrogating his responsibility?"[21] In this instance, however, board policy prevailed over staff objections, and the number of black principals increased from thirty-one in 1968 to ninety by September 1972, an increase from 7 to 18 percent.

The guidelines for local school councils, approved by the school board in June 1971, also provided more formal and substantive representation than previously. Formally, the local councils were much more representative than the district councils had been. Over 50 percent of a council had to be parents, and institutional representation was permitted only if community representatives approved of it. Also, not only was a long list of acceptable agenda topics, including school budgets and textbook selection, included within the purview of the councils, but the list, by being suggestive in character, left open to the councils themselves final determination of the matters which they could take up. Indeed, the authority to participate in the selection of principals was now for the first time clearly given to a permanent part of the local structure. Nonetheless, the administrative staff qualified the powers of the council in one crucially significant respect:

> It should be recognized that the principal will make every effort to comply with properly passed resolutions of the council,

but members of the council should also understand that the principal may not have the administrative power to comply with all such resolutions.[22]

Organizational Change

These organizational innovations occurred despite staff opposition because the board impinged on policy-making activities usually left to administrators. By establishing committees that included external, nonschool members, the board provided itself with information, expertise, and influences which countered the generally pervasive impact of the administrative staff on policy making. In other words, by altering its own organizational procedures the board was able to change the behavior of its staff. Even so, the board's success in this regard varied with the power position of various components of the administrative staff. The greatest community representation occurred at the lowest levels of the organization, in the local school, where the principal experienced a significant modification of the role he was expected to play. It was at this level that councils were chosen at community meetings, given a wide range of policies considered legitimate for council discussion, and assigned a somewhat authoritative role in the recruitment of a line administrator. Although the Principal's Club was opposed to these developments, its capacity to influence board decisions was limited by its distance from the centers of power. District superintendents, one step closer to the central office, were forced to accept education councils, but these councils worked within guidelines developed by the superintendents that sharply restricted their deliberations. The next higher echelon, consisting of the three area associate superintendents, had no advisory councils at all. In short, organizational resistance to sharing power with outsiders was increasingly successful the closer proposed changes approached real centers of power within the organization.

In sum, the modest quality of these changes is easily explained by organizational theory. Although the school system resisted decentralization for six years after it was originally proposed, even when finally implemented, the structure of authority was altered in only the most marginal fashion. As in most cases where change threatens organizational interests and values, it was token, incremental, and only slowly implemented.

POLITICAL BARGAINING: BOARD AUTHORITY AND GROUP LEGITIMACY

A school board, seeking to promulgate a policy contrary to the interests and values of its administrative staff, is likely to be frustrated by the latter's control over information, expertise, and capability for executing the policy. As seen from the perspective of the organizational model, this board-staff conflict shaped decentralization policy. Yet even from this perspective it was apparent that the board was not operating in a political vacuum, that its initiatives were prompted at least in part by external forces, such as the organized attempts to dismiss two white principals from schools serving two all-black communities and the effort by citywide reform groups, including the Citizens Schools Committee and the League of Women Voters, to open the policy-making processes to citizen groups. Although this was a minor theme in the district and local school council issues, the impact of external political forces was more apparent whenever citizen participation was a constituent component of a federal program.

In these cases, the dependence of an educational program upon an external governmental agency—whose financial support was conditional upon at least minimal compliance with specified guidelines—opened up an otherwise largely self-regulating decision-making system to third parties. As a result, the degree of political decentralization varied with different federally funded programs, depending upon the degree to which the federal and local forces pressured the school system to provide citizen participation.

Three federally funded programs called for some degree of citizen participation: ESEA Title I programs, whose funds were to be concentrated in low-income areas; the Model Cities Program, an effort to develop new comprehensive models for urban living in inner-city neighborhoods; and the Woodlawn Experimental Schools Project, an experimental program funded under Title III of ESEA, which authorized expenditures for innovative, experimental programs. Since ESEA's Title I during this period did not legislate a strong citizen participation requirement, and since the program was administered by the Office of Education, through the Illinois State Department of Education, neither of which were strongly committed to citizen participation, only haphazard structures providing minimal representation of neighborhood interests resulted from the implementation of this program. In the case of model cities, Congress required "widespread citizen participation," and the Department of Housing and Urban Development was more committed to involving community groups in program development; consequently, formal representation was provided through democratically elected citizen councils. Even so, these councils had little influence over model cities programs conducted by the school system. Finally, the highest level of citizen participation, even to the point of sharing authoritative power, occurred in the Woodlawn Experimental Schools Project, where the government had explicitly funded a program calling for substantial representation of the Woodlawn community. Because the degree of political decentralization in this instance was so unusually large, the bargaining processes bringing it into being deserve special attention.

Woodlawn Experimental Schools Project

In the South Side community adjacent to the University of Chicago where a strong community organization, the Woodlawn Organization (TWO), played an influential role in a special project funded by Title III and Title IV ESEA funds, we can identify the combination of political resources needed for community control advocates to win major concessions from the school system: the availability of federal funds for experimental programs, a strong community organization, and an external third-party advocate, the University of Chicago, whose access to the system and legitimacy among educators was extraordinarily high. Even then, political decentralization was not achieved without political struggle.

That Title III funds were to be spent for experimental purposes proved crucial. Since only a small number of Title III programs could be established across the country, these funds could be spent with great discretion by federal officials. Unless the Chicago school system could propose plans that were attractive to the Office of Education, it would lose its potential claim to other communities. As a result, even though no Title III guidelines required citizen participation, local officials were forced to be much more attentive to federal concerns than they had been in the case of Title I.

In this regard, the origins of the Woodlawn Experimental Schools Project are instructive. In the spring of 1966 a newly formed committee on urban education at the University of Chicago proposed to the Office of Education that it form an experimental school in the nearly all-black Woodlawn community adjacent to the university. When TWO objected that the proposal was made without consulting the Woodlawn community, the university's project was returned by the Office of Education for revision based on consultations with the public schools and with Woodlawn. After this rebuff, the university initiated discussions with both public school representatives and TWO, out of which emerged a tripartite planning board, representing each entity equally. When these developments were reported to the Office of Education, it encouraged the board to submit a Title IV developmental grant allowing them to work out a more comprehensive proposal for Title III funds. In short, experimental funds,

attractive to both the public schools and the university, were successfully manipulated by federal officials to entice these institutions
into working closely with a community organization.

Organized by Saul Alinsky several years earlier, TWO has established itself as a significant political force in its neighborhood by
vigorously opposing efforts of the University of Chicago to use
various portions of the northwestern edge of Woodlawn for institutional purposes.[23] By the mid-sixties, it had won sufficient concessions from both the university and city hall that it was generally
respected as the most potent, independent community group in
Chicago's low-income black neighborhoods. Under shrewd political
leadership with a flair for capturing newspaper headlines and the
sympathy of liberal easterners,[24] TWO had acquired a substantial
financial base by securing church and foundation support together
with an increasing number of grants from various federal agencies.
Moreover, the University of Chicago was learning that by providing
services to TWO members it could secure better relations with the
Woodlawn community. Had it not been for prior successes and a
relatively stable resource base, TWO, as a community organization,
would not have been taken seriously either locally or nationally.

Even the coincidence of available federal funds and a strong community organization would not have induced school officials to decentralize the control of a single school district, had not the prestige,
legitimacy, and resources of the University of Chicago supported the
experiment. From the beginning, the school system engaged only
reluctantly in planning the experiment. While the superintendent expressed verbal support for some form of collaboration, he took no
initiative to offer specific kinds of assistance and made it clear that
no local funds could be used to help finance the program. Moreover, the administrator selected by the superintendent to assist in the
planning personally expressed great reservations about community
involvement. As the project's first director put it, "the institution
which faced the greatest difficulty in entering into a collaborative
arrangement was the . . . public schools."[25] When the final plan was
prepared for submission to the board in December 1967, shortly
before a deadline for federal funding, the superintendent hesitated
to endorse it, avowing his personal support but arguing that the board
would not accept it. At a board meeting, the school attorney expressed doubts about the legal authority of the school board to
delegate its powers to a tripartite community board, on which the
school system had only one-third representation. When several board
members expressed their own doubts, consideration of the issue
was deferred to a later meeting, an action that would kill the experi-

ment unless a satisfactory solution could be found before the federal deadline.

It was at this point that the resources of the University of Chicago most crucially affected the outcome. Earlier, Redmond's willingness to let his staff help plan the project must be traced to his friendship with the university's dean of the School of Education, Roald Campbell, who had participated in Redmond's recruitment. And in the many sessions of the tripartite planning board, university representatives played a broker role, seeking compromises acceptable to the other sides. But after the school attorney questioned the proposal to be submitted to the Office of Education, the legal resources of the university proved to be of particular significance. When after the board meeting the attorney, in discussions of the legal question with the tripartite board, remained adamant that the board be the sole, ultimate authority, exceptionally able legal talent was recruited through university channels to combat the arguments. These lawyers countered that the Illinois School Code permitted a procedure in which the board of education would agree to take action only after concurrance had been obtained from a community board. After numerous conferences the school attorney agreed to this formulation, which was then passed by the board of education, with three dissenting votes, just in time for submission to the Office of Education. Significantly, Roald Campbell, invited as a special guest of the superintendent and seated within the area of the board room typically reserved for members and administrators, was invited to speak on behalf of the project at this board meeting. Since to our knowledge on no other occasion was a lay person allowed to speak at an official board meeting, access of an unusual order seems to have aided this effort at political decentralization.

When the Woodlawn Experimental Schools Project got underway, the arrangement whereby policies had to have the support of all three parties continued in effect. Significantly, the director of the program, a strong proponent of black power and community control, introduced numerous changes into the educational program of the Woodlawn schools and greatly increased the role of youth groups in the determination of school policy. However, the experiment in political decentralization could not be perpetuated without continued federal and university backing. As the director of the program became involved with the Woodlawn community, the University of Chicago, cut off from any significant research access to the project, grew increasingly distant from its operations. At the same time the advent of a Republican administration in Washington had an increasing effect on Office of Education policies. When funds from this source were cut off in 1973, Chicago's experiment in political decentralization came to an end.

Ideological Bargaining over Decentralization

This experiment in political decentralization provoked ideological conflict between machine and reform factions on the school board. Significantly, the debates focused on issues of authority and the legitimacy of TWO as a representative organization. Even after the board's attorney had grudgingly conceded that the school board could in fact delegate its authority to the Woodlawn Experimental Schools Project, Board President Frank Whiston, clearly unhappy about this sharing of authority, pointedly observed: "This is the City of Chicago public schools. . . . It is part of . . . the training of our system. And we are responsible for that."[26] Other machine-oriented board members also questioned the legitimacy of TWO: "Are you saying," Marge Wild asked of Superintendent Redmond, "that this is the only representative group in Woodlawn, when you are saying that there are no others who could have been part of this?"[27] To which reform-minded Warren Bacon replied: "Anybody in this city who is going to work in that community sooner or later is going to have to work with that organization or one similar to it."[28] Another reformer, Harry Oliver, asked: "If there is some activity of that organization that we are a little doubtful about today, isn't it possible that after we have worked with them in the kind of relationship being suggested here that maybe the direction that they seem to be going will be modified?"[29] Reformers on the board generally answered this question affirmatively, for most of them voted yes to the proposal for increasing participation. Whiston and Wild, however, together with Louise Malis, voted against the experiment, objecting that it shared board authority with an illegitimate, unrepresentative community organization.

A year later the board divided sharply and clearly for a second time over matters of board authority and group legitimacy. In the fall of 1968 a series of student boycotts and demonstrations broke out in a large number of all-black and racially integrated high schools. Organized groups of students, capable of sustaining disruptive political action over a period of several weeks, demanded more black teachers and administrators, more black studies courses, and more community and student involvement in local school policy formulation. Although no faction on the board was willing to concede policy innovations that came close to satisfying these demands, board members vigorously disagreed among themselves about whether student leaders should be given an opportunity to state their grievances directly to the board itself.

Significantly, the issue once again revolved around questions of the board's authority and the legitimacy of student groups. Machine-oriented board member Marge Wild questioned whether the organization was indigenous to the student body. "Kids didn't draw up those manifestoes they're passing around. There is an organized leadership behind this—the same thing that is going on all over the world." She approved of their demand for more vocational schools and more homework, but "otherwise," she said, "it's a question as to who's going to run the schools. This is ridiculous."[30] If the machine faction doubted the wisdom of admitting this interest into the pluralist bargaining process, reform-oriented board members, more concerned about the need for democratic participation, felt, as Jack Witkowsky put it, "the boycotts showed a real need for improved communication between district staffs, students and parents."[31] When Malis proposed that some kind of "citywide student forum" be set up to "open the channels of communication," Thomas Murray replied, "It won't work. You're putting the responsibility of education in the hands of the community and the students, and trying to take it away from the educators."[32] At the end of this debate, the machine-reform cleavage on the board emerged once again, as the board decided by a six-to-five vote to listen to student grievances. Five of the six board reformers were joined by Mrs. Green, a usually machine-oriented black, to pass the proposal over the opposition of four machine-oriented board members plus Harry Oliver, a usually reform-oriented white.

When the hearing for student leaders was finally held, the authority issue was raised in its sharpest form. During the course of the hearing, various speakers were interrupted by audience applause, much to the annoyance of President Whiston, who had opposed the hearing from the beginning. After a two-and-one-half-hour session at which various teachers and students had called for more black administrators, greater community control, and more black studies courses, James Harvey, a young adult who had helped students organize the boycott, exclaimed:

> We didn't come here today to play word games. We came here to emphasize that our demands must be met. . . . It's our meeting, not yours, baby.[33]

At which point President Whiston adjourned the meeting.

As these cases demonstrate, ideological conflict on the board was provoked whenever demands for decentralization involving a shift in the locus of authority came to its attention. Although the board could agree on local school councils that provided only marginal representation of community groups, when substantially significant decentralization was proposed or when black student leaders were disrupting school functioning, the ideological divisions among board members concerning the way in which citizens should participate in school affairs determined their responses to these issues. If the politics of decentralization in Chicago was relatively quiet, it was not because the issues that generated great conflict in New York and Detroit were not similarly perceived but because decentralizing forces in Chicago were generally very weak.[34]

RATIONAL DECISION-MAKING MODEL: CIVIL DISORDER AND SOCIAL CONTROL

If decentralization policy can be understood either as the output of an organization resistant to change or the outcome of a bargaining process in which prodecentralization forces had few political resources, it can also be seen as a rational plan for achieving a specific goal of concern to the school board, taken as a governing unit. Whatever the differences among individual board members, the board as a whole had an overriding objective of primary importance in the formation of decentralization policy.

Social Control

That objective was to maintain social order within the city and especially within the city's schools. In this respect, school board members were no different from most civic and political leaders in Chicago and other major American cities. Politicians, administrators, businessmen, civic group leaders all need a relatively high degree of social order to achieve their respective goals of exercising power, delivering services, maximizing profits, and initiating worthy causes.[35] Although in times of expansion and prosperity, social order can be taken for granted, American cities have more than once suffered hard times and social unrest. Indeed, since the Civil War, problems of ethnic and racial succession, economic dislocation, and labor unrest have required continual attention by civic leaders. In the late 1960s, urban demonstrations and riots, increasing crime rates, and interracial violence in public places focused elite attention once again on this recurrent problem. A wide range of public policies were subsequently developed, including increased support for police services, coordinated efforts to contain mass media discussion of civil disorders, expansion of training and employment opportunities in minority neighborhoods, and formation of such new structures linking government and inner-city minority groups as community action and model city programs, neighborhood centers, and little city halls.[36]

If social cohesion was a salient problem for urban elites in general, several characteristics of urban school systems magnified its significance in this particular setting. First, as compulsory institutions for all youths to the age of sixteen, schools had to serve almost the entire age cohort, including adolescents of all races and ethnic groups, all abilities, interests, and aptitudes, and varying degrees of alienation and interpersonal aggressiveness. Significantly, those compelled to utilize school services included the age cohort most prone to engage in violent and disruptive behavior and the most active participants in the civil disorders of the late sixties.

Secondly, because of the differentials in the age structure of the white and minority group populations and the disproportionate use of nonpublic schools by white children, the public schools in Chicago, as in other big cities, had particularly high proportions of those minorities actively discontented with urban conditions. Although in 1970 blacks composed only 34 percent of Chicago's population, the school system's pupil population was 55 percent black.

Thirdly, minority group pupils often did not have teachers and administrators of a racial background similar to their own. In Chicago, although a surprisingly high 34 percent of the teaching staff in 1968 was black, this was still 20 percent less than the percentage of pupils who were black. Moreover, only 7 percent of the 457 principals in all Chicago schools were black. As a result, the racial conflict in the city directly overlapped the authority conflict that divides teachers and administrators from their pupils, further accentuating problems of social cohesion.

Fourth, school systems were increasingly constrained from using the most direct forms of social control by their overt mission of educating the young. Many influential educators in the sixties were arguing that schools were both ineffective and inhumane; children, they said, should be enticed, encouraged, induced, but not forced into acquiring new skills and abilities. Moreover, courts began to narrow the latitude within which educators regulated the lives of students; the traditional privilege to act in loco parentis gave way to stricter rules according students procedural and substantive due process. While many school officials favored more traditional practices, it became more and more difficult to restrict behaviors to the same extent as prisons and youth homes. Although the Chicago schools had their own security force of over three hundred and enjoyed a cooperative relationship with the police department, this was, as Marge Wild once said, "obviously inadequate."

Civil Disorder

Civil disorder was clearly more than an abstract concern in the late sixties. During this period Chicago suffered two major instances of race-related civil violence, one in the summer of 1965 and the other at the time of Martin Luther King's assassination in April 1968. More significantly, for school board members, all-black and racially integrated schools experienced a continuous sequence of disturbances, lunchroom violence, boycotts, walkouts, sit-ins, mass marches, arson, vandalism, and the like. From even a cursory review of newspaper clippings covering school events during 1967–68, it is clear that a rapid upsurge in student and community unrest occurred during that school year. Numerous incidents occurred in the fall and winter months, and after King's funeral, black students, upon returning to their classrooms, displayed more political self-consciousness and militancy than ever before. For example, students at Hirsch High School protested postponing Afro-American day and against "Operation Snatch," a plan whereby teachers, to maintain order, were expected to grab loiterers in hallways and bring them into their classrooms until the end of the hour. Also, a group of black students at integrated Harrison High School formed a student organization called the New Breed, which requested that a black studies program be instituted the following year. "Rumors of terror and violence in Chicago's integrated high schools, . . ." the *Sun-Times* reported in late May 1968, "have grown increasingly widespread in recent months."[37] Daley, who had only recently ordered his police department to "shoot to kill" thieves and looters, ordered an investigating committee to pay special attention to "the role and responsibility of the schools" in fostering civil disorder.

The school system responded to these race-related, politically significant disturbances with strong reassertions of its authority. A black history teacher encouraging protest in one school was reassigned to another; a white principal remained at an elementary school in the face of community opposition, because, as Redmond said, "I am not going to sit idly by and have pressure groups determine the assignment of principals of Chicago schools"; and the New Breed was denied standing as a school organization at Harrison. Although the Woodlawn experiment was approved that year and two new black district superintendents were appointed, in most school districts not even the most minimal moves toward formal representation of community interests were taken by the Redmond regime.

When schools opened in the fall of 1968, racial conflict escalated dramatically. At Farragut High School students "sat in" on the principal in support of a demand for more black administrators and more adequate instruction in black studies. At Tilden High School whites boycotted to demand better police protection and dismissal of unruly students. But, most significantly, at Harrison, the New Breed organized a walkout on September 13, when told that three white instructors would teach a one-semester elective in black history. A larger walkout, involving an estimated five hundred students, occurred on September 15, even though the principal had now agreed to include two black teachers among the three history instructors. The boycott continued and expanded over the next three days. By the end of the month the New Breed had developed a comprehensive set of demands, including insistance that black schools be controlled by the black community. The school system responded by arranging for the arrest of Sharon Matthews and Victor Adams, the two most effective student leaders.

October became the month of Monday boycotts. As the events at Harrison gained citywide publicity, a specific community conflict grew to a disorder involving most of the school system. On October 14, 21, and 28, thousands of black students failed to report to classes, and a large number of the absentees marched to the board of education offices on North La Salle Street. On the first two Mondays, the absentee rate in the thirty-two high schools neared 28,000, but on the third Monday, it dropped to 15,000. On the first Monday, marchers were estimated at 3,000 but on the third Monday the total dropped to an estimated 250.[38] Faced with this declining participation rate, boycott leaders called for a 'sit-in' for the first Monday in November, which, they claimed, would disrupt polling in school houses on the following Tuesday, election day. Through concerted, well-organized joint action, school officials and police officers quickly broke up all sit-in efforts.

Although this serious challenge to the functioning of Chicago's schools gradually cooled down, racial incidents in many schools recurred continuously throughout the school year. Innumerable incidents were significant enough to warrant extensive attention by the news media, particularly as spring weather facilitated student organization and mobilization. But the magnitude of the problem is perhaps most concisely conveyed by the vandalism report issued by the school system. During the 1968–69 school year, vandals inflicted a

total of $1,943,000 in damage on the schools, compared with $1,
206,000 during the not-so-peaceful 1967–68. Fire damage caused
by arsonists increased from $69,000 in 1967–68 to $397,000 in
1968–69.[39]

Restoring Social Control

Given this chaotic atmosphere, board members and administrators
recognized that some steps had to be taken to quell unrest and to
reestablish the eroding authority of school officials. One might expect that divisions between machine and reform board members over
questions of authority and representation would preclude their acting in a strong, unified manner. And to be sure, machine members
favored a more repressive response. Not only did they oppose capitu-
lating to community groups seeking the ouster of school principals,
but they regarded meeting with student boycott leaders as a serious
mistake. On the other side, reformers, more enthusiastic about citizen participation, were more inclined to believe that both student
and community groups should have greater opportunities to communicate their opinions to school officials. But whatever their differences on these questions, both factions, recognizing the importance
of maintaining order in the schools, could accommodate the other's
special concerns. Reformers willingly accepted increasing numbers
of security guards, arrest of student boycott leaders, and cooperative
ties between school and police officials. On their side, machine members saw no harm in devices such as advisory councils and student
representation—provided these structures were advisory in character
and did not confer legitimacy on radical groups.

That the differences between the two factions were far from irrec-
oncilable is revealed by the statements of each side. Even in the
midst of the student boycotts, the most responsive board member,
Warren Bacon, in proposing a meeting with students was careful to
safeguard the board's authority: "The meeting would be 'informa-
tional and not a negotiating session.' "[40] Louise Malis, one of the
most vocal advocates of student and community participation, was
also one of the members most concerned about the legitimacy of
many such groups; on one occasion she expressed her fear that "people outside of the community are coming in and doing much of the
organizing."[41] At times, in fact, some of the board members who were
generally closely aligned with the machine were as willing to undertake the risks of decentralizing as the reformers. Marge Wild, while
obviously uneasy about giving communities even advisory power in
the recruitment of principals, in the end sighed: "I don't disagree. I
am willing to try it; anything would be better than today."[42] She had,

in fact, helped draft the committee recommendations on local school councils which gave these groups a significant advisory role. And John Carey, hardly a vigilant reformer, accepted greater community participation on the grounds that this might forestall the community control movement that had gained such strength elsewhere.[43] As much as the board members debated and bargained over various schemes for decentralization, their common recognition of the tensions under which the system was laboring unified their discussions.

In this regard, a moderate program calling for some degree of political decentralization made a good deal of sense to a board concerned about maintaining order in its schools. In a highly centralized system conflict in any school can become a problem for the center, as disturbances ripple throughout the system. Decentralizing authority not only relieves the center's burden of responding to the problem, but, more importantly, increases the probability of containing a conflict within a specific neighborhood. When student boycotts began in the fall of 1968, Superintendent Redmond insisted they were local problems to be handled by local administrators under his recently inaugurated plan for administrative decentralization. While this stance reveals the advantages of any decentralization scheme, the strictly administrative plan implemented by Redmond lacked necessary legitimating institutions. In the fall of 1968, most principals and district superintendents lacked even formally constituted advisory councils where the demands could be discussed and compromises reached.

As unrest mounted, Redmond pressured his associate superintendents to establish an interschool council in each of the three administrative areas. Redmond wished to answer board members who felt that more communication was needed between the professional staff and students. He hoped the councils would give militants a place to state their grievances while moderating their views. However, the staff implemented Redmond's demands so slowly and reluctantly that the councils were not even partly operational for many months. In the end, a board meeting with student boycotters proved necessary, because the central school board was the only agency of political legitimation.[44] Significantly, it was only after the board heard student leaders that the boycott lost its mass support. A plan for formal representation of local parent and community groups might have helped contain the conflict within specific neighborhoods and permitted system response to vary with the pressures placed upon it.[45]

Secondly, formal representation of community opinion could be most effective in reducing racial tensions if the authority conflict did not directly overlap the racial division in the city. From the point of view of the school board, recruting blacks and other minorities to positions of responsibility within the school system was a relatively painless means of reducing school disruptions. Whatever threats this policy posed to the interests of existing members of the administrative staff, the board, by changing the racial composition of its higher echelons, could, without sacrificing the structure of authority itself, alleviate a primary cause of the disruptions it was experiencing. Any rational response to the disorders the board faced, therefore, was likely to involve (1) changes in the formal, not the substantive, structures of representation and (2) changes in the racial composition of supervisory staff. As we have seen, this is precisely what the school board did.

In short, the Chicago school board was committed to maintaining social order in its classrooms, and, when that order was seriously threatened, it introduced token measures for student discussion of grievances, formal representation of community groups in school decision making, and changes in the racial composition of its administrative staff. Of course, other mechanisms for restoring social cohesion were also utilized, not excluding expansion of the school system's security force and, it seems, widespread, systematic police surveillance of dissident groups. And it probably can never be shown whether the declining levels of civil violence in Chicago during the 1970s were due to more effective police controls, more opportunities for citizen participation, more black faces in administrative positions, or environmental factors beyond the influence of any governmental agency. Yet it remains clear that school officials perceived a common problem, rationally sought efficient mechanisms for alleviating that problem, and quite reasonably concluded that a measure of decentralization was to be included among the means explored. As Louise Malis said when urging that channels of communication be opened, "We may be tending to alienate the youth at a time when this tremendous energy might be channeled in constructive directions."[46] Structures for formal and symbolic representation of parent and community groups were the constructive channels that the board finally chose.

CONCLUSIONS

Each of the three models of policy formation used in this chapter contributes to our understanding of Chicago's politics of decentralization. The organizational model identified the manner in which an administrative staff can undermine innovations that threaten its interests, values, and operating routines. Autonomous as the staff was, external political forces, identified by the political bargaining model, at times penetrated the decision-making structure. Indeed, when community and student groups on two occasions—the Wood-lawn experiment and the student boycotts—were able to place pro-posals for substantive decentralization schemes on the board's agenda, the board divided into two ideological factions that debated the na-ture of the board's authority and the legitimacy of the community and student groups in question. But even though reformers favored greater responsiveness to community pressures than did machine-oriented members, both were sufficiently committed to maintaining social order in the schools that much of the board's actions could be understood simply as the product of the board's unified, instrumen-tally rational pursuit of this objective.

Some might wish to interpret events strictly from a bargaining per-spective. From such a perspective, it might be said that the school board was caught between intense demands of racial minorities for greater community participation and equally strong opposition to such demands from its own administrative staff. Other participants in-cluded reform-oriented citizen groups, such as the League of Women Voters and the Citizens Schools Committee, as well as local news-papers. Since Mayor Daley chose not to influence policy, the power-ful Democratic organization removed itself from the conflict. In the circumstances, the board chose a compromise which gave community groups more black administrators and some formal access to the system but saved its staff from any wholesale restructuring of the decision-making system. A consensual, pluralist decision-making pat-tern was dominant except when minority groups chose boycotts and demonstrations to state their case, at which time the board divided ideologically between the machine and reform factions.

Although this interpretation has much to recommend it, we be-lieve that in the end it is misleading, for several reasons. First, the board regularly denied the legitimacy of the prodecentralization forces. It refused to negotiate with them, questioned the legitimacy of their representatives, and often found their language and manner of expression offensive. Since community groups had a reciprocal view of the board, there was little basis for bargaining between the two sides. Secondly, the community groups lacked either direct or indirect political resources sufficient to win concessions from the school board. Board members, appointed by the mayor, were under no obvious pressure from that office to decentralize their governing structure; in fact, the sole attempt of city hall to alter policy involved opposition to the Woodlawn experiment. To be sure, agitation for community control had stirred some reform groups to back decen-tralization, but these reformers were too weak to be effective third-party "reference groups" acting on behalf of the protesters.[47] Politically, the board had wide discretion in selecting the manner of its response to the civil violence that had occurred. Thirdly, the board responded to these events not openly in the course of community discussions but covertly—developing its own plans quietly and then announcing them at a time of its own choosing.

Yet if student and community groups could not bargain successfully, conditions could be created by such organizations in local schools that threatened the stability of the school system, a primary objective of Chicago's school board. In the late 1960s, turmoil and demonstrations reached just such a peak. Given the board's objective of restoring social order, it had a limited set of options, and these were discussed among board members themselves, not with any set of external actors. One alternative was harsh, strict, coercive control. Although strong punishments, including suspensions, expulsions, fines, and imprisonment might have crushed the unruly, such authoritarian measures often backfire. Indeed, at Harrison High School, when the two leaders, Victor Adams and Sharon Matthews, were suspended, the boycott expanded. Confronted by mass upheaval, authorities often respond by both threatening coercive force and providing opportunities for civilized discussion, and that was what happened in Chicago. In the words of one newspaper, the board took a "careful middle course" in dealing with student discontent. On the one hand, it instructed principals "to enforce truancy laws against students . . . and to dock the pay of teachers who join them."[48] On the other hand it decided that "there is no need to shut off communication." That the school board chose a more sophisticated pacification technique than crude use of force does not mean it bargained with the discontented. On the contrary, it rationally maximized its chances for achieving the social order it earnestly desired.

Most notably, the rational decision-making model accounts for changing school board policies over time. When disturbances first occurred in 1967, the school board responded with reassertions of its authority. Only after civil disorder steadily increased and expanded in 1968 did the board insist that its staff expand opportunities for student and community participation. As the turmoil continued in 1969 and 1970, the board took steps to increase the number of black administrators. In the four years from the fall of 1968 until the fall of 1972, the percentage of black principals increased from 7 to 18 percent. However, as discontent subsided in the seventies, board concern over citizen participation noticeably declined. Even though the political strength of the black community in Chicago politics seemed to expand in the 1970s, this had little impact on board decentralization policies. In the absence of threatening disorder, the board allowed its administrative staff to shape school-community relations. And from 1972 to 1975, the percentage of black principals increased by only one percent.

As fundamentally important as these considerations were, the rational decision-making model still did not account entirely for all aspects of decentralization policy. First, board response to protest, boycotts, and demonstrations was inordinately slow. Although the school disruptions reached their peak in 1968–69, major decentralizing moves were not finally implemented until 1971–72. Although the board took action in the heat of the community unrest, the organization, eagerly defending its own interests and routines, resisted implementation for another two years. To that degree, an organizational analysis must supplement any interpretation that sees the board efficiently maximizing its objectives. Secondly, the board did respond to external pressures whenever the bargainer had sufficient resources to induce action. In the case of the Woodlawn experiment, a powerful university and a well-organized community group came to share in the governance of certain schools. Here the final outcome must be seen as a bargain struck among several parties, none of whom maximized their goals. Indeed, the bargaining was so clear and explicit in this exceptional case that it points up once again how inadequately such a model characterizes Chicago's overall policy-making for mostly symbolic political decentralization.

In the end, the relative significance of the three models depends on the observer's opinion concerning what outcomes were most important. If one wishes to account for the difficulty the board had in establishing buffering mechanisms to alleviate distress to the system, one must begin by using the organizational model, focusing on staff resistance to board initiatives. Or if one wants to explain the structure, location, and duration of decentralization "experiments," as in Woodlawn, one must look closely at the bargaining relationships among school system, community groups, the federal government, and the university. But from our perspective, the reluctance of the school board as a whole, including both its machine and reform factions, to decentralize politically in any other than the most formalistic and symbolic terms is of central significance. Accordingly, the rational decision-making model identifies the preeminent factors. Since conflicts between staff and board and among board members themselves were carried out within exceedingly narrow parameters, the vigors of these disputes should not disguise the underlying consensus that unified school leaders. At no point did Superintendent Redmond deny the need for some symbolic gestures to community groups. And though the board pushed Redmond and his subordinates further than they may have liked, at no point were decentralization plans like those of Detroit and New York ever seriously considered.

This opposition to significant decentralization was a function of two reinforcing factors. First, the board acted to protect its own authority, seeking to maintain legitimacy for a school system whose direction rested in its hands. At the same time, board members were linked to an array of interests with a great stake in the central institutions of the city, including Mayor Daley and his Democratic organization, downtown businessmen, the Chicago Federation of Labor, other municipal bureaucracies, and citywide reform groups such as the Citizens Schools Committee. Although some of these groups could accept some decentralization, major restructuring of power relations within the school system would seriously threaten them all. Political decentralization involved a potential shift in the locus of control away from central, citywide elites to black and white neighborhood groups and politicians with local, not metropolitan, concerns. Whereas PTAs and school advisory councils posed little threat to citywide interests, new local elites, if given too much authority or power, might pursue racial segregation and traditional curricular policies; others might introduce black nationalist ideas or use school resources to enhance independent black or Latin political organizations. Both developments threatened dominant interests, who consequently sought to insure that Chicago's basic framework for running its schools remain intact. To this end the board rationally pursued a path that effectively blocked most decentralization reforms.

Part Four

CONCLUSIONS

Ten

MAKING POLICY FOR THE DECLINING CITY

School politics in Chicago had in its essentials a style characteristic of big-city school systems. Chicago's school board, like those in most big cities, was in the late sixties plagued by civil rights cries for integration, teacher organization demands for improved salaries and working conditions, and neighborhood group insistence on greater involvement in local school policy. Or, to state the issues in their fundamental terms, big-city schools were beset by racial migration, worker dissatisfaction, falling pupil performance levels, and bureaucratic isolation. Our three case studies of policy making in Chicago thus identify a school board's response to core issues faced by school policy makers in the largest of our central cities.

In certain ways Chicago's policy-making processes had their own special character. Bargaining over school policy by machine-oriented and reform-minded board members could take place only in a city with a powerful political machine challenged by a weaker reform drive that had had some success, historically, on school issues. Also, machine influence in Chicago's black neighborhoods handicapped civil rights efforts, labor's close ties to Chicago's Democratic party aided teachers, and decentralization was easily scuttled in this city because neighborhood groups autonomous of the Democratic organization were weak and widely scattered. But Chicago's school board, like most big-city school boards, governed through a massive, inbred, ponderous administrative structure. And Chicago's school board, again like most big-city school boards, was responsible for schools in an aging central city whose economic and social future remained at best uncertain.

After applying both bargaining and unitary models to this board's policy-making processes, we argued in concluding sections to earlier chapters that the relative utility of the models was in part a function

247

of the analyst's purposes. Since these contain an irreducible element of subjectivity, the matter of the relative utility of unitary as compared to bargaining models, which has provoked great scholarly debate, cannot be resolved altogether in strictly scientific terms. Nonetheless, it is still possible to specify for what purposes each model proved most useful.

Bargaining models help identify policy-making influences peculiar to a specific decision-making system. In this study bargaining models —either pluralist or ideological—proved crucial for specifying the significance of such matters as the power of the political machine, mayoral influence on board behavior, internal conflicts within the board of education, and group pressures of teachers, neighborhood organizations, and citywide school reformers. In all cases, Chicago's specific political history had its own impact on the schools. But as richly as these bargaining models have elaborated Chicago's style of school politics, their utility for generalizing about big-city school politics as a whole was limited. What Chicago shared with other once-great central cities was school system entropy and a relative decline in its socioeconomic status. When looked at in historical perspective, it is all the more clear that this second factor, the transformation in the economic and social well-being of the city, overlooked in most studies of school politics but strikingly captured by the rational decision-making model, significantly constrained the making of school policy.

THE EXPANDING CITY

Cities of the nineteenth century were at the heart of America's rapid industrial development. By controlling critical points in the nation's transportation system, cities grew with every turn in the country's upward economic spiral. As new technologies were introduced, cities found their capabilities for absorbing immigrants from rural areas at home and abroad constantly increasing. First, horse-drawn streetcars, next electric trolleys and subways, then buses and paved roads, finally the automobile and expressways expanded the arteries through which goods and people could move to and from the central business district. Equally important, elevators, steel girders, and concrete pillars permitted skyscraper construction that multiplied daytime densities in the heart of the city.

So powerful was the center of nineteenth-century American cities that the influential Chicago school of urban sociology, using Chicago as their primary laboratory, could contend that the "natural" ecology of a city was a series of concentric rings flowing outward from the central business district.[1] Adjacent to this core of industry and commerce were transition zones, which gave way to workingmen's homes, then to more middle-class areas, and finally to an outer ring of commuters, who lived in spacious and pleasant garden suburbs. Each ring's status was dependent upon its distance from the center of economic and political power, the central business district. As a result, whenever technology enabled the core to expand, its dominating position forced all other zones outward, thereby producing patterns of succession and neighborhood change which have fascinated urban sociologists ever since.[2] Although largely implicit in the Chicago school's own studies, their concentric circle model specified the manner in which the center's monopolistic control over the region's most valuable land enabled it to dominate the surrounding hinterland.

Not surprisingly, this great economic and social power easily translated itself into political successes. Perhaps the best example was the ease with which big cities absorbed adjacent areas. During the period from 1900 to 1910 cities were so successful in annexing open areas that they grew by 37 percent, while their suburban ring grew by only 24 percent.[3] Chicago itself provides an excellent example of successful central-city annexation of areas of future growth. During the ten years between 1880 and 1890 Chicago expanded from an area of 35 square miles to 170 through annexation of numerous suburbs.[4] As a result, 81.5 percent of the population in 1900 living within the Chicago area's standard metropolitan statistical area, as defined by the U.S. Bureau of the Census, resided within the central city.[5]

With these economic and political resources, cities supplied services to their residents on a scale which, if not up to contemporary levels, far surpassed anything offered in outlying towns and villages. Specifically, big city schools led the country in prestige, innovativeness, and financial resources. In terms of expenditures alone, cities of over 300,000 in 1910 spent $41.41 per pupil in average daily attendance, while the average for the United States as a whole was only $27.85.[6] Even though Chicago trailed behind other, more progressive cities in the East, it still spent 53 percent more than the national average on current educational expenditures per pupil.[7] So outstanding were urban schools that educational reformers focused on problems in rural areas.

URBAN DECLINE

As a result of trends which became increasingly apparent after World War II, central cities lost the monopolistic advantage and therefore the fiscal capabilities they once enjoyed. Technological advance that once had insured their mastery of the countryside now undermined central city preeminence. As private-car registration increased from twenty-seven million in 1940 to almost ninety million in 1970, the automobile became the primary mode of travel.[8] As the number of trucks rose from five million in 1940 to over nineteen million in 1970,[9] commerce and industry were freed from excessive dependence upon those few acres of land near water and rail intersections. During the ten years after 1950, suburbs grew by 46 percent (compared with only 11 percent within the central cities themselves), and economic decentralization took a course which the core city could not control.[10] With these innovations, land once of peripheral value became highly competitive with declining central city real estate.

As fundamental as these changes have been, their importance should not be overstated. Central cities still have access to water routes and rail lines that are of great value. Their towering skyscrapers and prestigious addresses are eagerly sought as home-office locales by the largest of America's corporations. Many manufacturing and commercial companies, with substantial fixed investments, cannot migrate as easily as newer, more capital-intensive industries. With such possible exceptions as Newark and Detroit, most central cities are not immediately becoming reservations for the poor or "sandboxes" in which children play but which productive adults ignore.[11] As aptly as those concepts might have been applied to small towns a generation ago, it is misleading, however compelling at times, to treat these metaphors as descriptive of central cities within which millions are employed, where art museums, opera companies, and symphony orchestras flourish, where restaurants and theaters abound, and which contain luxury highrise apartments with spectacular views of nearby rivers and shorelines. Central cities remain important economic, social, and cultural centers. What they have lost is their virtually monopolistic control over land use in the surrounding region.

In the competition with the central city, suburban areas now have many advantages. Although they lack access to rail lines, subways, and port facilities, many suburbs have convenient access to airports and are relatively free of the automobile congestion that plagues core areas. Although suburbs do not frequently possess high-quality cultural amenities, they characteristically have had new schools, green grass, spacious homes, cleaner air, lower crime rates, and homogeneous, middle-class neighborhoods. Even though many suburbs have had to build and supply a host of new public services, tax rates too are to their competitive advantage. In 1966–67 the total tax for central cities in the thirty-seven largest metropolitan areas averaged $219 per capita, while in the outlying suburbs of these same metropolitan areas, the average was only $170.[12] Local taxes consumed 6.1 percent of personal income in central cities, only 3.4 percent in the suburbs.[13] At the same time, cities have experienced population declines, aging housing, racially changing neighborhoods, increasing crime rates, withdrawal of investments by banks and savings and loan associations, abandonment by private hospitals, nursing homes, and other charitable institutions, and an influx of black and Spanish-speaking citizens with access only to the margins of the market economy.

POLICY-MAKING TO SAVE THE CENTRAL CITY

As a consequence of their severely declining competitive position, cities have a clearly defined set of interests which significantly constrain their political and economic leaders. Just as in a highly competitive market economy all firms, in order to survive, must follow certain pricing policies, cities, in competition with other political jurisdictions, can survive only by pursuing a delimited set of objectives. Whatever differences among elites, whatever disagreements between machine politicians and urban reformers, all have a common stake in the socioeconomic prosperity of their political territory. As long as the larger political system permits capital and labor to migrate freely from one subunit to another, as long as regional or national governments use neither regulatory powers nor tax incentives to direct economic investment, central cities must struggle as best they can to entice both industry and desirable labor into their political jurisdictions. To do this, they must provide quality amenities uncontaminated by the presence of undesirable groups, pursue fiscally responsible public policies, and maintain social order. In short, it is the competition among cities that establishes a unified set of objectives for cities taken as a whole, that is, which defines a recognizable set of public interests, making useful a rational decision-making model in the study of local policy formation.

In each of the three case studies where the rational decision-making model has been applied, its utility derived from Chicago's need to maintain parity with its hinterland. Most obviously, plans for allocating minority pupils among the system's schools were consciously constructed by machine and reform board members alike with an eye to their consequences for white and black migration patterns. Since whites were regarded as the more productive members of the territory, every effort within the political capacity of the school board was necessary to retard, if not reverse, their outward migration. Therefore, no scheme for wholesale desegregation of Chicago's schools was ever considered. On the other hand, integration programs that were perceived to have stabilizing consequences were given careful consideration, and even implemented in the most promising places.

All these efforts may in the long run have been in vain. Since cities can only induce, not control, movements of capital and labor, the school board or any other unit of local government may not be able to contain the centrifugal socioeconomic forces discussed above. But the need to try establishes a unitary set of objectives which limits the alternatives board members can consider. Thus a rational decision-making model, once thought appropriate only for considering policies of a nation-state in a highly competitive international political system, is equally appropriate to the analysis of local politics.

Similarly, school boards must be fiscally responsible. Their powers of taxation and their capacity for issuing bonds is limited not only by state law but by the marketplace. What was well known during the great Depression was forgotten until recently: cities can borrow money only if financiers regard municipal bonds as relatively safe investments. In a period in which central cities dominated the valuable land of a region, these constraints, though not unimportant, were minimized by the recognition that the cities' prosperity went hand in hand with that of the economy as a whole. In a crisis situation legal constraints could be modified, and the city could tax the great wealth within its boundaries. Next to those of the United States Treasury, big-city municipals were considered safer than any other bonds on the market. However, as cities have slipped to simply one among many competitive local government jurisdictions, their credit has also been jeopardized. It must now be recognized that over the long run an increase in taxes may not yield an increase in tax revenue. Central cities, which already employ more public servants per capita and tax at a higher per capita rate than the surrounding suburban areas, are constrained from raising taxes greatly on productive capital and labor within their boundaries.

Chicago's school expenditures, which in 1910 were 59 percent more than the national average, by 1966 equaled only 94 percent of that average.[14] Even by 1971, despite the spectacular budgetary expansion of the late sixties, the figure was only 31 percent more than the national average, a position still well below its 1910 standing. Any further increases would presumably only hasten the outward movement of productive families and businesses. As a result, collective bargaining between school boards and teachers cannot over the long run be a strictly political bargaining process, in any narrow sense. School boards, like firms, function in a competitive context, which requires that they keep costs from rising too far above the level necessary to obtain qualified labor. Given these considerations, the anomalies between the rational model and the board's collective bargaining behavior, as discussed in chapter 8, raise serious issues explored below.

Finally, decentralization policies had to be constructed so as to sustain social order in schools while allowing for central direction of vital school policies. Even when cities held monopolistic control over valuable land, a minimal degree of social order had to be maintained. But in the early 1970s, with central city crime and racial conflict seemingly potent deterrents to the inward flow of productive capital and labor, orderly maintenance of public systems was especially critical. The violence and disruption that haunted urban schools in the late sixties could not be tolerated for long by any rational school board concerned about Chicago's long-range survival. It therefore coupled a stringent set of security precautions with a series of advisory councils that ventilated local problems and facilitated minority recruitment to administrative positions. At the same time, no significant element among the city's leadership, on or off the school board, ever considered wholesale decentralization of financial, curricular, and pupil-placement authority to autonomous neighborhood groups, along the lines proposed by some decentralizing enthusiasts.[15] Instead, the board was careful to retain most of its authority so that these responsibilities would be centrally exercised. Once again, the city's competitive position with its hinterland so sharply constrained the alternatives that made sense to leaders that a unitary model of policy formation proved of considerable utility.

Indisputably, bargaining—even ideological bargaining—marked the processes by which policies in these critical areas were formulated. Both representatives of the political machine and its reform opposition had coherent political ideologies that shaped their views of the city's interests. Board members associated with Chicago's political machine believed that policies should be developed through traditional channels with due consideration to important vested interests. They also believed that neighborhood interests and parochial values deserved protection. They therefore were suspicious of integrationist claims that any desegregation plan, no matter how carefully formulated, could stabilize Chicago's white population. Moreover, so long as the mayor felt he had requisite financial resources, machine-oriented members believed that schoolteachers, now a vested part of Chicago's institutionalized bargaining process, should be awarded as substantial wage settlements as necessary to avoid a strike. Also, they felt that coercive police powers should be the city's primary response to those black parents and students who used illegitimate, disruptive techniques to press their claims for school decentralization.

Chicago's reformers were more committed to rationalized administrative processes and citizen participation than were machine-oriented board members. Specifically, they disliked both making ascriptively based distinctions among pupils and bargaining over school financial policies. Reformers therefore were more responsive to arguments that integration could foster, not inhibit, racial stabilization, and that strikes were less debilitating than unbalanced budgets. Finally, reformers, more interested in citizen participation, were more willing to encourage experiments in school decentralization and more willing to listen to parent groups and student leaders protesting school conditions.

As differentiated as these two factions were across all the major issues the board faced, the bargaining, though defined in ideological terms, was still always constrained by a common concern for the interests of the central city. Although the participants themselves may have believed they were locked in bitter conflict, both sides could deeply commit themselves to their competing views only because both could sensibly claim that their program was in Chicago's interest. Common objectives, as identified by the rational decision-making model, were not just rhetorical shibboleths used to justify particular group interests. They structured the debate within clearly defined parameters.

Although the school board had a set of common objectives which unified its approach to school policy formation, it was nonetheless constrained in carrying them out by the fact that it executed these policies through a large, complex organization. In each of the case studies, organizational behavior modified specific programs in such a way as to handicap the board's pursuit of its objectives. The school board abandoned its racial stabilization plan for South Shore and, perhaps, for many other parts of the city because the administrative staff had constructed an unworkable mechanism for implementing them. Political decentralization was delayed and undermined by a staff committed to maximizing its own discretionary powers. The board's bargaining position vis-à-vis the union was weakened by the staff's recruitment of inexperienced bargainers, its commitment to old certification policies, its traditional means of compiling a budget, and its fear of a strike. Indeed, the deviation from what a school board might rationally be expected to do in this policy area was so great that Chicago's school board came near to acting in a fiscally irresponsible fashion, a matter worthy of more general attention.

During the past decade central cities have greatly increased their budgets, taxed their property heavily, imposed new sales taxes and user charges, and allowed their bonded indebtedness to swell. In part, these financial changes have enabled cities to improve their services, especially to low-income residents. But as a number of urbanologists have stressed, increasing costs are also due to the pressures for higher pay, earlier retirement, improved pensions and other special benefits for municipal employees.[16] After the Kennedy administration allowed collective bargaining in the public sector and civil rights groups legitimized civic disruption as a political tactic, municipal employees, including policemen, firemen, welfare workers, hospital employees, sanitation engineers, and many more, have found a new, very effective mechanism for enhancing their economic position. In this regard, big-city teachers, especially in Chicago and New York, have led the way. Indeed, the power of teachers and other employees to win financial concessions has proved so substantial that, in the light of their declining competitive position, big central cities, even in a healthy economy, may someday be rescued from bankruptcy only by outside intervention.

Perhaps the current fiscal crisis is only a passing phenomenon, due to mistakes made by governing institutions during a transition period when they were adjusting to collective bargaining techniques. Or, perhaps concessions to public employees were necessary only in the late sixties when racial unrest so disturbed the cohesiveness of central cities that unusual financial outlays were necessary to avoid urban social disintegration. As a measure of social order has been restored in the seventies, governing elites may negotiate fiscally more responsible settlements with municipal unions. But the power of municipal employees to wrest concessions from political leaders may rest on a more enduring base. As economic elites have recognized that the geographic mobility of their own more capital-intensive enterprises limits their dependence on any particular territorial space, they have attended less to community affairs. Although New York City bankers have a suddenly renewed interest in their city's affairs, it remains unclear whether this signals a new trend in business influence. In the meantime, elected officials, looking for alternative sources of political support, have discovered that the one group with an abiding interest in government policy are their own employees. Now organized into strong unions and sophisticated professional associations, these employees influence elections, are accepted as legitimate participants in policy-making processes, and regularly threaten to withdraw their services. In a showdown leaders must balance the immediate crisis induced by uncollected garbage, unpatrolled streets, or unopened schools against a longer-range crisis of bankruptcy. If a mayor as verbally committed to the welfare of big cities as John Lindsay perceived the labor rather than the financial crisis as the more pressing, other politicians, with closer ties to labor leaders, can be expected to reach similar conclusions.

It is easy at this point to call for the federal government, the deus ex machina, to enter with largess to resolve the vicious circle of increasing demands, decreasing resources, and increasing taxes. But that ignores the federal government's own contributions, as expressway builder and mortgage supplier, to central city decline. With that history, one cannot expect a federal government, elected by a suburban hinterland, to undertake the Herculean measures necessary to reverse accelerating socioeconomic processes.

The federal government's response to change in rural America is instructive. When farms disappeared in the face of mechanized agriculture, the federal government responded with farm advisory committees and subsidies to productive farmers.[17] When small towns dependent on rural America were eclipsed by big cities, the government created a small business bureau, which dispensed favors and patronage to politically connected businessmen.[18] Only ruralists and hometown preachers mourned the debris and sorrow progress left behind.

The federal government's response to the urban crisis has been remarkably similar. To meet the needs of poor racial minorities, it sponsors citizen participation in community action, model cities, and other programs that serve as dispensers of patronage to middle-class administrators and politically connected neighborhood leaders. To slow deterioration of inner-city housing, the Department of Housing and Urban Development has subsidized developers and mortgagers. To alleviate the fiscal crisis, the government has promulgated revenue sharing—at the price of many grants-in-aid. To rationalize transportation policy, it projected an increase in mass transit outlays, but only up to 31 percent of its highway construction budget.[19]

As central cities have declined, the urban ministry has grown and universities have expanded their urban studies programs. Since cities still have great resources, it will be some time before these new professions, though already waning, take their place alongside the rural sociologist and country parson. The latter professions, by the way, may some day have new growth potential. After all, land in the small towns of Minnesota is now about as valuable as more desirable portions of the South Side of Chicago.

NOTES

NOTES TO THE PREFACE

1. Andrew MacFarland, *Power and Leadership in Pluralist Systems* (Stanford, Cal.: Stanford University Press, 1969).

2. Cf. J. Greenstone and Paul E. Peterson, *Race and Authority in Urban Politics* (Chicago: University of Chicago Press, reprint, 1976), chapter 5. See also Paul E. Peterson and J. David Greenstone, "Two Competing Models of the Policy-making Process: The Community Action Controversy as an Empirical Test," in Michael Lipsky and Willis Hawley (eds.), *Theoretical Perspectives on Urban Politics* (Englewood Cliffs, N.J.: Prentice-Hall, 1976).

3. Peter Bachrach and Morton S. Baratz, "Two Faces of Power," *American Political Science Review* 57 (December 1962): 947–52; Edward C. Hayes, *Power Structure and Urban Policy: Who Rules in Oakland?* (New York: McGraw-Hill, 1972); Edward S. Greenberg, *Serving the Few: Corporate Capitalism and the Bias of Government Policy* (New York: John Wiley, 1964).

4. Matthew A. Crenson, *The Un-Politics of Air Pollution: A Study of Non-Decisionmaking in the Cities* (Baltimore: Johns Hopkins Press, 1971).

5. Graham Allison, *Essence of Decision* (Boston: Little Brown, 1971).

6. The classic example, of course, is Floyd Hunter, *Community Power Structure* (Chapel Hill: University of North Carolina Press, 1953). For a convenient collection of readings and an accompanying bibliography, see Willis D. Hawley and Frederick M. Wirt (eds.), *The Search for Community Power* (Englewood Cliffs, N.J.: Prentice-Hall, 1968).

NOTES TO CHAPTER ONE

1. The conversation concerning the trophy case is taken from a transcript of board meetings made available to this study by the Chicago Board of Education. Where data have been obtained from confidential or inaccessible sources, no citation is given.

2. An analysis of board member voting is presented in chapter 3.

3. The political realignment of the thirties, which made the Democratic party overwhelmingly popular in urban areas, has been discussed in Walter Dean Burnham, *Critical Elections and the Mainsprings of American Politics* (New York: W. W. Norton, 1970), chap. 5. See also V. O. Key, "A Theory of Critical Elections," *Journal of Politics* 17 (February 1955): 3–18; and Duncan MacRae, Jr., and James A. Meldrum, "Critical Elections in Illinois: 1888–1958," *American Political Science Review* 54 (September 1960): 669–83. In Chicago, supporters of the national Democratic ticket were very likely to be supporters of Mayor Daley as well. The ward-by-ward correlation for the Democratic mayoral vote in 1955 and Democratic presidential vote in 1956 was .86; the 1959 mayoral vote correlated at the .93 level with the 1960 presidential vote; the 1963–64 correlation was .91, and the 1967–68 correlation, .88. I thank Stanley Goumas for providing me with these figures. Clearly, local Democrats benefited from the popularity of national Democrats in urban areas, and vice versa.

4. Alex Gottfried, *Boss Cermak of Chicago* (Seattle: University of Washington Press, 1962), chaps. 10 and 11.

5. Ibid., chaps. 9–11. For data on the patterns of voter support in the thirties, see the classic study of the Democratic organization in Chicago, Harold Gosnell, *Machine Politics: Chicago Model*, 2d ed. (University of Chicago Press, 1968), chap. 5.

6. Mike Royko, *Boss: Richard J. Daley of Chicago* (New York: E. P. Dutton, 1971), pp. 63–64. See also Milton Rakove, *Don't Make No Waves, Don't Back No Losers* (Bloomington, Indiana: University of Indiana Press, 1975), chap. 4, and the description of the organization of the machine in Martin Meyerson and Edward Banfield, *Politics, Planning and the Public Interest* (Glencoe, Ill.: Free Press, 1955), chap. 3.

7. This is documented in Leo Snowiss, "The Metropolitan Congressman," (doctoral dissertation, Department of Political Science, University of Chicago, 1965).

8. Francis Fox Piven and Richard Cloward, *Regulating the Poor* (New York: Random House, 1971), p. 336.

9. The data are from J. David Greenstone and Paul E. Peterson, "Machines, Reformers and the War on Poverty," in James Wilson (ed.), *City Politics and Public Policy* (New York: John Wiley, 1968), p. 280.

10. James Wilson, *The Amateur Democrat* (Chicago: University of Chicago Press, 1962), p. 65.

11. Meyerson and Banfield, pp. 66–68.

12. Gilbert Steiner and Samuel Gove, *Legislative Politics in Illinois* (Urbana: University of Illinois Press, 1960), and Daniel Elazar, *American Federalism: A View from the States* (New York: Thomas Y. Crowell, 1966), provide two perspectives on Illinois politics. For the case of educational politics see Nicholas Masters, Robert Salisbury, and Thomas Eliot, *State Politics and the Public Schools* (New York: Alfred Knopf, 1964).

13. Snowiss, p. 403.

14. J. David Greenstone and Paul E. Peterson, *Race and Authority in Urban Politics: Community Participation and the War on Poverty* (New York: Russell Sage, 1973), pp. 19–24.

15. Gary Orfield, *The Reconstruction of Southern Education* (New York: John Wiley, 1969), chap. 4.

16. J. David Greenstone, *Labor in American Politics* (New York: Alfred Knopf, 1969), especially chap. 3.

17. Meyerson and Banfield, pp. 66–68.

18. Edward Banfield, *Political Influence* (New York: Free Press, 1961); Mike Royko, *Boss: Richard J. Daley of Chicago.*

19. If Royko had wished to use psychoanalytic categories, he might have compared Daley to Chicago's other great mayor, Anton Cermak, who was power-centered, meticulous, ill at ease in the company of women, and endured frequent inflammations of the colon, characteristics Gottfried considered to be manifestations of an "anal" personality. Gottfried, passim, but especially Appendix 2.

20. James David Barber, *The Presidential Character* (Englewood Cliffs, N.J.: Prentice-Hall, 1972) provides a psychological interpretation of American presidents which, among other things, distinguishes between active-positive and active-negative presidents, the latter determined to do their duty without realizing any deep satisfaction from the effort. Barber thinks the latter are likely to pursue rigidly a policy line, even after its disastrous consequences should be obvious. On the basis of the Royko material, Barber would have to classify Daley as one of the "active-negatives."

21. Royko, pp. 19–20.

22. The following interpretation of the machine politician's ideology follows closely Greenstone and Peterson, *Race and Authority*, chap. 4. See also Paul E. Peterson and J. David Greenstone, "The Community Action Controversy as a Test of Two Competing Models of the Policy-making Process," in Michael Lipsky and Willis Hawley (eds.), *Theoretical Perspectives on Urban Politics* (New York: Prentice-Hall, 1976).

23. See James Bryce, *The American Commonwealth* II (New York: Macmillan, 1910), especially chaps. 60–68; and M. Ostrogorski, *The Organization and Development of Political Parties II: The United States* (New York: Macmillan, 1910), especially chaps. 11 and 12.

24. Besides Banfield's *Political Influence*, see Edward Banfield and James Wilson, *City Politics* (Cambridge: Harvard University Press, 1963), and Robert K. Merton, *Social Theory and Social Structure* (New York: Free Press, 1957), pp. 71–81.

25. An early theoretical defense of this principle can be found in James Madison, *The Federalist No. 10*. Political scientists such as Herbert Agar, in *The Price of Union* (New York: Houghton-Miflin, 1950), and E. Pendleton Herring, in *Group Representation before Congress* (Baltimore: Johns Hopkins Press, 1929), carried the theme forward in the earlier part of the twentieth century. Besides Banfield, the best contem-

porary theorist in this tradition is Robert Dahl. See especially *Who Governs?* (New Haven: Yale University Press, 1961); *A Preface to Democratic Theory* (Chicago: University of Chicago Press, 1956); and, with Charles Lindblom, *Politics, Economics and Welfare* (New York: Harper & Row, 1953).

26. Edward J. Flynn, *You're the Boss* (New York: Viking Press, 1947), p. 17.

27. The brotherly imagery was suggested to me by Michael Rogin. See his "Liberal Society and the Indian Question," *Politics and Society* 1 (May 1971): 305–12.

28. The three school referenda are analyzed in J. David Hood, "Issues and Response: A Causal Analysis of Voting on Chicago School Finance Referenda in the 1960's" (M. A. paper, Department of Political Science, University of Chicago, June 1972).

29. The phrase, as applied to the Chicago schools, is taken from Mary J. Herrick's excellent history of *The Chicago Schools* (Beverly Hills, Cal.: Sage Publications, 1971), the heading to chapter 15. Her discussion of this period, informed by personal experience, is particularly detailed and interesting.

30. Gosnell's *Machine Politics: Chicago Model* and Charles Merriam's *Chicago: A More Intimate View of Urban Politics* (New York: Macmillan, 1929) were not friendly accounts of machine-style politics. Merriam not only fathered the 1955 candidate against Richard Daley but had himself twice been a Republican reform candidate for mayor.

31. See James Wilson, *The Amateur Democrat*, chap. 12; Meyerson and Banfield, chap. 11; Eugene C. Lee, *The Politics of Nonpartisanship* (Berkeley: University of California Press, 1960), pp. 76–84, 139–40. Also, Oliver P. Williams and Charles R. Adrian, "The Insulation of Local Politics under the Nonpartisan Ballot," *American Political Science Review* 53 (December 1959): 1059–61. See also Willis Hawley, *Nonpartisan Elections and the Case for Party Politics* (New York: John Wiley, 1973); Banfield and Wilson, *City Politics*, chap. 21.

32. The phrase is taken from Wallace Sayre and Herbert Kaufman, *Governing New York City* (New York: Russell Sage, 1960), pp. 710–16.

33. Following Robert Agger, Daniel Goldrich, and Bert Swanson, *The Rulers and the Ruled* (New York: John Wiley, 1964), David Greenstone and I have labeled the more conservative reformers Progressive Conservatives and the more liberal reformers Community Conservationists. (Greenstone and Peterson, *Race and Authority*, chap. 4). In Chicago school politics, the two elements combined frequently enough to make this distinction unnecessary.

34. Stephen D. London, "Business and the Chicago Public School System, 1890–1966," (Ph.D. dissertation, Department of Education, University of Chicago, 1968), chap. 4.

35. Rakove, chap. 6. Snowiss, p. 92. For a discussion of these practices in an earlier period, see Gosnell, p. 44.

36. The Chicago Standard Metropolitan Statistical Area, as defined by the U.S. Bureau of the Census, grew from 4,569,600 in 1940 to 6,978,947 in 1970, an increase of 55 percent.

37. Philip Rees, "A Factorial Ecology of Metropolitan Chicago" (Master's thesis, Department of Geography, University of Chicago, 1968), p. 69.

38. As a result, blacks paid higher prices for comparable housing. See H. L. Molotch, *Managed Integration: Dilemmas of Doing Good in the City* (Berkeley: University of California Press, 1972).

39. Of twenty-eight major cities surveyed by the National Advisory Commission on Civil Disorders, Chicago, with 17 percent of its policemen black, ranked third in this dimension. Only Washington, D.C., with 21 percent black officers (as compared with a total population estimated to be 63 percent black), and Philadelphia, with 20 percent black officers (and, like Chicago, a machine city with approximately the same proportion of blacks in its population) ranked higher than Chicago. Other cities' recruitment of blacks was very poor by comparison: Detroit's police force, for example, was only 5 percent black, although blacks comprised an estimated 39 percent of the population. These and other data can be found in U.S. National Advisory Commission on Civil Disorders, *Report* (New York: Bantam, 1968), p. 321.

Data on racial composition of Chicago teachers are given in chapter 8 of this volume.

40. Ira Katznelson, *Black Men, White Cities* (New York: Oxford University Press, 1973), p. 118. Katznelson's quotation comes from Harold Baron, "Black Powerlessness in Chicago," *Trans-Action* 4 (November 1968): 28, 33.

41. Peter Rossi and Robert Dentler, *The Politics of Urban Renewal* (New York: Free Press, 1961).

42. This short account of a long, complex struggle follows Herrick, p. 316. See also the bibliography contained therein.

43. Samuel Lubell, *White and Black: Test of a Nation* (New York: Harper and Row, 1964), pp. 157, 160.

44. This occurred, most notably, when Warren Bacon sought to become president of the school board. All minority group candidates voted for him plus one white board member (see chap. 4).

45. On Chicago black politics in the fifties, see James Wilson, *Negro Politics* (New York: Free Press, 1960); in the thirties, Harold Gosnell, *Negro Politicians*, 2d ed. (Chicago: University of Chicago Press, 1968). See also Ira Katznelson, *Black Men, White Cities* (New York: Oxford University Press, 1973), chap. 6.

46. One example illustrates the general problem well. In 1970 Illinois held a constitutional convention, and each senatorial district was to elect two representatives. In the area around the University of Chicago two liberal, antimachine candidates ran, one black and one white. The white was associated with a prestigious, reform-oriented law firm and had

worked for many years wih the Independent Voters of Illinois. The black had been head of the Co-ordinating Council of Community Organizations that had led the anti-Willis battle. Although IVI endorsed both candidates, it concentrated its efforts on the white candidate—even though the racial composition of the area gave the black much the better chance of winning. The black candidate won, the white one lost. See also Wilson, *The Amateur Democrat*, pp. 277–88.

47. Banfield, *Political Influence*, pp. 256–59.

48. Biographical information is taken from *Who's Who in America* 1971.

49. Robert Crain, *The Politics of Desegregation* (Chicago: Aldine, 1968), pp. 264–87.

50. City of Chicago, Board of Education, General Superintendent of Schools, "Can the Schools Be an Instrument in Social Change?" Speech to Principals Club Education Conference, Chicago, Illinois, March 29, 1969, as quoted in James Cibulka, "Administrators As Representatives: The Role of Local Communities in an Urban School System" (doctoral dissertation, Department of Education, University of Chicago, 1973), p. 272.

NOTES TO CHAPTER TWO

1. Andrew MacFarland argues that bargaining is "an overly general concept for many explanatory purposes," for it refers to almost the entire universe of political interactions, except when an absolutely clear hierarchical relationship exists. Even prisoners can be said to "bargain" with their guardians. See his *Power and Leadership in Pluralist Systems* (Stanford, Cal.: Stanford University Press, 1969), p. 43.

2. The ensuing discussion of the pluralist bargaining and ideological bargaining models is closely related to the discussion of electoral interests, organizational interests, and political ideologies in J. David Greenstone and Paul E. Peterson, *Race and Authority in Urban Politics* (New York: Russell Sage, 1973); Chicago: University of Chicago Press, Phoenix paperback, 1976; pp. 125–32. Because of differing purposes, the labels used to make the distinctions differ somewhat. In *Race and Authority* our purpose was to characterize the interests of the decision makers; here the purpose is to characterize more generally the policy-making process. Also, see Paul E. Peterson and J. David Greenstone, "Two Competing Models of the Policy-making Process: the Community Action Controversy As an Empirical Test," in Willis Hawley and Michael Lipsky (eds.), *Theoretical Perspectives on Urban Politics* (Englewood Cliffs, N.J.: Prentice-Hall, 1976).

3. The argument has been developed most elegantly and in greatest detail by Anthony Downs, *An Economic Theory of Democracy* (New York: Harper and Bros., 1957). The perspective was set forth in 1942 by Joseph A. Schumpeter, *Capitalism, Socialism and Democracy* (New York: Holt, Rinehart and Winston, 1960); See also V. O. Key, *The*

Responsible Electorate (Cambridge: Harvard University Press, 1966);
Robert Dahl, *Who Governs?* (New Haven: Yale University Press, 1961),
and Joseph Schlesinger, *Ambition and Politics* (Chicago: Rand, McNally,
1966). Empirical data showing that many local politicians do not appear
to be ambitious and a discussion of the problems this raises for political
representation in local communities can be found in Kenneth Prewitt and
Heinz Eulau, "Political Matrix and Political Representation: Prolegom-
enon to a New Departure from an Old Problem," *American Political
Science Review* 63 (June 1969): 427–41.

4. The best and most relevant statement of this position is contained
within Edward Banfield, *Political Influence* (New York: Free Press,
1961). An early classic developing this perspective is Robert A. Dahl
and Charles E. Lindblom's *Politics, Economics, and Welfare* (New York:
Harper and Row, 1953). See, especially, chap. 12. See also Charles E.
Lindblom, "The Science of Muddling Through," *Public Administration
Review* 19 (1959): 79–88. The model is applied to urban politics in
Norton E. Long, "The Local Community as an Ecology of Games,"
American Journal of Sociology 64 (November 1958): 251–61, which is
reprinted in Edward Banfield (ed.), *Urban Government* (New York:
Free Press, 1969), pp. 465–79.

5. Robert Dahl, *Who Governs?*

6. Ibid., p. 94.

7. Ibid., p. 214.

8. Edward Banfield, *Political Influence.*

9. Ibid., p. 273.

10. Ibid., pp. 337–38.

11. This same point has been made more critically by Grant McConnell, *Private Power and American Democracy* (New York: Alfred Knopf,
1966). See also Mancur Olson, *The Logic of Collective Action* (Cambridge: Harvard University Press, 1965).

12. For an analysis of voting behavior from this perspective, see Bernard R. Berelson, Paul F. Lazarsfeld, and William N. McPhee, *Voting*
(Chicago: University of Chicago Press, 1954).

13. Robert Dahl, *Pluralist Democracy in the United States: Conflict
and Consent* (Chicago: Rand McNally, 1967), pp. 338–39.

14. Ibid., p. 338.

15. Aaron Wildavsky, *Leadership in a Small Town* (Totowa, N.J.:
Bedminster Press, 1964), p. 342.

16. A careful empirical study indicates that relationships vary con-
siderably from issue area to issue area and are generally rather marginal.
See Warren E. Miller and Donald E. Stokes, "Constituency Influences in
Congress," *American Political Science Review* 57 (March 1963): 45–56.

17. It might be argued that decision-making processes are quiet simply
because policy makers keep them within the bounds acceptable to the
public at large. Otherwise, a new issue will arise threatening the position
of established elites. In Wildavsky's words, "competing sets of leaders

have a stake in not pursuing policies which will lead to the entry of new participants who will make a bid for leadership that may upset prevailing patterns. The more extreme the policy, the greater the departure from the *status quo*, the more likely that interest will be created and potential leaders motivated to make their bid, thus threatening the powers that be" (Leadership, p. 342). Little research has been conducted on the ease with which new political elites can enter into the bargaining system through independently constructed organizational structures. Much of Wildavsky's argument—and Dahl's claim that the political stratum "is easily penetrated" (*Who Governs?*, p. 91)—depends on what research might discover on this point. We would hypothesize that barriers to entry are high enough so that existing elites have considerable latitude in policy formation.

18. Robert Agger, Daniel Goldrich, and Bert Swanson, *The Rulers and the Ruled* (New York: John Wiley, 1964), pp. 761–65.

19. David Minar, "Ideology and Political Behavior," *Midwest Journal of Political Science* 5 (November 1961): 317–31.

20. We are developing in this section an understanding of ideology consistent with the one given in Greenstone and Peterson, pp. 128–31. Further rationale for this definition of ideology is presented therein.

21. Dahl, *Who Governs?*, p. 94.

22. Ibid.

23. For a detailed discussion of these authority structures that characterize the American political regime, see Greenstone and Peterson, pp. 100–111; Appendix A.

24. James Wilson, *The Amateur Democrat* (Chicago: University of Chicago Press, 1966), p. 161. See also Agger, Goldrich, and Swanson, pp. 773–76.

25. Ibid., p. 427.

26. Theodore Lowi, "American Business, Public Policy, Case Studies and Political Theory," *World Politics* 16 (July 1964): 711.

27. On the use of ideology for vote maximization, see Downs, pp. 100–102.

28. J. David Greenstone, *Labor in American Politics* (New York: Alfred Knopf, 1968), p. 9.

NOTES TO CHAPTER THREE

1. Norman Kerr, "The School Board As an Agency of Legitimation," *Sociology of Education* 38 (1964): 34–59. See also M. Kent Jennings and Harmon Zeigler, with Wayne Peak, *Governing American Schools* (North Scituate, Mass.: Duxbury, 1974).

2. David Rogers, *110 Livington Street* (New York: Random House, 1968), pp. 216–39. See also James Andrews, Luvern Cunningham, and Raphael Nystrand, "The Changing Politics of Education—Columbus,

Ohio," paper prepared in Department of Education, Ohio State University, Columbus, Ohio (mimeographed).

3. On this point, see Peter Bachrach and Morton S. Baratz, "Two Faces of Power," *American Political Science Review* 56 (December 1962): 957–62; Matthew Crenson, *The Unpolitics of Air Pollution* (Baltimore: Johns Hopkins Press, 1971).

4. Cf. Nelson Polsby, *Community Power and Political Theory* (New Haven: Yale University Press, 1963), pp. 95–96; Andrew MacFarland, *Power and Leadership in Pluralist Systems* (Stanford: Stanford University Press, 1969), chap. 5.

5. Although the extent of conflict on the board could be measured by the nonunanimous percentage of all roll calls, this figure would be misleading. The Chicago Board of Education includes within a category called "omnibus" nearly all of its noncontroversial business. One roll call is taken to cover all these items. But the number of specific items included in the omnibus category varies substantially from one meeting to the next. One roll call vote on the omnibus item can therefore cover a large but varying number of items of business. Analyzing variation in simply the number of split roll calls assumes that the amount of business with which the board deals does not vary substantially from year to year; this assumption is more likely to be valid than any assumptions necessary for computing the data in percentage terms.

6. Joseph Pois, *The School Board Crisis: A Chicago Case Study* (Chicago: Educational Methods, 1964), pp. 81–82.

7. Andrews, Cunningham, and Nystrand describe a similar increase in board conflict in their study of school politics in Columbus, Ohio.

8. The cluster analysis of the roll call data follows the technique developed by Duncan MacRae, Jr. For a theoretical and practical presentation of the various steps taken in such an analysis, see his *Issues and Parties in Legislative Voting: Methods of Statistical Analysis* (New York: Harper and Row, 1970), pp. 39–74. The coefficient of correlation used in the computation was Yule's Q.

9. Duncan MacRae, Jr., "A Method for Identifying Issues and Factions from Legislative Votes," *American Political Science Review* 59 (December 1965): 909–26; see also his *Parliament, Parties and Society in France, 1946–1958* (New York: St. Martin's Press, 1967).

10. Our analysis interprets the data in the same way as those who have used intercorrelation among items in survey questionnaires in order to identify consistency in belief systems. See Philip Converse, "The Nature of Belief Systems in Mass Publics," in David E. Apter (ed.), *Ideology and Discontent* (New York: Free Press, 1964), pp. 206–61; Norman Nie and Kristi Andersen, "Mass Belief Systems Revisited: Political Change and Attitude Structure," *Journal of Politics* 36 (August 1974): 540–91; Robert Dahl, *Pluralist Democracy in the United States: Conflict*

and Consent (Chicago: Rand McNally, 1967), pp. 360–63; James S. Coleman, *Introduction to Mathematical Sociology* (New York: Free Press, 1964), chap. 12.

11. It should be noted, however, that scales are more likely to have high intercorrelations with one another than are single items. Scales are constructed on the basis of a number of items; minor inconsistencies and errors in data recording disappear and the underlying pattern emerges more sharply.

12. The summary measure for board members for the period 1946–54 was constructed by averaging the score on the machine-reform dimension that each board member received for each single board on which he served. Board members ranged from extreme and consistent support of reform to extreme and consistent support of the machine. Their score on the summary measure reflected their pattern of voting for the entire 1946–54 period.

13. Significantly, this was the historical period which provided the data base for Robert Dahl's and Edward Banfield's studies, which emphasized the pluralist, consensual character of American politics.

14. MacRae, *Issues and Parties*, p. 74.

15. Converse makes a similar argument, pp. 239–41.

16. Chap. 1.

17. These points are developed in detail in chap. 1.

18. Fred Muskal, "The Mayor's Advisory Commission on School Board Nomination: History and Appraisal," paper submitted to the Project on Society and Education in Chicago, Department of Education, University of Chicago, March 1966. I have reanalyzed this data.

19. This 1957–58 board's major dimension of cleavage, which did not correlate highly with the major dimension of the other boards, was excluded from the data used to build the machine-reform index on which each member was ranked.

20. For one member there was insufficient information to permit classification. Also the number of individuals in each of these two factions does not give valid information about the power relations between the two groups on the board. Members did not vote as a bloc but were distributed over a continuum. More important, different board members served for various lengths of time, and it is necessary to examine the composition of each board to determine which tendency is in the majority.

21. Muskal.

22. The evidence for this is in table 6, where the .50 correlation between the reform-machine conflict dimension on the 1958–61 board and the one dealing with civil rights issues in 1961–62 is due more to *reform* than to *machine* member opposition to civil rights demands. In the beginning, reform members seem to have been especially sensitive to criticisms of the professional school superintendent, whereas at least some machine members treated black demands for integration as another

special interest to be considered, and a legitimate part of the bargaining process. It was only as the conflict intensified that reformers became more supportive of integration, less supportive of Superintendent Willis, while machine-oriented members became strong defenders of the neighborhood school.

23. See Edward C. Banfield and James Q. Wilson, *City Politics* (Cambridge: Harvard University Press, 1963) and James Q. Wilson and Edward C. Banfield, "Public-Regardingness as a Value Premise in Voting Behavior," *American Political Science Review* 58 (December 1964): 876–87. See also Wilson and Banfield's more recent "Political Ethos Revisited," *American Political Science Review* 65 (December 1971): 1048–62.

24. *City Politics*, p. 41.

25. Richard Hofstadter, *The Age of Reform* (New York: Random House, 1955), p. 9.

26. James Q. Wilson, *The Amateur Democrat* (Chicago: University of Chicago Press, 1966), p. 258.

27. Ibid., pp. 262–65.

28. Hofstadter, p. 9.

29. Elmer E. Cornwell, Jr., *Annals of the American Academy of Political and Social Science* 353 (May 1964): 28.

30. See n. 23.

31. Raymond E. Wolfinger and John O. Field, "Political Ethos and the Structure of City Government," *American Political Science Review* 60 (June 1966): 306–26.

32. Ibid., p. 326 n.

33. Robert L. Lineberry and Edmund P. Fowler, "Reformism and Public Policies in American Cities," *American Political Science Review* 61 (September 1967): 702–3. Also, see Daniel Elazar, *Cities of the Prairie* (New York: Basic Books, 1970), and *The Politics of Belleville* (Philadelphia: Temple University Press, 1971).

34. James Q. Wilson and Edward C. Banfield, "Communications," *American Political Science Review* 60 (December 1966): 999.

35. Many studies have documented the overrepresentation of high status occupations in all phases of political activity. See, for example, Lester Milbrath, *Political Participation* (Chicago: Rand McNally, 1965); Sidney Verba and Norman Nie, *Participation in America* (Boston: Little Brown, 1972); Heinz Eulau and Kenneth Prewitt, *Labyrinths of Democracy* (Indianapolis: Bobbs-Merrill, 1973), chap. 13. What could be said in this context is that some appraisals of the machine tend to disregard these findings when they insist on the machine's close ties to the immigrant poor. The poor may have provided the votes, but it is quite doubtful that they contributed disproportionately to the leadership of either machine or reform movement.

36. J. David Greenstone, *Labor in American Politics* (New York: Alfred Knopf, 1969), chap. 3. Greenstone's distinction between the old

AFL craft unions and the CIO industrial unions in Chicago illuminates some differences in the behavior of union officials on the Chicago board. Union officials affiliated with the craft unions were uniformly allies of the machine faction on the board, whereas the three representatives of the industrial unions were less predictable in their voting. One industrial union official's voting record on the school board contradicted informed judgments of his views; another industrial union member was the only board member of the sixties whose voting record was so erratic he could not be classified along the integrationist neighborhood-school dimension; and the third representative, Raymond Pasnick, contributed to the racial controversy that Mayor Daley and his machine wanted to avoid.

37. Board members were classified into integrationist-minded reformers and neighborhood-school-oriented machine members by averaging their score on this dimension of cleavage for all the boards during the 1961–68 period on which they served. The ensuing rank order of board members was then dichotomized.

38. Earl Latham, *The Group Basis of Politics* (Ithaca: Cornell University Press, 1952), p. 36.

NOTES TO CHAPTER FOUR

1. Edward Banfield, *Political Influence* (New York: Free Press, 1961), pp. 235–38.

2. Christopher Chandler, "How the Democratic Party Captured Schools," *Free Press*, n.d., p. 16.

3. *Chicago Tribune*, September 14, 1969.

4. Mike Royko, *Boss: Richard J. Daley of Chicago* (New York: E. P. Dutton, 1971), p. 201.

5. Mary Herrick, *The Chicago Schools: A Social and Political History* (Beverly Hills, Cal.: Sage Publications, 1971), p. 380.

6. Laurence Iannaccone and Frank Lutz, *Politics, Power and Policy: The Governing of Local School Districts* (Columbus, Ohio: Charles Merrill, 1970), chap. 2; Robert Wood, *Suburbia: Its People and Their Politics* (Boston: Houghton Mifflin, 1958), pp. 186–97.

7. For an interesting comparison with European developments, see Arnold Heidenheimer, "The Politics of Public Education, Health and Welfare in the United States and Western Europe: How Growth and Reform Potentials have Differed," paper prepared for delivery at the 1972 Annual Meeting of the American Political Science Association, Washington, D. C., September 5–9, 1972.

8. *Chicago Daily News*, October 5, 1963, p. 1.

9. Mike Royko, "Maybe We Should Pray!" *Chicago Daily News*, May 20, 1968.

10. *Chicago Daily News*, May 21, 1968, p. 1.

11. *Chicago Tribune*, April 2, 1969, p. 5.

12. On the interwar period, see George Counts, *School and Society in Chicago* (New York: Harcourt, Brace, 1928). Counts's data is imag-

inatively interpreted in Robert Salisbury, "Schools and Politics in the Big City," *Harvard Educational Review* 37 (1967): 408–24.

13. Herrick, pp. 141–42.

14. Ibid., p. 167.

15. Ibid., p. 169.

16. Ibid.

17. J. Stephen Hazlett, "Crisis in School Government: An Administrative History of the Chicago Public Schools, 1933–1947," doctoral dissertation, Department of Education, University of Chicago, December 1968), p. 212.

18. The specific issues raised are discussed by Hazlett in chaps. 2–4.

19. Joseph Pois, *The School Board Crisis: A Chicago Case Study* (Chicago: Educational Methods, 1964), p. 15.

20. Murray Edelman, *The Symbolic Uses of Politics* (Urbana: University of Illinois Press, 1964); Michael Lipsky, *Protest in City Politics* (Chicago: Rand McNally, 1970); Michael Lipsky and David J. Olson, *Commission Politics: The Processing of Racial Crisis in America* (New Brunswick, N.J.: Trans-Action Books, 1976).

21. J. David Greenstone, *Labor in American Politics* (New York: Alfred Knopf, 1968), pp. 58–70; 387–408.

22. Ibid., p. 66.

23. William L. Riordon, *Plunkitt of Tammany Hall* (New York: Alfred Knopf, 1948), p. 23.

24. Philip Selznick, *Leadership in Administration* (New York: Harper and Row, 1957), p. 57.

25. Richard O. Carlson, *Executive Succession and Organizational Change: Place-Bound and Career-Bound Superintendents of Schools* (Chicago: Midwest Administration Center, University of Chicago, 1962), p. 19.

26. Ibid., p. 21.

27. Ibid., p. 14. This finding is confirmed by Joseph Cronin, "The School Superintendent in the Crucible of Urban Politics," in Frank Lutz (ed.), *Toward Improved Urban Education* (Worthington, Ohio: Charles Jones, 1970), p. 154. Cronin does note further that appointed boards are more apt to recruit outsiders than are elected boards. In this respect, Chicago follows the norm. It is not easy to see how recruitment from the outside could have been sustained throughout the postwar period had the school board been an elected one.

28. On Calvin Gross's short tenure as superintendent of the New York City school system, see David Rogers, *110 Livingston Street: Politics and Bureaucracy in the New York City School System* (New York: Random House, 1968), pp. 243–52; Bert E. Swanson, *The Struggle for Equality: A Report on the School Integration Controversy in New York City* (New York: Hobbs, Dorman, 1966); and M. Gittell and T. E. Hollander, *Six Urban School Districts: A Comparative Study of Institutional Response* (New York: Praeger, 1968), p. 174. On Mark Shedd's

experience in Philadelphia, see Peter Binzen, "Philadelphia: Politics Invades the Schools," *Saturday Review* 55 (February 5, 1972): 44–49.

29. Marshall Langberg, "The Politics of Appointments," doctoral dissertation, Department of Political Science, University of Chicago, 1974).

30. Herrick, pp. 138–39.

31. *Chicago Sun*, June 3, 1947, p. 3.

32. Doherty is identified as a reformer, according to his voting behavior on the board. But he may be the one case where the voting behavior of the board member does not reflect accurately his other behavior. Doherty is the *only* board member where all other data runs counter to his voting behavior. A union official appointed by Kelly before the 1946 crisis, Doherty did not have a college education and came from a Catholic ethnic background. He favored insiders for the superintendency both in 1947 and in 1953, and he was adjudged to be one of the machine-oriented board members by the informants interviewed by Muskal, as reported in chap. 3.

33. *Official Report of the Proceedings of the Board of Education of the City of Chicago*, June 25, 1947, p. 1246.

34. The board formally voted unanimously in favor of Willis, but the five Lubera supporters initially passed their votes, later changing them to Willis votes. Their speeches made it clear that a "pass" was an expression of support for Lubera.

35. Doherty was the reform "exception." See n. 33.

36. *Board of Education Reports*, June 10, 1953, p. 1697.

37. Ibid., p. 1699.

38. Whiston, who was board president when Redmond was hired in 1965, had been favorably impressed with him during the earlier service with the Chicago school system. In opposing Willis's appointment in 1953 Whiston remarked, "Unfortunately, for us, Dr. Redmond, whom I think might have been Dr. Hunt's successor, left us just about the time that Dr. Hunt did." (Ibid., p. 1705.) Ironically, Whiston later came to be a firm Willis friend and supporter; however, after backing Redmond as Willis's successor, Whiston grew dissatisfied with the administrator he had admired for so many years.

39. Hazlett, p. 278.

40. The Illinois Congress of Parents and Teachers had remained neutral during the schools crisis of 1946, but the Chicago locals of the PTA had actively supported the reform forces. This created tensions within the Illinois PTA, and the Chicago locals eventually formed the Chicago Region of the Illinois Congress of Parents and Teachers, which has continued to ally itself with the Citizens Schools Committee throughout the postwar period. See Hazlett, pp. 248–50.

41. *Chicago Tribune*, June 18, 1946, p. 4., as quoted in Fred Muskal, "The Mayor's Advisory Commission on School Board Nominations:

History and Appraisal" (paper presented to the University of Chicago Project on Society and Education in Chicago, March, 1966).

42. Two other board members had resigned and declared themselves uninterested in serving another term on the board.

43. The vote against Whiston and Murray by the representative from De Paul University remains an unexplained deviant case.

44. One of Daley's friends on the advisory commission (probably Dr. Oldberg) commented: "I told them if they just left it up to him, and quietly let him know how they felt, that maybe, just maybe, he might drop those two. But they didn't listen to me, and they made their recommendations public, so he did as just what I expected. He turned right around and reappointed them. He's not letting anybody tell him what to do" (Royko, *Boss*, p. 202).

45. *Chicago Tribune*, n.d.

46. Ibid., May 3, 1968, p. 2.

47. Ibid., March 2, 1969.

48. Ibid., n.d.

49. Ibid., May 2, 1968.

50. Ibid., May 1, 1968.

51. *Chicago Sun-Times*, May 17, 1968, p. 4.

52. Ibid.

53. *Chicago Daily News*, May 2, 1968.

54. Ibid., May 18, 1968.

55. *Chicago Tribune*, May 1, 1968.

56. Ibid.

57. Theodore J. Lowi, *At the Pleasure of the Mayor* (New York: Free Press, 1964), pp. 193 ff.

58. Chicago's Urban League was generally thought to be more militant than the Chicago chapter of the NAACP. See James Wilson, *Negro Politics* (New York: Free Press, 1960), pp. 111–17.

59. *Chicago's American*, May 1, 1968.

60. *Chicago Daily News*, May 18, 1968.

61. *Chicago Tribune*, March 2, 1969.

62. The education panel consisted of the seven universities represented on the old commission; the professions included the two bar associations, the two medical associations and the technical society represented on the old commission as well as the dental society and the Association of Social Workers; the human relations panel including the NAACP, National Conference of Christians and Jews, and the Leadership Council of Metropolitan Chicago; the welfare panel included the Federation of Settlements, Welfare Council, YMCA, YWCA, and the social welfare departments of Catholic Charities, the Jewish Federation, and the Church Federation of Greater Chicago; the public affairs panel included the Civic Federation, the City Club of Chicago, the American Association

of University Women, and the League of Women Voters. Each panel elected one representative from their membership to serve on the advisory commission.

63. It seems Malis would support Witkowsky but not Bacon, and Boutte would support Bacon but not Witowsky.

64. The changing composition of the Chicago board demands increasing emphasis on the racial composition of the two factions. As late as 1968 the board consisted of nine whites and two blacks, one of whom voted with the machine faction, the other with reformers. By 1970 minority group representation had increased to four, and all of them tended to oppose the machine faction—though Boutte was the least dependable of the reform-minority coalition.

65. The correlations between earlier conflicts on the board and the dominant ones on the two boards that served during 1971 fell dramatically. As measured by the procedures discussed in chapter 3, the median value of the correlation between the conflicts of the 1960s and those in 1971 was only .25, very low as compared with the better than .7 median correlation value among conflict dimensions in the 1960s reported in table 7.

66. Theodore J. Lowi, "American Business, Public Policy, Case Studies and Political Theory," *World Politics* 16 (July 1964): 677–715. Although Lowi's distributive, regulative, and redistributive categories are useful, he exaggerates the degree to which the nature of a policy "determines" the type of politics provoked by it. See the comments on his scheme in J. David Greenstone and Paul Peterson, *Race and Authority in Urban Politics* (New York: Russell Sage, 1973), pp. 278–85, and in James Wilson, *Political Organizations* (New York: Basic Books, 1973), pp. 327–32. In the instance discussed in the text, however, it does seem that the type of policy gave an advantage to the actor (Mayor Daley) who wanted to reduce the level of controversy.

NOTES TO CHAPTER FIVE

1. Among the more recent classics of organizational theory, we note Talcott Parsons, *Structure and Process in Modern Societies* (New York: Free Press of Glencoe, 1960); Herbert A. Simon, *Models of Man, Social and Rational* (New York: John Wiley, 1957); James G. March and Herbert A. Simon, *Organizations* (New York: John Wiley, 1958); James G. March (ed.), *Handbook of Organizations* (Chicago: Rand McNally, 1965); Philip Selznick, *Leadership in Administration* (Evanston, Ill.: Row, Peterson, 1957), *TVA and the Grass Roots* (Berkeley: University of California Press, 1949); Amitai Etzioni, *Complex Organizations* (New York: Free Press, 1961). See the useful distinction between the "rational" and "natural system" model of organizational analysis drawn in Alvin W. Gouldner, "Organizational Analysis," in Robert K. Merton, Leonard Broom, and Leonard S. Cottrell, Jr., *Sociology Today* (New York: Basic Books, 1959), pp. 400–428.

2. Gouldner criticizes this "tendency of the natural-system model . . . [to] focus on the system as a whole and to overstate the degree of mutual interdependence and integration among its parts" (p. 420). Gouldner would emphasize more the bargaining within the organization, a move which, in our opinion, would simply replace an organizational model with one or another of the bargaining models we elaborated earlier. It is better to keep the various analytical lenses distinct than to mix them together in a haphazard manner.

3. H. H. Gerth and C. Wright Mills (eds.), *From Max Weber* (New York: Oxford University Press, 1958), pp. 196–244.

4. The rational model of organizational behavior is discussed in Gouldner. Also, see Amitai Etzioni, "Two Approaches to Organizational Analysis: A Critique and a Suggestion," *Administrative Science Quarterly* 5 (September 1960): 257–78; James D. Thompson, *Organizations in Action* (New York: McGraw-Hill, 1967). The unitary models we are developing could in fact be presented as two alternative models of organizational behavior, but because the rational model, as we are using it, does not need to take into account any specifically organizational characteristics and because in recent years organizational theory has emphasized the limits on rationality, we have treated what Gouldner calls the "natural system" model as coextensive with what we label the organizational model of policy formation.

5. Graham Allison, "Conceptual Models and the Cuban Missile Crisis," *American Political Science Review* 63 (September 1969): 689–718. All citations of Allison in this chapter are from this article. But for a full discussion of the use of rational decision-making models in the literature on international relations, see his *Essence of Decision: Explaining the Cuban Missile Crisis* (Boston: Little, Brown, 1971).

6. *Ibid.*, Allison, "Conceptual Models," p. 700.

7. Social roles are analytical constructs and thus only in a certain sense can it be said that roles have interests. However, in ordinary language we make such attributions continuously. Class interests, union interests, judicial interests, and school interests are all commonly used and accepted phrases. In every case, the reference is not to any particular individual but to the role which the individuals are performing. In applying these labels we take into account what members of a particular social role tell us about what they need and want. A judge can be a valuable source of information about the interests of the judiciary, a union leader about trade union interests, school superintendents about the needs of their schools. But we do not rely solely on the opinions, desires, and evaluations of any particular incumbents of a social role in order to determine what is in the interest of that role. Indeed, we are willing to assert from time to time that certain role incumbents are not serving that role's interests well. A union leader may not be serving his own union's interests, certain judges might not be acting in a manner consistent with judicial interests, and any given superintendent may be-

tray the interests of his organization. We can understand such judgments because we identify interests inherent in a social role which are independent of the desires of any particular role incumbent. By and large, in making these judgments, we equate role interests with those things that improve the long-range chances that role incumbents will enjoy more wealth, power, prestige, and other perquisites. The matter is discussed more fully in J. David Greenstone and Paul E. Peterson, *Race and Authority in Urban Politics* (Chicago: University of Chicago Press, Phoenix paperback, 1976), chap. 2. Also, see Richard Flathman, *The Public Interest* (New York: John Wiley, 1964); Pitkin, chaps. 7–9.

8. Charles Perrow, "Organizational Prestige: Some Functions and Dysfunctions," *American Journal of Sociology* 66 (January 1961): 335–41.

9. Union recognition, not pay increases, was the key issue in the first major New York City schoolteacher's strike in November 1960. See Stephen Cole, *The Unionization of Teachers* (New York: Praeger, 1969), pp. 170–72.

10. By values, we mean the expressed beliefs and commitments of organizational members, whether or not they are in the long-run interest of the organization itself.

11. On the evolution of values important to educational administrators, see R. E. Callahan, *Education and the Cult of Efficiency* (Chicago: University of Chicago Press, 1962).

12. Paul E. Peterson, "The Politics of American Education," in Fred N. Kerlinger and John B. Carroll (eds.) *Review of Research in Education* (Itasca, Ill.: F. E. Peacock, 1974), pp. 350–66.

13. Illinois, *Revised Statutes* (1967), c. 122, sec. 34.

14. In fact the percentage of educational resources raised by the state (as distinct from localities within the state) was lower for Illinois than for all but six other states in 1960–61. Nicholas Masters, Robert Salisbury, and Thomas Eliot, *State Politics and the Public Schools* (New York: Alfred Knopf, 1964), p. 288. Generally speaking, it is the wealthier states that leave educational finance to local communities. Thomas Dye, *Politics, Economics and the Public: Policy Outcomes in the American States* (Chicago: Rand McNally, 1966), p. 89.

15. U.S. Bureau of the Census, *Census of Governments, 1967, VII: State Reports Illinois, no. 13.* (Washington, D.C.: Government Printing Office, 1970), p. 79. In that year revenue sources totaled $375,193,000. Sixty-one percent came from local sources, 2 percent from federal programs, and 5 percent from charges, other local governments, and miscellaneous sources.

The contribution of state aid to Chicago's school budget in 1972 increased only slightly, to 33 percent. The contribution from local taxes declined substantially, to 50 percent. Federal aid's proportion of the budget increased to 10 percent, proceeds of school bonds provided 4.5 percent, and 2.5 percent came from miscellaneous sources. Chicago

Board of Education, *Facts and Figures: Chicago Public Schools, 1972–1973*, p. 100.

16. Joseph Pois, a former Chicago school board member, has expressed in writing the commonly held feeling of professional educators toward the office of State Superintendent of Public Instruction: "In practice, the role of the state with respect to Chicago's public schools has been primarily of a fiscal character; the state superintendent does inspect the schools, but his actual influence is nominal, and the Chicago Board does not look to him for either guidance or leadership in connection with educational policies and programs. . . . The situation can be better understood if it is remembered that this official is chosen on a political basis and his prestige and professional standing, particularly in relation to those expected of the Chicago superintendent, would ordinarily be such that a board would view with some trepidation any deep intrusion by the state superintendent into its affairs." Joseph Pois, *The School Board Crisis: A Chicago Case Study* (Chicago: Educational Methods, 1964), p. 37.

17. Masters, Salisbury, and Eliot, p. 177. See also Laurence Iannaccone, "Norms Governing Urban-State Politics of Education," in Frank Lutz (ed.), *Toward Improved Urban Education* (Worthington, Ohio: Charles Jones, 1970), pp. 233–54.

18. The story is a bit more complex, since it took some time to get unity within Chicago. See Herrick, pp. 277–78.

19. Masters, Salisbury, and Eliot, p. 154.

20. Laurie Wasserman, "The Impact of the Political Culture of Illinois on Public Education" (unpublished A.B. paper, Department of Political Science, University of Chicago, 1970).

21. Local school districts differ in their fiscal independence or dependence. Some, such as New York City, must seek the approval of another municipal body for their annual budget. Others can tax, raise revenues, and allocate funds quite independently. Chicago, in essence, has the second type of arrangement, for the Illinois code states that "the sole duty of the [City] Council is to pass the necessary ordinances and spread the tax levy on the tax rolls."

22. Illinois, *Revised Statutes*, sec. 34–17.

23. The following observations on board procedures are taken from Fred Muskal, "City School Boards at Work: Chicago" (unpublished paper, Department of Education, University of Chicago, n.d.). Muskal's discussion was based on close observation of board proceedings over several years.

24. Ted Harp, Conrad Briner, and George Blair, "Political Costs and Educational Benefits" (unpublished paper, Claremont Graduate School, Claremont, Cal., 1975).

25. Board members were thus unable to employ one of the simplifying techniques that scholars have found to be a standard procedure used by most bureaucracies to guide their decisions. See C. E. Lindblom, "The

Science of 'Muddling Through,'" *Public Administration Review* 18 (1959): 79–88; Aaron Wildavsky, *The Politics of the Budgetary Process* (Boston: Little, Brown, 1964).

26. Howard S. Becker, "The Nature of a Profession," in *Education for the Professions*, Sixty-first Yearbook of the National Society for the Study of Education, part 2 (Chicago: University of Chicago Press, 1962), p. 35.

27. Callahan, *Education and the Cult of Efficiency.*

28. American Association of School Administrators, "Report of the Resolutions Committee," Official Report, 1963 (Washington, D.C.: American Association of School Administrators, 1963), p. 202.

29. Interview, December, 1969, as quoted in James Cibulka, "Administrators As Representatives: The Role of Local Communities in an Urban School System" (doctoral dissertation, Department of Education, University of Chicago, 1973), p. 340.

30. Interview, April 1969, as quoted in Cibulka, p. 340.

31. Interview, January 13, 1970, as quoted in Cibulka, p. 340.

32. Interview, May 1968, as quoted in Cibulka, p. 342.

33. Chicago Board of Education, "Tentative Staffing Formulas," November 1968.

34. Jesse Burkhead, *Input and Output in Large-City High Schools* (Syracuse: Syracuse University Press, 1967), chap. 3.

35. Chicago Board of Education, General Superintendent of Schools, "Statement on Student Demands," October 17, 1968, as quoted in Cibulka, p. 343.

36. The facts reported in this paragraph are taken from Chicago Board of Education, *Facts and Figures: Chicago Public Schools, 1972–1973.*

37. We do not have figures for nonteaching employes for 1970, but in October 1967 there was a full-time equivalent of 25,836 teachers, 14,257 other employees. In that month nonteaching salaries comprised 24 percent of the total payroll. U.S. Bureau of the Census, *Census of Governments, 1967, IV: State Reports, no. 13: Illinois* (Washington, D.C.: Government Printing Office, 1970), p. 66.

38. This is the view taken by Booz, Allen and Hamilton, Inc., "Organizational Survey for the Chicago Board of Education," May 1967 (mimeographed); and by Robert J. Havighurst, *The Public Schools of Chicago: A Survey for the Board of Education of the City of Chicago* (Chicago: Board of Education of the City of Chicago, 1964), chap. 19.

39. Interview, March 12, 1970.

40. Interview, March 5, 1970.

41. Charles E. Bidwell, "The School as a Formal Organization," in James G. March (ed.) *Handbook of Organizations* (Skokie, Ill.: Rand McNally, 1965), p. 976. As applied to Chicago, see Robert Crain and David Street, "School Desegregation and School Decision-Making," *Urban Affairs Quarterly* 2 (1966): 64–82.

42. The concept is taken from Wallace Sayre and Herbert Kaufman, *Governing New York City* (New York: Russell Sage, 1960), pp. 709–16.

NOTES TO CHAPTER SIX

1. Graham Allison, "Conceptual Models and the Cuban Missile Crisis," *American Political Science Review* 63 (September 1969): 689–718. Allison's own definition of rationality is somewhat confused. At times he seems to utilize a highly subjectivist definition: An actor has "one set of *perceived* options, and a single estimate of the consequences that follow from each alternative," (p. 694—my emphasis). But in the same sentence Allison also talks of objective rationality: the "actor has one set of specified goals (the equivalent of a consistent utility function)." And later, in elaborating the rational decision-making model, he speaks of "rational choice" as "value-maximizing." The rational agent selects the alternative whose consequences rank highest in terms of his goals and objectives" (p. 694). And still later, Allison says that decisions which in retrospect are obviously in error cannot be subsumed within the model but "are essentially appendages to [its] basic logic" (p. 696). But "mistakes" cannot be subsumed within a rational model only if one has an objective definition of rationality, which is contrary to Allison's previous use of words like "perceive" and "estimate."

2. Profit-maximizing and utility theories, as used by economists, are discussed in Julian Feldman and Herschel E. Kanter's "Organizational Decision-Making," in James G. March (ed.), *Handbook of Organizations* (Chicago: Rand McNally, 1965), pp. 629–36.

3. E. W. Kelley, "Utility Theory and Political Coalitions: Problems of Operationalization," in Sven Groennings, E. W. Kelley, and Michael Leiserson (eds.), *The Study of Coalition Behavior* (New York: Holt, Rinehart and Winston, 1970), p. 473.

4. Norman Frolich, Joseph Oppenheimer, and Oran R. Young, *Political Leadership and Collective Goods* (Princeton, N. J.: Princeton University Press, 1971).

5. Talcott Parsons, *The Structure of Social Action* (New York: Free Press, 1968), p. 59.

6. Ibid.

7. Ibid.

8. The example is taken from Feldman and Kanter, pp. 615–17.

NOTES TO CHAPTER SEVEN

1. Although the pattern has remained the same for decades, the figures change from year to year. These percentages were for 1971. David J. Kirby, T. Robert Harris, and Robert L. Crain, *Political Strategies in Northern School Desegregation* (Lexington, Mass.: Lexington Books, 1973), p. 243.

2. Thomas Dye, "Urban School Segregation: A Comparative Analysis," *Urban Affairs Quarterly* (1968): 141–65; J. S. Greene (ed.), *Standard Education Almanac, 1972* (Orange, N. J.: Academic Media, 1972).

3. Frederick M. Wirt, "The Politics of Education," in T. Bentley Edwards and Frederick M. Wirt (eds.), *School Desegregation in the*

North: The Challenge and the Experience (San Francisco: Chandler, 1967), p. 305.

4. Ibid., p. 323.

5. Ibid., p. 329. The pluralist model is also assumed in a projection of future developments in northern school desegregation in Thomas F. Pettigrew, "Extending Educational Opportunities: School Desegregation," in Marilyn Gittell (ed.), *Educating an Urban Population* (Beverly Hills, Cal.: Sage Publications, 1967), pp. 300–302.

6. Robert Crain, *The Politics of School Desegration* (Chicago: Aldine, 1968), chaps. 10, 11.

7. Ibid., p. 151.

8. Ibid., p. 157.

9. Ibid., p. 156.

10. Ibid., p. 162.

11. Ibid., p. 162. A quite similar argument has been made more recently in Kirby, Harris, and Crain, *Political Strategies in Northern School Desegregation.* For other studies of school desegregation that illustrate the ideological flavor of the controversy, see Thomas Vittulo-Martin, "The Role of Public Conflict in the Reordering of Local Communities" (doctoral dissertation, University of Chicago, 1972). Also, see Lilian Rubin, *Busing and Backlash* (Berkeley: University of California Press, 1972).

12. Crain, pp. 115–31.

13. David Rogers, *110 Livingston Street: Politics and Bureaucracy in the New York City School System* (New York: Random House, 1968), chaps. 3–6.

14. Ibid., p. 267.

15. Stokely Carmichael and Charles V. Hamilton, *Black Power: The Politics of Liberation in America* (New York: Vintage, 1967), p. 41.

16. *Chicago Sun-Times*, January 11, 1968.

17. *Chicago's American*, January 10, 1968.

18. *Chicago Tribune*, February 13, 1968.

19. *Chicago's American*, September 10, 1967.

20. Ibid., August 24, 1968.

21. *Chicago Daily News*, November 25, 1967.

22. *Chicago's American*, January 17, 1968.

23. *Chicago Daily Defender*, February 27, 1968.

24. Ibid., February 29, 1968.

25. See the discussion of the changes in the goals of black leaders in Paul E. Peterson, "The Political Functions of Ideologies: Black Power and British Socialism." Paper presented before the Conference on Urban Protest: Retrospect and Prospect, Stanford University, May 1974.

26. *Chicago Defender*, January 24, 1968.

27. *Chicago Sun-Times*, October 23, 1967.

28. *Chicago Tribune*, January 18, 1969. Note the reference to the "good of the entire city," an indication of the continuity of the older reform tradition and the integrationist drives of the 1960s.

29. *Chicago Sun-Times*, February 27, 1968.

30. E. E. Schattschneider, *The Semi-Sovereign People* (New York: Holt, Rinehart and Winston, 1960).

31. *Chicago Sun-Times*, February 28, 1968.

32. Ibid., February 27, 1968.

33. There is an apparent but not genuine exception to this generalization. In South Shore both integrationists and neighborhood school supporters criticized the school administration's proposals. However, their criticisms were directly opposed in character, the former saying the proposals did not go far enough, the latter saying they went too far. The zero-sum nature of the conflict only meant that compromise proposals tend to be attacked from both sides. The point is discussed below in this chapter.

34. *Chicago Tribune*, December 27, 1967.

35. Ibid., January 25, 1968.

36. Examples of this bias included: (1) background stories on instances of successful busing experiences elsewhere (with no stories about negative consequences in other cities); (2) a story which emphasized Robert Havighurst's criticism of CCCO's attack on Redmond's plan with hardly a mention of black civil rights concerns; (3) use of highly selective quotes from neighborhood school groups that tended to portray them as "racist" and "bigoted"; and (4) the identification of the two communities where busing was to occur as South Shore and Austin, systematically ignoring the fact that the receiving schools, where opposition to the scheme came from, were for the most part located in two quite different communities, South Chicago and Belmont-Cragin.

37. *Chicago Sun-Times*, January 11, 1968.

38. *Chicago Daily News*, March 1, 1968.

39. The one citywide political force lending its support to neighborhood school groups was Chicago's conservative newspaper, the *Tribune*, which editorialized that the school board was "rezoning families . . . out of their home neighborhoods and into alien ones. Their street addresses may remain the same, but their children are scattered about like seeds from a dandelion." *Chicago Tribune*, January 11, 1968. But the *Tribune*'s reporting was not heavily biased in the direction of neighborhood groups; for example, it ran no stories on the dangers and disasters of busing in other cities. Moreover, its sister paper, the evening *Chicago's American*, took a rather equivocal position. On the one hand, it observed that "the neighborhood school system has great advantages for children and parents, and should not be scrapped in favor of sociological experiments." On the other hand, "the one thing the neighborhood school system can't do is stabilize neighborhoods." *Chicago's American*, January 12, 1968.

40. *Chicago Sun-Times*, February 16, 1968.

41. *Chicago Sun-Times*, October 21, 1967.

42. Bob Terpstra, "Day the Antibusers Came," *Chicago's American*, Jan. 14, 1963, p. 1.

43. *Chicago's American*, December 27, 1967. Judge Edward Scheffler, who had been the only member to abstain from approving the Redmond plan even "in principle" and who indicated that he was opposed to busing, was ailing and absent on vacation in Florida throughout the controversy, leaving the voting membership of the board at ten. He resigned from the school board the following spring. In the meantime neighborhood school forces might have prevailed upon him to return for a meeting if they thought his vote was crucial; as it turned out, his vote against busing would not have changed any of the outcomes (except for an early procedural matter which seems not to have had any long-range consequences).

44. This was the procedural question which would have been affected by Scheffler's vote. Had he been present, his fourth vote to defer would have been sufficient—given the two-thirds margin necessary to overrule a request for deferral—to have blocked the budgetary allocation at the December meeting.

45. Quotation from the transcript of the general committee meeting of the Chicago Board of Education, August 23, 1967. Parts of these quotations can be found in *Chicago's American*, August 24, 1967, p. 1.

46. Transcript of the general committee meeting of the Chicago Board of Education, August 23, 1967.

47. *Chicago Daily News*, December 28, 1967.

48. *Chicago Tribune*, December 28, 1967; the first part of this quotation was indirect, the second part, direct.

49. Transcript of the General Committee meeting of the Chicago Board of Education, August 23, 1967. See also *Chicago's American*, August 24, 1967, p. 1.

50. *Chicago Daily News*, January 11, 1968, p. 8.

51. *Chicago Tribune*, January 13, 1968, p. 1.

52. *Chicago Daily News*, January 12, 1968, p. 1.

53. Ibid.

54. *Chicago Tribune*, September 6, 1967.

55. Ibid.

56. Ibid.

57. Ibid.

58. *Chicago's American*, January 11, 1968, p. 1.

59. Ibid.

60. Ibid.

61. *Chicago Sun-Times*, January 12, 1968.

62. *Chicago Tribune*, January 30, 1968.

63. My emphasis. Note that the board member is hinting here at the distinction between pluralist bargaining, which the mayor is engaged in, and ideological bargaining, which involves the nonelected board.

64. Graham Allison, *Essence of Decision* (Boston: Little, Brown, 1971), p. 85.

65. For the attitudes of Chicago school administrators toward busing plans, see James Cibulka, "Administrators As Representatives: The Role of Local Communities in an Urban School System," (doctoral dissertation, Department of Education, University of Chicago, 1971). For an analysis of a similar reluctance to implement desegregation plans among field administrators in New York, see Rogers, *110 Livingston Street*, pp. 346–49.

66. Harvey L. Molotch, *Managed Integration: Dilemmas of Doing Good in the City* (Berkeley: University of California Press, 1972), pp. 9, 41–43. This monograph is an excellent in-depth study of the processes of racial change in South Shore during the period just before the announcement of the Redmond plan.

67. Ibid., p. 72.

68. *Chicago Daily Defender*, November 9, 1967.

69. Ibid.

70. *Chicago Tribune*, February 6, 1968.

71. *Chicago Sun-Times*, February 6, 1968.

72. *Chicago Tribune*, January 10, 1968.

73. *Chicago Sun-Times*, February 6, 1968.

74. Christopher Chandler, "School Busing Presents Large Issue, Small Plan," *Chicago Sun-Times*, January 15, 1968.

75. *Chicago Sun-Times*, January 15, 1968.

76. At a later meeting, Louise Malis commented on the board's lack of information about these negotiations: "It is my understanding from what I have read in the newspaper, and this is the only thing I can base it on, that the staff has gone to the community already. Now I don't know."

77. Patterns of communication between board and staff are discussed in chapter 5.

78. Crain, *Politics of School Desegregation*, pp. 126–28.

79. Rogers, p. 267.

80. Longer-range solutions to racial stabilization included the formation of magnet schools and educational parks.

81. This and the following quotations from board members are taken from the transcript of the general committee meeting of the Board of Education, August 23, 1967.

82. *Chicago Daily News*, December 26, 1967.

83. The latter point is made in Francis Fox Piven, "The Urban Crisis: Who Got What, and Why," in Robert Paul Wolff (ed.), *1984 Revisited* (New York: Random House, 1975).

84. *Chicago Tribune*, October 25, 1967.

85. Mary Ullrich, "Reaction to Redmond Plan Varies," *South Central Neighborhood News*, September 3, 1967.

86. *Chicago Tribune*, February 7, 1968.

87. *Chicago Sun-Times*, January 17, 1968.

88. See chapter 4.

NOTES TO CHAPTER EIGHT

1. Salary data in figure 5 are taken from Chicago Board of Education, Bureau of Research, Development and Special Projects, *Facts and Figures*, Chicago Public Schools, September 1968; Department of Systems Analysis and Data Processing, Bureau of Administrative Research, *Facts and Figures, Public Schools, 1972–73*; and, for information on recent contracts, from David Peterson, Chicago Teachers Union, telephone conversation, July 1974.

The value of salaries in constant dollars was determined by the following formula:

$$\frac{(\text{actual salary}) \times 100}{100 + (\% \text{ increase in CPI})},$$

where CPI is the Consumer Price Index for the year in question as compared to 1965. Changes in Consumer Price Index were calculated from information on Chicago contained in U.S. Department of Labor, Bureau of Labor Statistics, *Handbook of Labor Statistics*, 1973, and *Consumer Price Index*, April 1974.

Per capita disposable personal income in constant (1958) dollars is given in Office of the President, Council of Economic Advisers, *Annual Report to the President*, 1973, Appendix C. Since this data is given in 1958 dollars and teachers' salaries are given in 1965 dollars, comparisons should be made between the two trend lines over time rather than between actual dollar figures. Salaries are presented in the figure for odd-numbered years only in order to eliminate short-term fluctuations in the overall trend.

2. Chicago teacher organizations have had a long and fascinating history. See Mary J. Herrick, *The Chicago Schools: A Social and Political History* (Beverly Hills, Cal.: Sage Publications, 1971), and sources cited therein.

3. Herrick, chap. 12.

4. Ibid., p. 268.

5. Ibid., p. 280.

6. Ibid., pp. 290–91.

7. On the basis of interviews with some thirty-seven "teacher-leaders," Alan Rosenthal concluded that in the early sixties, "Willis exhibited the type of personal, political, and professional domination seldom found on the American educational scene." Alan Rosenthal, *Pedagogues and Power: Teacher Groups in School Politics* (Syracuse, N.Y.: Syracuse University Press, 1969), p. 151.

8. Reformers also opposed in 1967 the inclusion of school clerks within the CTU, endorsing instead formation of a separate association for that group. After considerable maneuvering, in which control of the president's chair by the machine faction was critically important, clerks became part of CTU's constituency. Inasmuch as it did not involve any financial issues, the case illustrates well an antiunion bias among reformers.

9. In 1970, reform-oriented Carey Preston voted for a contract that gave only limited concessions to the unions. In 1971, Warren Bacon and Gerald Sbarboro cast the only two negative votes.

10. Union supporters were Frank Whiston, John Carey, Thomas Nayder, Mrs. Wendell Green, Alvin Boutte, Gerald Sbarbaro, Marge Wild, and Thomas Murray. Opponents were Carey Preston, Cyrus Adams III, Warren Bacon, Harry Oliver, Louise Malis, Jack Witkowsky, Mrs. David Cerda, and Mrs. William Rohter. Members are classified into machine and reform categories according to the procedures set forth in chapter 3.

11. This and following quotations are from personal interviews with school board members conducted in 1969.

12. *Chicago Daily News*, January 8, 1968.

13. See J. David Greenstone, *Labor in American Politics* (New York: Alfred Knopf, 1968), pp. 94–95.

14. One of the antiunion, reform-oriented board members, Warren Bacon, discussed the transformation in the attitude of the machine faction towards the CTU in the following way: "All the good board members who normally vote as a block with the establishment [i.e., the machine faction] were adamant against granting the union the right of collective bargaining. . . . In addition to wanting more money, they also wanted the right to hold an election to determine the sole bargaining agent. Bill Lee (president of the Chicago Federation of Labor) and one or two other top leaders very closely identified with the so-called 'power structure' of this city were sent over to the Board meeting, and those Board members who were adamant against granting the union this right changed just like that." Warren Bacon, "Comments," in Sol Tax (ed.), *The People vs. the System: A Dialogue in Urban Conflict* (Chicago: Acme Press, 1968), p. 167.

15. The phrase in quotation marks is from Edward Banfield and James Wilson, *City Politics* (Cambridge: Harvard University Press, 1963), chap. 1.

16. Martin Meyerson and Edward Banfield, *Politics, Planning and the Public Interest* (Glencoe, Ill.: Free Press, 1955), p. 264.

17. The incident is discussed in note 43, below.

18. *Chicago Sun-Times*, January 12, 1971.

19. *Chicago Tribune*, January 13, 1971.

20. Later Whiston resigned from the committee but then appointed John Carey, another labor leader, to serve on it.

21. J. David Hood, "Issues and Response: A Causal Analysis of Voting on Chicago School Finance Referenda in the 1960's," (M.A. paper, Department of Political Science, University of Chicago, June 1972).

22. See Grant McConell, *Private Power and American Democracy* (New York: Alfred Knopf, 1966), chap. 5, for an excellent discussion of the oligarchical pattern that characterizes the internal politics of unions.

23. Discussed in note 43, below.

24. Barry Shapiro, "The Chicago Teachers Union and the Ghetto," (M.A. paper, Department of Political Science, University of Chicago, 1968), p. 43.

25. Besides the FTB issue, there were a number of other issues that divided black from white teachers. In the first place, white teachers tended to be more interested in salary increases at the expense of educational improvements than black teachers, who were concentrated in inner-city schools with more difficult working conditions. As one leader of the Black Caucus demanded, the CTU must "bring about fundamental changes in Black schools" (Shapiro, p. 40). Secondly, schemes for desegregating the faculty, which the federal government was trying to impose on the school board, created racial tensions among teachers. It is true that a number of black teachers did not want to be forced to teach in white schools, but the long fight that CTU led against federal proposals was clearly of greater concern to white than to black teachers. Thirdly, community control of schools posed a much greater threat to whites than to blacks. Indeed, community control could well give new administrative opportunities to black educators. Perhaps it was the sizable black minority within the union that softened CTU opposition to community control experiments. Certainly, the Chicago union leadership was not interested in making this a major issue, as it was in New York. Even when a community-control experiment in Woodlawn became involved in gang problems, pitting one black administrator against another and receiving citywide newspaper attention, Desmond adopted a moderate, mediating stance towards the matter.

26. Chicago's board of education would not reveal the racial composition of FTBs. Concerned FTBs claimed that 95 percent of the category were black. Other informed sources quoted by Shapiro suggest that 90 percent were black; Shapiro himself says 80 percent is a conservative figure (Shapiro, p. 37).

27. *Chicago Tribune*, February 13, 1969.

28. Since 85 to 90 percent of most black teachers were FTBs, who were not allowed to participate as union members with full voting rights until 1966, it can be expected that many blacks were either not union members at all or, at the most, nominal members only. In 1966 and 1968, the Desmond's slate did not feel that it had to run any black candidates for the three important, full-time union offices, and even TAC, the liberal opposition, ran only one black for these positions during this period. No systematic data are available on the number of black delegates to the union house of representatives, but Shapiro counted only 15 at a meeting at which 114 union representatives were present (Shapiro, p. 37).

29. On the general problem of sustaining an organization without powers to compel members to contribute, see Mancur Olson, Jr., *The Logic of Collective Action* (Cambridge: Harvard University Press, 1965).

30. Hope Justus, "Schools Here Face Teacher Demand for $50 Million Package," *Chicago's American*, November 2, 1967.

31. *Chicago Tribune*, November 23, 1968.

32. Shapiro, p. 23.

33. Ibid., p. 22.

34. For example, *Chicago's American* gave Desmond's speeches calling for educational improvements such headlines as "Raise for New Teachers Sought" (November 1968—no specific date available) and "Teacher Squabble over Pay Starts on a Polite Note" (November 23, 1968).

35. Nicholas Masters and Robert Salisbury, *State Politics and the Public Schools* (New York: Alfred Knopf, 1964).

36. A sample of the way in which the slogan is used in debate occurred at the November 22, 1968 meeting of the school board, as recorded in the transcript of the meeting:

President Whiston: "If you go out now and ask for 115 million dollars and 35 million dollars . . . that is a quarter of a billion dollars on the taxpayers of this city in addition to what the city is asking for . . . I don't know where they are going to get the money to pay for it."

Harry Oliver: "These are parents, Frank, and they are themselves highly concerned about the education of their children."

Whiston: "I am just as concerned as those parents are."

Oliver: "Therefore, I think we should ask them. I think it is our responsibility to ask them. If they turn us down cold, they turn us down cold."

37. *Chicago Sun-Times*, January 6, 1968.

38. In his analysis of school factors related to verbal ability scores, Coleman finds almost no correlation between length of school year and performance. James Coleman et al., *Equality of Educational Opportunity* (Washington, D.C.: U.S. Government Printing Office, 1966). On the other hand, David Wiley, in some research in progress at the University of Chicago, has found a positive association between the number of days a pupil is in school and his score on verbal ability tests.

39. That 8 percent increase becomes part of the salary base from which negotiations begin in future years; teachers in the long run are still ahead if they strike for eight days for a gain of only four percent.

40. Discussed earlier in this chapter.

41. The budget, which by law could not anticipate expenditures in excess of anticipated revenues, was based on the calendar year (January through December) rather than on the state's fiscal year (September 1-August 31). As a result, it was impossible for the board to anticipate how much state aid, granted on a fiscal-year basis, the district would receive in the second half of its budgetary year. Presumably, it would not be less than amounts allocated previously, though the state had every legal right to cut school aid. The amount of increase, on the other hand, could only be anticipated by guessing the outcome of political processes in the legislature.

42. Confidential interview with informed observer of school board–union negotiations in Illinois.

43. Collective negotiations engaged not just one but two large, complex organizations. Although in the early years, the teachers' union bargained astutely, in 1969 pressure by union activists forced the leadership to call for both a mass lobbying effort in Springfield and its first strike against the school board. Both actions proved counterproductive. State legislators were only antagonized by teachers' pressure techniques, and the school board discovered for the first time that school strikes were not a disaster after all. Although Desmond resisted both measures, he was unable to prevent them. The decline in CTU success in the 1970s was thus due not only to more astute bargaining on the part of the board but also to this costly error by the CTU.

44. Data on U.S. public elementary and secondary day school enrollments were taken from U.S. Department of Health, Education and Welfare, Office of Education, National Center for Educational Statistics, *Statistics of Public Elementary and Secondary Day Schools*, Fall 1971; *Statistics of State School Systems*, 1963–64, 1965–66, 1967–68; and *Digest of Educational Statistics*, 1971, 1973. Data on earned B.A. degrees in the area of education awarded by U.S. colleges and universities is taken from U.S. Department of Health, Education and Welfare, Office of Education, *Earned Degrees Conferred by Higher Educational Institutions*, 1955–56—1970–71.

45. These measures of supply and demand are obviously only very approximate indicators of the actual market situation in any given year. We prefer them to other more complex indicators used by the National Education Association and other analysts, because we are interested primarily in demand and supply factors that are relatively unresponsive to price changes. School board decisions to reduce class size or hire specialized staff may well be influenced by salary costs, but the number of children for whom they are responsible is beyond the board's control.

On the supply side, the rate at which teachers, especially women, leave teaching for other occupations and the reentry rate of former teachers into the teaching market will obviously fluctuate according to salaries paid teachers. But in the short run the number of students earning B.A. degrees in education may well be as much a function of the size of an age cohort in the population and the proportion of that age cohort who attend college as it is a response to immediate employment opportunities in the field of education.

In short, as imprecise as these indicators of demand and supply are, we feel they are the best quantitative measures of exogenous forces affecting prices within the teacher labor market.

46. We compared the national trend line in elementary education with the national trend line for all education graduates to see whether or not the elementary education data for Illinois would provide a reasonable basis for estimating trends in the supply of teachers taken as a whole.

We found that at the national level the two trend lines were very similar in shape during the period 1955 to 1965, but that the elementary education trend line rose less steeply in the late sixties and early seventies than did the trend line for the number of education B.A.'s taken as a whole. Evidently, during this later period, a higher percentage of teachers were preparing for secondary education and for other specialized fields than in previous years. Assuming that similar patterns were occurring within the state of Illinois, data on total number of education B.A.'s would reveal an even sharper increase in Illinois teacher supply in recent years than is indicated in figure 7.

47. These figures were calculated from data published in the National Education Association's *Salary Schedules and Fringe Benefits for Teachers, 1972–73*, Research Report 1973-R-2.

48. Paying all teachers the same salary regardless of their working conditions was economically not rational. As a result, many school board members urged that special "combat pay" be paid teachers in inner-city schools. One can readily understand the union's unrelenting opposition to such a policy, for differential pay for inner-city schools would allow the system to reduce the pay of other teachers working in more attractive situations.

49. "Four largest cities" are New York, Los Angeles, Detroit, and Philadelphia. "Fourteen cities" are those four plus Washington, D.C., Baltimore, Cleveland, Indianapolis, San Diego, Atlanta, St. Louis, Milwaukee, Dallas, and Houston. "AFT cities" are New York, Detroit, Philadelphia, Washington, D.C., Baltimore, and Cleveland.

Salary data on all cities other than Chicago (see n. 1) are taken from American Federation of Teachers, *Survey of Teachers' Salaries*, 1965, 1968, 1969, 1970, 1973–74; and from National Education Association, *Salary Schedules and Fringe Benefits for Teachers, 1972–73*, Research Report 1973-R-2.

Salary figures for each city were first corrected for differences in the Consumer Price Index among cities in spring 1970, as stated in U.S. Department of Labor, Bureau of Labor Statistics, *Three Budgets for an Urban Family, 1969–70*, Supplement to Bulletin 1570-5. These corrected dollar figures were then transformed into constant 1965 dollar figures by using procedures described in note 44.

Chicago salaries are graphed for odd-numbered years only in order to eliminate short-term fluctuations from graph. Data for other cities presented for each year it was readily available (1965, 1968, 1969, 1970, 1972, 1973). For these cities, short-term fluctuations in specific cities are eliminated in the process of averaging.

NOTES TO CHAPTER NINE

1. But see Robert Crain and David Street, "School Desegregation and School Decision-making," *Urban Affairs Quarterly* 2 (1966): 64–82.

2. This can be concluded from a careful reading of F. W. Bertolaet,

"The Administrative Functions of the District Superintendent in Chicago As Related to Decentralization" (doctoral dissertation, University of Wisconsin, 1964).

3. Thomas Williams, "Administrative Decentralization," (unpublished paper, Department of Education, University of Chicago, 1968), p. 5.

4. On the distinction between political and administrative decentralization, see William Boyd and David O'Shea, "Theoretical Perspectives on School District Decentralization," *Education and Urban Society* 7 (August 1975): 357–76.

5. Chicago Board of Education Proceedings, April 15, 1965, p. 2465.

6. On other cities, see the careful, comprehensive work by G. R. LaNoue and B. L. R. Smith, *The Politics of School Decentralization* (Lexington, Mass.: D. C. Heath, 1973); also, the entire August issue of *Education and Urban Society* 7 (1975).

7. Hanna Pitkin, *The Concept of Representation* (Berkeley: University of California Press, 1967); Paul E. Peterson, "Forms of Representation: Participation of the Poor in the Community Action Program," *American Political Science Review* 64 (June 1970): 491–507.

8. Since we find that most council members had little influence, their orientation is of little significance in this investigation. On the orientations of representatives, see Peterson, "Forms of Representation," 492–93.

9. Chicago Board of Education, "District Superintendent's Education Councils," March 26, 1969.

10. Ibid.

11. Ibid.

12. Ibid.

13. Ibid.

14. Field notes of participant observer.

15. Ibid.

16. Chicago Board of Education, "Report on District Superintendent's Education Councils and Other Means of Communication with School Patrons," September 10, 1969 (my emphasis).

17. For a fuller elaboration of procedures and findings, see James Cibulka, "Administrators As Representatives: The Role of Local Communities in an Urban School System," (doctoral dissertation, Department of Education, University of Chicago, 1973).

18. City of Chicago, Board of Education, "Calumet-Hess Report," January 15, 1970.

19. City of Chicago, Board of Education, "District Superintendent's Education Councils," March 25, 1970.

20. *The Reporter*, spring 1971, pp. 7–8. We are indebted for this information on the principals' reaction to Jeffrey C. Powell, whose unpublished paper on local school councils also provided us valuable information on the early stages of their establishment.

21. Ibid.

22. City of Chicago, Board of Education, "Revised Guidelines for Local School Councils," June 16, 1971.

23. Charles Silberman, *Crisis in Black and White* (New York: Random House, 1964).

24. Ibid.

25. William Congreve, "Institutional Collaboration to Improve Urban Public Education . . ." Office of Education, Bureau of Research, Urban Education Developmental Project, Project no. 7-0346, March 15, 1968, p. 35.

26. City of Chicago, Board of Education, Transcript of Board Meeting, December 27, 1967.

27. Ibid.

28. Ibid.

29. Ibid.

30. *Chicago Tribune*, October 17, 1968.

31. Ibid.

32. *Chicago Sun-Times*, October 24, 1968.

33. Ibid., October 31, 1968.

34. For an elaboration of this point, see James G. Cibulka, "School Decentralization in Chicago," *Education and Urban Society* 7 (August 1975): 412–38.

35. Peterson has stated portions of the argument developed here in "Afterword:: The Politics of Decentralization, *Education and Urban Society* 7 (August 1975).

36. Michael Lipsky and David J. Olson, *Riot Commission Politics: The Processing of Racial Crisis in America* (New York: Dutton, 1976); National Advisory Commission on Civil Disorders, *Supplemental Studies for the National Advisory Commission on Civil Disorders* (Washington, D.C.: Government Printing Office, 1969); Francis Piven and Richard Cloward, *Regulating the Poor: The Functions of Public Welfare* (New York: Random House, 1971).

37. *Chicago Sun-Times*, May 19, 1968. The subsequent article then sought to deny the validity of the rumors, ending with the interesting request: "If you have a story to tell, the *Sun-Times* would like to hear it. Of particular interest would be constructive experiences relating to interracial situations that have been resolved in a positive manner." Apparently, the *Sun-Times* was not sure whether its mission was to report news or "positively" to influence public opinion. Events the following fall indicated the rumors had probably been valid.

Much of our information on the student boycott and the subsequent board response is taken from Francis M. Landwermeyer, "Student Disorders in the Chicago Public School System, Fall, 1968" (unpublished paper, Department of Education, University of Chicago, 1969).

38. Information reported in *Chicago Tribune*, October 15 and 29, 1968; *Chicago Daily News*, October 28, 1968.

39. *Chicago Tribune*, August 25, 1969.

40. *Chicago Sun-Times*, October 24, 1968. Quotation is partially direct, partially indirect.

41. Chicago Board of Education Proceedings, November 18, 1970. Transcript of General Committee meeting.

42. Ibid.

43. Ibid.

44. Norman Kerr, "The School Board As an Agency of Legitimation," *Sociology of Education* 38 (1964): 34–59.

45. J. D. Thompson, *Organizations in Action* (New York: McGraw-Hill, 1967).

46. *Chicago Sun-Times*, October 24, 1968.

47. Cf. Michael Lipsky, *Protest in City Politics* (Chicago: Rand McNally, 1970).

48. *Chicago's American*, n.d.

NOTES TO CHAPTER TEN

1. Louis Wirth, *On Cities and Social Life* (Chicago: University of Chicago Press, 1964); Harvey Warren Zorbaugh, *The Gold Coast and the Slum* (Chicago: University of Chicago Press, 1929).

2. Excellent recent studies include Peter Rossi and Robert Dentler, *The Politics of Urban Renewal* (New York: Free Press, 1961); Harvey Moloch, *Managed Integration: Dilemmas of Doing Good in the City* (Berkeley: University of California Press, 1972); William Kornblum, *Blue-Collar Community* (Chicago: University of Chicago Press, 1974).

3. Murray S. Stedman, Jr., *Urban Politics* (Cambridge, Mass.: Winthrop, 1975), p. 32.

4. Mary Herrick, *The Chicago Schools: A Social and Political History* (Beverly Hills, Cal.: Sage Publications, 1971), p. 71.

5. Seymour Sacks, *City Schools/Suburban Schools* (Syracuse: Syracuse University Press, 1972), p. 50.

6. Ibid., p. 31.

7. Ibid., p. 31.

8. Jay S. Goodman, *The Dynamics of Urban Government and Politics* (New York: Macmillan, 1975), p. 49.

9. Ibid., p. 49.

10. Ibid., p. 53.

11. George Sternlieb, "The City As Sandbox," *Public Interest* 25 (Fall 1971): 14–21; Norton E. Long, "The City as Reservation," *Public Interest* 25 (Fall 1971), 22–38.

12. Goodman, p. 144.

13. Werner Z. Hirsch, "The Fiscal Plight: Causes and Remedies," in Werner Z. Hirsch et al., *Fiscal Pressures on the Central City* (New York: Praeger, 1971), p. 30.

14. Sacks, p. 31.

15. Milton Kotler, *Neighborhood Government: The Local Foundations of Political Life* (Indianapolis: Bobbs Merrill, 1969).

16. See Sterlieb, "The City as Sandbox"; Long, "The City as Reservation", and Frances Fox Piven, "The Urban Crisis: Who Got What, and Why," in Robert Paul Wolff (ed.), *1984 Revisited* (New York: Alfred Knopf, 1973).

17. Grant McConnell, *The Decline of Agrarian Democracy* (Berkeley: University of California Press, 1953); Philip Selznick, *TVA and the Grass Roots*, (Berkeley: University of California Press, 1949).

18. See John Bunzel, *The American Small Businessman* (New York: Alfred Knopf, 1962.)

19. *Congressional Quarterly Weekly Report* 33 (February 1, 1975): 278.

INDEX OF PERSONS

INDEX OF SUBJECTS

298